A Letter from Ana Maria Araújo Freire

Very few times have I felt touched by the effort and solidarity of a group of intellectuals who, as teachers, share with Paulo Freire what they are doing in their reflective practices—practices inspired by what Paulo thought, what he did, what he said, and what he wrote.

These letters bear witness to Paulo's presence among us, his joy, his coherence, and his generosity. Even when he was denouncing the barbarities of this world, he understood that only by denouncing could one announce a new world. The loving testimonies recorded through these letters represent a communication form Paulo liked so much because he believed it was a way to better dialogue with readers. Through letters one could more truthfully and easily reach the very marrow of the heart and reason. The letters contained in this book—whose title is happily foretelling—use Paulo himself as preamble and the names of his books as a point of departure so that they will reach all readers but, above all, my husband, Paulo. I am certain that God will not deny him the great happiness and joy along with the humble and restrained pride that this book would have unleashed in him.

Sonia Nieto is daring for having dreamt and realized a project that "not even she nor anyone else could have imagined" without the complicity of dozens of people—some of whom I know personally and to whom I feel radically linked and, hence, I ask permission to name: Dean Birkenkamp, Ira Shor, Tom Wilson, Donaldo Macedo, and the legendary Maxine Greene—individuals who most definitely felt and became involved in Paulo's extraordinary critical-humanistic-political-ethical comprehension of education, a comprehension that served as a foundation for this book of rare beauty and extreme importance. It is a must read for all those who want to continue re-creating a philosophy of reading the world that will make them want to transform it, making it more just, more beautiful, and more ethical.

We should all congratulate ourselves: Paulo is smiling with us.

Nita
Ana Maria Araújo Freire
São Paulo, Brazil
March 5, 2008

Series in Critical Narrative

Donaldo Macedo, Series Editor

University of Massachusetts Boston

Now in Print

DEAR PAULO
LETTERS FROM THOSE WHO DARE TEACH

edited by

SONIA NIETO

Foreword by Donaldo Macedo

PARADIGM PUBLISHERS
Boulder & London

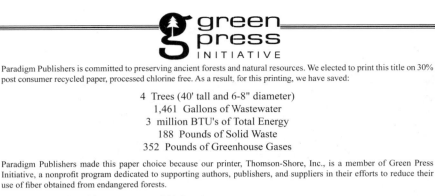

green press
INITIATIVE

Paradigm Publishers is committed to preserving ancient forests and natural resources. We elected to print this title on 30% post consumer recycled paper, processed chlorine free. As a result, for this printing, we have saved:

4 Trees (40' tall and 6-8" diameter)
1,461 Gallons of Wastewater
3 million BTU's of Total Energy
188 Pounds of Solid Waste
352 Pounds of Greenhouse Gases

Paradigm Publishers made this paper choice because our printer, Thomson-Shore, Inc., is a member of Green Press Initiative, a nonprofit program dedicated to supporting authors, publishers, and suppliers in their efforts to reduce their use of fiber obtained from endangered forests.

For more information, visit www.greenpressinitiative.org

Environmental impact estimates were made using the Environmental Defense Paper Calculator. For more information visit: www.papercalculator.org.

Copyright © 2008 Paradigm Publishers
Eating, Talking, and Acting: The Magic of Freire Copyright © 2008 Herb Kohl

Published in the United States by Paradigm Publishers, 3360 Mitchell Lane Suite E, Boulder, CO 80301 USA.

Paradigm Publishers is the trade name of Birkenkamp & Company, LLC,
Dean Birkenkamp, President and Publisher.

Library of Congress Cataloging-in-Publication Data

Dear Paulo : letters from those who dare teach / [edited by] Sonia Nieto.
    p. cm. — (Series in critical narrative ; 7)
Includes bibliographical references and index.
ISBN 978-1-59451-535-4 (paperback : alk. paper)
    1. Freire, Paulo, 1921–1997—Influence.   2. Critical pedagogy.   3. Teaching—Social aspects.   4. Teachers—Conduct of life.   5. Social action.   I. Nieto, Sonia.
    LB880.F732D43 2008
    370.11'5—dc22

                                                                                        2007052428

Printed and bound in the United States of America on acid-free paper that meets the standards of the American National Standard for Permanence of Paper for Printed Library Materials.

Designed & Typeset by Straight Creek Bookmakers in Adobe Caslon.

12 11 10 09 08   1 2 3 4 5

Contents

Foreword

⊸ Donaldo Macedo ⊷

One of Paulo Freire's constant preoccupations toward the end of his life had to do with the mechanization of his work—a process that even well-meaning liberal educators use to reduce his leading ideas into a method. Freire often shared with me his concerns that even educators who embrace his work do so selectively and, in the end, mistakenly transform his notion of dialogue into a reductionistic method, thus losing sight of the fact that the fundamental goal of dialogical teaching is to create a process of learning and knowing that invariably involves theorizing about the experience shared in the dialogue process.

Sonia Nieto's book, *Dear Paulo: Letters from Those Who Dare Teach,* is a refreshing affirmation that Freire's pedagogical proposals cannot be reduced through a method of epistemological relationship by dialogue to a vacuous, feel-good comfort zone where teachers, in their eagerness to democratize power in the classroom, relinquish their roles as teachers to become facilitators. Becoming a facilitator signals, in the view of many liberal educators, the creation of pedagogical spaces that can lead to the empowerment of students. What is often left unexamined in this process is that the classroom, as well as the society within which the classroom is inserted, is shaped and guided by power asymmetries that, ultimately, undermine the pretense of divesting from the teacher's authority. Although the facilitator posture continues to inform many educators who blindly advocate the dialogical model, these educators selectively ignore Freire's own pronouncement when he cautioned educators by categorically saying that "I consider myself a teacher and always a teacher. I have never pretended to be a facilitator. What I want to make clear also is in being a teacher, I always teach to facilitate. I cannot accept the notion of a facilitator who facilitates so as not to teach."[1]

Dear Paulo: Letters from Those Who Dare Teach makes it abundantly clear that dialogue cannot be mechanized into a controlled turn-taking where all students are expected to speak and share their experience, where the rules guiding the sharing of experience become the main object of knowledge. This form of dialogical encounter was referred to by Freire as "the same as the dialogue about a walk up the street, for example, which becomes no more than the object of mere conversation with friends in a bar. In this case, people are not necessarily engaged in a search for the delimitation of a knowable object."² In other words, the dialogue as conversation about individuals' lived experiences does not truly constitute dialogue. The appropriation of the notion of dialogical teaching as a process of sharing experiences creates a situation in which teaching is often reduced to a form of group therapy that focuses on the psychology of the individual. Although some educators may claim that this process creates a pedagogical comfort zone, in my view it does little beyond making the oppressed feel good about their own sense of victimization. Simply put, I do not think that the sharing of experiences should be understood in psychological terms only. It invariably requires a political and ideological analysis as well. For example, the very notion of comfort zone implies privilege, thus it cannot be created outside those social and political factors that shape and maintain privilege for certain groups of people, while other groups are interminably locked out of any sort of privilege. That is, the sharing of experiences must always be understood within the social praxis that entails both reflection and political action. Such action must view dialogue as a process of learning and knowing that interrogates the power asymmetries that shape privilege in the first place, to be followed by a political project with the objective of dismantling oppressive structures and mechanisms prevalent in our society.

The insightful letters to Paulo included in *Dear Paulo: Letters from Those Who Dare Teach* demonstrate that dialogue must not necessarily require verbalization and coordinated turn-taking. These inspirational teachers have been engaged with Freire's leading ideas for many years, and their copious journals exemplify both the breadth and depth of intellectual engagement with Freire's many pedagogical proposals. In fact, these educators embrace Freire's dialogical teaching by taking up letter writing as another form of dialogical engagement expertly used by Freire to apprehend an object of knowledge where important educational practices are theorized and where the distance between theory and practice is significantly diminished. Freire brilliantly used letter writing throughout his career to revisit his major pedagogical proposals and to maintain conviviality with educators as they are challenged to engage in "theoretical reflections and practical strategies [that] can demonstrate the potential of teachers to be what Henry Giroux (1988) has called 'transformative intellectuals.'"

Dear Paulo: Letters from Those Who Dare Teach honors Freire in another significant manner by becoming an example, par excellence, of what it means to dismantle academic borders designed to produce an arrogant elitism that excludes, dismisses, and devalues other bodies of knowledge. That is, this excellent text unmasks the false division between theory and practice, teachers and researchers, and so-called high knowledge versus low knowledge. The authors of these letters to Paulo teach in multiple settings that range from universities to K–12 classrooms. They demystify the belief that research and books are written only by researchers and university professors and that community and K–12 teachers are merely consumers of knowledge—knowledge generated by the so-called experts in the field. In addition, these authors also honor Paulo by adhering to his constant call for humility, for, without humility, our progressive discourse about social justice, equity, and equality is summarily undermined by arrogance, false belief in stardom, and elitism that is a form of hiding ignorance. Freire succinctly emphasized the importance of humility when he stated:

> My respect as a teacher for the student, for his/her curiosity and fear that I ought to curtail or inhibit by inappropriate gestures and attitudes, demands of me the cultivation of humility and tolerance. How can I respect the curiosity of the students if, lacking genuine humility and a convinced understanding of the role of the unknown in the process of reaching the known, I am afraid of revealing my own ignorance? How can I consider myself to be an educator, especially in the context of open-minded and enlightened teaching practice, if I cannot learn to live—whether it cost little or much—with what is different? How can I be an educator if I do not develop in myself a caring and loving attitude toward the student, which is indispensable on the part of one who is committed to teaching and to the education process itself?[3]

Notes

1. Paulo Freire and Donaldo Macedo, "A Dialogue: Culture, Language, and Race," *Harvard Educational Review* 65, no. 3 (fall 95): 377–402.

2. Ibid.

3. Paulo Freire, *Pedagogy of Freedom: Ethics, Democracy, and Civic Courage* (Boulder, CO: Rowman and Littlefield Publishers, 1998), p. 65.

Introduction

Paulo Freire was timeless. That is why when he died suddenly on May 2, 1997, not only his family and close friends and colleagues but also his admirers all over the world found his death difficult to accept. While it is true that he was seventy-five years old, his was a young seventy-five, a seventy-five years full of love and hope and life. In one of the final books he wrote shortly before his death, Paulo Freire characterized age not by chronology but rather by the quality of one's life:

> The main criterion for evaluating age, youth, and old age cannot be that of the calendar. No one is old just because he or she was born a long time ago or young just because he or she was born a short time ago. People are old or young much more as a function of how they think of the world, the availability they have for curiously giving themselves to knowledge (Freire, 2004a, p. 72).

Judging Paulo's seventy-five years in this way, one must conclude that he was very young indeed. Thus his death, although inevitable, was nevertheless a jarring and cruel jolt because the world was not yet ready to see him go.

Paulo Freire loved and lived life deeply and powerfully, and this intensity is visible in his writing and in the international work to which he dedicated himself for more than half a century. A dozen years before his death, he had reflected on his love for life:

> I like to live, to live my life intensely. I am the type of person who loves his life passionately. Of course, someday I will die, but I have the impression that when I die, I will die intensely as well. I will die experimenting with myself intensely. For this reason I am going to die with an immense longing for life, since this is the way I have been living (Freire, 1985b, p. 195).

This "immense longing for life" is one of the greatest legacies left by Paulo Freire, a living legacy that is carried on not only by university academics who follow his work but also by teachers who have been influenced by it. My hope is that you will see this same level of intensity and passion through the letters written to Paulo in this book, letters full of love, fear, uncertainty, joy, and commitment.

The Genesis of This Book

Paulo Freire was a constant companion throughout my time at the University of Massachusetts, first when I became a doctoral student in 1975 and later as a faculty member from 1980 to 2005 in what was subsequently to become the Language, Literacy, and Culture (LLC) Program in the School of Education. When I arrived as a doctoral student, the School of Education was an exciting place, buzzing with energy and experimenting with many different ways to prepare progressive teachers and other educational leaders. It is no accident that I was introduced to Paulo Freire at this time. His ideas, so new to me then, were pervasive throughout the School of Education, whether through courses in language, international education, multicultural education, or in the many conferences, symposia, and other stimulating activities available to students and faculty. As a doctoral student, I read *Pedagogy of the Oppressed* (1970) and anything else written by Paulo that I could get my hands on. His ideas had a profound impact on my thinking, on my graduate studies, and, ultimately, on how I envisioned the life I would carve out for myself in the years ahead.

In 1980, when I became an assistant professor, Paulo Freire was invited by Dean Mario Fantini of the School of Education and Professor Peter Park, then a faculty member in the Sociology Department and a close colleague of Paulo's, to be a Visiting Scholar with a joint appointment in Education and Sociology. Elza, Paulo's first wife, accompanied him on this and subsequent visits, and they resided in a small apartment on campus. This first month-long visit from early January until the very end of the month, when most classes began, presented a unique opportunity for graduate students and faculty to get to know and interact with him personally. As one of the organizers of the event for the School of Education, I helped schedule Paulo's time with seminars, public events, community visits, and a few classes during the final week of his visit. We also arranged for meals and other informal activities, usually with students, faculty, or community members, and Elza frequently attended those and other events with him. This initial trip was followed by three or four visits over several winters at the University of Massachusetts in the early 1980s. It was only after the death of Elza, which left Paulo heartbroken, that he was unable to return to our campus for a number of years. After marrying Nita, his second wife, Paulo once again came to life, resuming a full and exhausting schedule and traveling all over the word.

From the beginning of my tenure as a faculty member, *Pedagogy of the Oppressed* (1970) was a required text in some of my teacher education classes. Even though most of my students were master's and doctoral students—many already classroom teachers and others preparing for the profession—some found the text difficult to understand; others questioned why I would choose this book rather than a more conventional textbook. After all, the courses I taught focused on multicultural education, and that term was never even used by Paulo in any of his writings. Yet it was clear to me that his philosophy was profoundly multicultural in that it focused on equality, freedom, hope, and critical pedagogy. It was for those reasons that I chose Freire's books as foundational texts.

Given the students' difficulty with the text, and because I thought it was important to enter into critical dialogue together about Freire's ideas, I decided early on to use a letter format to have students reflect on their reading of Paulo's work. As a result, one of the course assignments was to write a "Dear Paulo" letter in their journals after they had completed their readings. I thought that doing so would personalize Paulo and allow students to "talk" with him directly about their reactions to his text, at the same time helping them clarify their own ideas about teaching and learning, and about the nature of education in general. I wanted them to see Paulo Freire as a person, not as a distant academic with no understanding of the classroom context. Once, after he had been to the campus the previous winter, I even mailed my students' letters to Paulo, who by then was back in Brazil after having been in exile for sixteen years.

When in the 1980s I started asking them to write a "Dear Paulo" letter, most of my students were keeping handwritten journals. Some came to me with coffee and food stains, telltale signs of early-morning or late-night entries. The letters were often moving and heartfelt; some were laudatory, others questioning or critical. They usually related Paulo's words to their own classrooms and contexts, trying to puzzle through how a pedagogy developed among peasants in Brazil might help them in their urban, rural, or suburban U.S. contexts. Later, in the late 1990s, I substituted *Teachers as Cultural Workers: Letters to Those Who Dare Teach* (1998c) as the required text, since it was a book directed specifically to teachers. No matter what they said, and whether or not they agreed with him, the students invariably revealed how much, in reading and rereading the text and then writing about it, they had learned in the process. It was a transformative activity for some students, and for me it was a joy to see how they connected Paulo Freire's words to their emergent ideas about education and their practices in teaching.

In late 1999, in my twice-yearly ritual of reading the "Letters to Paulo" in students' journals (by now, most were typed directly on computers), I read the letter written by Mary Cowhey, a new first- and second-grade teacher in Northampton, Massachusetts. Mary had been a community organizer for fourteen years before deciding to enter teaching, which she saw as a more hopeful profession. She was, and still is, fiercely committed to teaching, to her students and their families, and to social justice. Her letter was beautiful and eloquent, insightful in its interpretation of Paulo Freire's ideas for her specific classroom context, something he would have loved. It was while reading it that a "Dear Paulo" book occurred to me. What more fitting tribute to Paulo's legacy, I thought, than a collection of letters from teachers—novices and veterans, teachers of children and of adults, of various experiences and sociocultural realities? The epistolary genre was, after all, one of Paulo's favorite and most common forms of communicating complex ideas in a personal way, beginning with *Pedagogy in Process: Letters from Guinea-Bissau* (1978), and continuing with *Letters to Cristina: Reflections on My Life and Work* (1996), *Teachers as Cultural Workers: Letters to Those Who Dare Teach* (1998c), *Pedagogy of Indignation* (2004b), and the letter to North American teachers in Ira Shor's *Freire for the Classroom* (1987). Paulo Freire's "talking books" (Freire and Macedo, 1987; Shor and Freire, 1987) and articles (Freire and Macedo, 1995; Freire and Macedo, 1997) offered another model of constructing knowledge from dialogue and study, a key objective I had for my students.

That was the genesis of this book.

Why Letters to Paulo? Why Now?

Sharing letters that teachers have written to Paulo Freire is not simply a private endeavor, however. Our world needs Paulo Freire now more than ever, and the sociopolitical context in which we find ourselves at the moment demands that we reread and converse with him. Thus reasons beyond personal experience make *Dear Paulo* for me a worthwhile, and even necessary, project. Given the widespread denigration and disrespect that teachers face in many nations around the globe, a book celebrating educators' theoretical reflections and progressive practical strategies can demonstrate the potential of teachers to be what Henry Giroux (1988) has called "transformative intellectuals."

Yet it is becoming increasingly difficult to be a progressive educator, much less a "transformative intellectual," not only in the United States but also in many other countries. A glaring example: right-wing neoliberal and neoconservative ideologies have had a powerful and negative impact on public education internationally. The new right, according to Michael Apple (2006), is not a unitary force, but rather a coalition of sometimes strange bedfellows. It includes neoliberals (defined by Apple as "capitalism with the gloves off," p. 15), who believe in a weak state and view the world through a market lens, defining freedom as little more than individual choice; neoconservatives, who believe in a strong state and tend to hold a vision of an idyllic past to which they yearn to return; and religious fundamentalists, who want to bring God (or, more accurately, *their* version of God) into public institutions. Together, this amalgam of ideologies forms the "new right," or what Apple calls "conservative modernization" (p. 4). A growing standardization, bureaucratization, and privatization define the international sociopolitical context.

There are numerous examples of how neoliberal and neoconservative policies have impeded progress in public education, particularly as such policies relate to social justice, or its lack thereof. In the United States, the education reform movement that began in 1983 after the publication of *A Nation at Risk* has been backed by a broad coalition of conservatives and liberals, although their reasons for supporting reform are often at odds. Many liberals, for instance, are sincerely concerned about the long-term and seemingly intractable inequality in learning outcomes for the most vulnerable and marginalized students, particularly students of color and those who live in poverty. A key component of the articulated rationale for high-stakes testing, for example, has been a demand for high standards and accountability for all students, regardless of race, ethnicity, social class, or other differences. Conservatives and others representing business interests, on the other hand, while ostensibly supporting this goal, often favor the privatization of education, including vouchers and other schemes that would eventually wipe out public schools.

One result of the educational reform movement was the No Child Left Behind (NCLB) law, a law characterized primarily by a rigid definition of "accountability," the blaming of students and teachers for school failure, and a string of high-stakes tests to which students are subjected throughout their educational careers. The law, in fact, has had an effect opposite to its purported goal of equality of educational outcomes: dropout rates among the poor and among black and Latino students have increased, and both pedagogical approaches and curriculum choices have been constricted, especially in classrooms serving the most educationally disadvantaged students (Meier and Wood, 2004; Nichols and Berliner, 2005; Johnson and Salz, 2008). As a result, educational achievement, originally espoused as the goal of NCLB, has not improved achievement measurably. In the end, what ostensibly began as a policy to improve educational outcomes has become discriminatory in practice.

The No Child Left Behind legislation is a perfect amalgam of neoliberal and neoconservative agendas in the United States, but our nation is not alone in forging such policies. Australia is another nation where the reversal of progressive and inclusive educational policies has been felt. There, the introduction of community languages in urban secondary schools in the 1980s had very positive effects not only at the school level but also in the community (Kalantzis, Cope, Noble, and Poynting, 1990). Notwithstanding that success, many of these programs were dismantled in the 1990s when neoliberal educational policies began to be implemented in the country (Castles, 2004). England, New Zealand, Canada, Australia, and other nations have also felt the effects of the rigid accountability agenda (Apple, 2006; Gillborn and Youdell, 2000). And in Brazil, Freire's own country, educational policies have continued to privilege the elite at the expense of blacks, indigenous people, and others marginalized by poverty (Gonçalves e Silva, 2004). It would seem, then, that because education throughout the globe has experienced similar agendas, the reflections in *Dear Paulo* speak to teachers and other educators throughout the world. In writing of Freire that "his ideas are in the world and from the world," Martin Carnoy (2004, p. 8) captures the appeal of Freire's work for teachers in many different contexts. Even though he was first and foremost Brazilian. Paulo Freire is, according to Carnoy, "an anomaly among educators because he is truly international" (p. 8).

The situation in which teachers and other educators around the world currently find themselves is precarious indeed. Subjected to privatization and rigid accountability agendas, de-skilled and robbed of autonomy, teachers need the voice of hope and critique offered by Paulo Freire. Ira Shor, writing near the beginning of the current reform movement in the 1980s, predicted: "The mechanical, authoritarian remedies offered by the new reformers cannot solve the current dilemmas in education" (Shor, 1987, p. 1). Instead, it will take serious reflection and concerted action to tackle these problems. For Paulo Freire, serious study meant, first of all, a deep connection with the text. In his "talking book" with Ira Shor, Paulo mused, "I say that reading is not just *to walk on the words*, and it is not *flying* over the words either. Reading is re-writing what we are reading" (Shor and Freire, 1987, p. 10). In the spirit of Paulo Freire, I invite readers to engage with this text, to listen to the teachers and academics who wrote the letters, and to dialogue with them.

Organization of the Book

Dear Paulo: Letters from Those Who Dare Teach consists of the reflections of classroom teachers, teacher educators, and other academics relating to Paulo Freire's writings, specifically *Pedagogy of the Oppressed* (1970) and *Teachers as Cultural Workers: Letters to Those Who Dare Teach* (1998c), from which it borrows its subtitle. In it, teachers enter in dialogue with Paulo, debate his ideas with him, share their own teaching stories, and suggest classroom applications for these ideas. They also let him know how his words and ideas have changed them, as people and as teachers.

After making the decision to begin work on the book a number of years ago, I contacted former students and also collected letters from students in subsequent years. Most of those who had written the first letters were by now teachers, and many were enthusiastic about sharing their reactions with other teachers and readers. Some who had been doctoral students were now teacher educators. It was at this point that I decided to expand my original idea of including only letters from classroom teachers to also include teacher educators and Freirean scholars, because I thought that their letters would illustrate the range of Paulo Freire's thinking and the tremendous influence he has had throughout education, from K-12 and community settings to higher education and teacher preparation.

The names of some of the letter writers will be known to you; most will not. They represent a wide range of educators and intellectuals, from first-time teachers to seasoned academics. They teach students from preschool to graduate school in urban, suburban, and rural schools, in small liberal arts colleges and large universities, and in community settings. They teach elementary, middle, and high school, and their subject matters range from English to art to science, and more. They teach students living in poverty, privileged students, and troubled youth, as well as first-time and veteran teachers. Their ages range from twenty-two to octogenarians. They represent a vast spectrum of the cultural and ethnic diversity in the United States and the world. They are, in a word, an amalgamation of the teachers to be found in many nations.

Following this introduction, the body of the book commences, as it should, with Mary Cowhey's letter, the one that inspired the idea for the book in the first place. In her letter, Mary reflects on all of the major themes addressed by Freire in his letters in *Teachers as Cultural Workers* (1998c). Mary Cowhey's letter is followed by a letter from Mary Ginley, a teacher who has lived through thirty-nine "first days." Following these two initial letters are eight sections related to themes that characterized Freire's work throughout his career. These include courage, love, praxis, and freedom, among others. The nearly seventy letters in the text are grouped according to these nine themes, although, naturally, many of the letters encompass not only one theme but many of the ideas that Freire considered in his work. I introduce each part, along with a brief description of the letters in the section. The book concludes with final reflections that highlight some of the issues addressed in the letters, focusing especially on such questions as these: What does it mean to use Paulo Freire's work in courses with teachers? How can his ideas help classroom teachers in the United

States think about and transform their work? How can the insights in this book—which run dramatically counter to the current discourse that views education as a market enterprise—position education as a tool to promote the public good?

Acknowledgments

When I first contacted Donaldo Macedo with the idea for this book, he was immediately enthusiastic. I am thrilled to have the book included in his Paulo Freire series, and I thank him for his help and encouragement throughout the process. Equally supportive from the moment he heard about the book was Dean Birkenkamp, President and Publisher of Paradigm Publishers. He has been, it seems to me, even more excited about it than I, and he has been patient and understanding about the many delays in getting it to production. Beth Davis, Education Editor, has been delightful to work with and has given me helpful advice as we saw the book to fruition. I also want to thank Carol Smith, Senior Production Editor, and Sharon Daugherty, Cover Design Coordinator, for their great support and flexibility throughout the final phases of the prodcution of this book. I thank them all for making the process such a satisfying one.

Dear Paulo: Letters from Those Who Dare Teach became a much more extended project than I or anyone else could have imagined. Although I received a contract for the book in 2004, I was unable to proceed with it because of many complications, including a bout with cancer and preparations for my retirement from the University of Massachusetts, both of which have now been completed. Donaldo, Dean, and Beth were champions of the book, and of me, throughout, and I am sincerely appreciative of them all.

I extend my heartfelt gratitude to the many teachers and academics whose letters are included in this book. Despite their busy and complicated lives, some took the time to search for the letters they had written years before, while others crafted letters from scratch. Their insights and reflections will, I am certain, enlighten, entertain, and push readers to think critically about education and about how Paulo Freire's ideas can be instrumental no matter their context or experience. I also want to thank Nita Freire for her endorsement of the book. Her words mean a great deal to me, especially knowing the close and collaborative relationship she had with Paulo.

Finally, my deepest gratitude goes, of course, to Paulo Freire. Although I was familiar with much of his work, editing this book gave me the opportunity to read his newer work, and, in a sense, to sit down and dialogue with him once again. Through his books we talked, agreed, disagreed, and talked some more. Whether in my study at home, on vacation, or on airplanes or trains as I traveled about the country and beyond, Paulo has been with me for a number of years since I began this book. Our conversations have made me realize anew how profound his influence has been on my life.

Part 1: Beginnings

We must dare so that we can continue to teach for a long time under conditions that we know well: low salaries, lack of respect, and the ever-present risk of becoming prey to cynicism. We must dare to learn how to dare in order to say no to the bureaucratization of the mind to which we are exposed every day.
—Paulo Freire, *Teachers as Cultural Workers: Letters to Those Who Dare Teach* (1998c), p. 3.

Whether we teach preschoolers or doctoral students, the word *beginnings* brings forth images of the first days of school: backpacks and books, crayons and art supplies, exciting ideas and new discoveries, falling leaves and crisp weather. These are, of course, idealized images that are sometimes far from the reality of the first days experienced by many. For some, the first day of school means returning to decrepit schools with no materials, little excitement, and ill-prepared teachers. For older students, it may mean boring lectures and what Paulo Freire (1970) called "banking education." In spite of the reality, the idea of *beginnings* is enticing because it promises hope in the face of the cynicism to which Freire refers above. It is fitting, then, that we begin this book of letters to Paulo with letters about beginnings, not only the first day of school but also the first day of teaching and a new way to "read the class."

In her letter, Mary Cowhey responds to the themes of each of the letters Paulo wrote in his book *Teachers as Cultural Workers: Letters to Those Who Dare Teach* (1998c). She illustrates, through her musings and stories, what it means to "read the class," and, in the end, what it means to be a critical and loving teacher of young children. Following is Mary Ginley's poignant reflection of her "thirty-nine first days," reflections that underline her commitment to teaching after so many years.

∾

⮞ *Mary Cowhey* ⮜

Reading the Class

There is something mysterious, something called "vocation," that
explains why so many teachers persist with so much devotion in spite
of the immoral salaries they receive. Not only do they remain, but they
fulfill as best they can their commitment. And do it with love.
— Paulo Freire, *Pedagogy of Freedom* (1998a), p. 126.

October 17, 2000
Dear Paulo,

When I first read "I do not have the truth; this book contains truths, and my dream is that those truths challenge or question the positions taken by the book's readers" (Freire, 1998c, p. 47), I thought about a question my class of first- and second-graders struggled with for most of last year: "How do you find the truth in history?" It started with a discussion about Columbus after I had read two different books, one portraying Columbus in pure, simple, and heroic terms and the other portraying him in a less flattering light as an invader and thief. When I asked students which version they thought was more accurate, they chose the latter, a book entitled *Encounter* by Jane Yolen (1992). When I asked them how they could find out which was truer, they said they could read more books.

I told them that most of the other books about Columbus in our school library would fall into the heroic category. Would that convince them that the heroic one was true? They said they would ask a teacher. I told them that from now until they graduate, they will have at least ten more teachers. What if all of the other teachers said Columbus was a hero? Would that make me a liar? They said no, that other teachers might not know this other story.

Eventually we got around to the idea of primary source documents, including journals, letters, and eyewitness accounts, but then a student raised the idea that people could lie in their letters or journals. She suggested interviewing people who were there, but another student pointed out that they could change the story to make themselves look better in it, because no one wants to look bad (this was before they realized that the people they wanted to interview were long dead).

They puzzled over this question all year, returning to it again and again. Many times I was tempted to cut to the chase, to say, "Look, kids, it's all about multiple perspectives," but I bit my tongue and let them sort it out. Eventually, Julius Lester, a well-known writer of children's books and professor at the local university, came to visit us, and the students asked him about this question. He said, "There are many truths in history." He talked with the students about different ways he pursues the truth in his historical writing.

Paulo, I like how you encourage questioning. As a child I was a good and well-behaved student. The one thing I consistently got into trouble for was questioning and contradicting my teachers. My father was a teacher, and he thought that this behavioral flaw of mine was particularly outrageous. Luckily, the questioning voice was never successfully silenced. I liked the quotation from the foreword: "What? Why? How? To what end? For whom? Against whom? By whom? In favor of whom? In favor of what? These are questions that provoke literacy learners to focus on the substantiveness of things, that is, their reasons for being, their purpose, the way they are done, and so on" (Macedo and Araújo Freire, quoted in the foreword, p. xi).

One of my very best questioners is a second-grader named Jimmy. Jimmy is great at philosophy and logic; he also has a reading disability. He has such a passion for learning that he single-handedly started a fad within our classroom culture to "do research."

Jimmy came up to me breathlessly on the first day of school this year, saying, "Ms. Cowhey, you know how last year in first grade we learned there was slavery and there was even slavery in Puerto Rico? Well, I was in Puerto Rico this summer to visit my cousins and I got a coin, a real old Spanish coin, like from the time of slavery, and I lost it in my house, but I'm gonna find it and bring it in so you could see it because I think maybe someone coulda used it to buy a slave in them days!"

A few days later Jimmy found the coin (a museum facsimile) and brought it in. Our student teacher brought him to the library, and he took out a couple of books on coins. I observed how he interested other students in the project, inviting them to sit beside him as he studied the pictures. When he found one that resembled his coin, he asked the partner to read the caption to him. He listened closely, then continued studying in this manner.

The next day I observed two first-grade girls (who had been hiding out in the classroom library playing house during quiet reading time the day before) carrying a huge stack of nature encyclopedias to their table. Michelle dropped her books with a dramatic sigh. "Oh, I have so much *research* to do! Look at all these books I have to read!" Her friend, Angelina, dropped her stack and imitated the sigh. "Me too! We have to do so much *research* today. Well, we better get started!"

Another boy brought in two foreign coins and requested to go to the library to get more books with which to research his coins. Three other students joined him. In the midst of this, there was Jimmy the trend-setter, dutifully replacing the forty-year-old set of nature encyclopedias on the shelves in numerical order, scouring the class for missing volumes like a worried shepherd, or squinting through a magnifying glass to count the legs on an insect a classmate had brought in from the playground and flipping through the pages of a Peterson's field guide to identify it.

Reading about the first day of school, I thought back to my very first day of teaching a first day of school. I remember I showed my lesson plans to a more experienced first-grade teacher for her advice. She glanced at my plan, which included a morning meeting, a math lesson to introduce materials and assess students, a read-aloud of *Santiago,* a shared reading of *I Went Walking* with a dramatization and introduction of the pocket chart, an introduction of the ABC center, reading aloud a chapter of *My Father's Dragon* after lunch, a discussion of student goals, a choice time period after gym, and some quiet reading at the end of the day. She cackled and said, "You're not really thinking you're going to *teach* the first day, are you?" I was so mad and embarrassed that I wanted to cry. My face burned. She walked out of my room, still laughing at me. I went back to taping up Romare Bearden artwork from an old calendar over the coat hooks and thought, "Damn straight I'm going to teach the first day!"

At the end of the first day, I was in tears. I loved my class and had, in fact, begun to teach, but I had one student who troubled me greatly. From my home visit a couple of days earlier, I knew that he had been abused as a young child and had been placed in foster care and then adopted earlier that summer. He was a bright boy who moved and talked constantly. He was physically very aggressive with other children and demanded constant attention. I felt overwhelmed by my inability to work with this child. I thought, "They knew this boy in kindergarten. They know I am a brand new, inexperienced teacher. Why did they assign such a challenging student to a novice?" I quickly learned that it wasn't an accident or an oversight. The most difficult students had been deliberately placed in the classes of the two new first-grade teachers, neither of whom was involved in making the class assignments.

The principal observed and was very concerned but didn't want to force the issue with the other teachers by reassigning him to another class where the teachers were clearly reluctant to accept him. The guidance counselor told me that she was sure it would work out. I asked his adoptive parents, two moms, to come in so we could talk. At first his parents said they thought he would do better if he sat at his own desk, in rows, and did work sheets. I said that I didn't teach that way. I explained that while he was strong in many academic areas, he was challenged in his social development, the area that would present his greatest challenge in first grade. One of his mothers was skeptical about my teaching methods but began volunteering in my classroom one day a week. That helped, having another adult in the classroom and having her make her own conclusions about the effectiveness of my teaching methods. I quickly recruited more parent volunteers. We worked on some behavior modification and some classroom adaptations. The boy flourished in the class. At the end of first grade, his mother was concerned about his class placement for second grade. I asked her what she would do. She said, "I'm going to recommend to the principal that you loop up to second grade." I was shocked, but she was serious. I began teaching the multiage looping model the next year [n.b.: "looping" means that a teacher goes up to the next grade with her students], with this wonderful, challenging boy again.

When I read "The best is to tell the learners, in a demonstration of being human and limited, how one feels at the time. It is to speak to them about the very right to fear, which cannot be denied to the educator. Teachers have as much right to fear as the learners do" (Freire, 1998c, p. 48), I thought about the first day of school this year.

Sweet little Lucia, a five-year-old first-grader, raised her hand during the morning meeting and said, looking around at everyone, "I feel kind of scared." Spontaneously, the other students and I began to share how we were feeling at that moment: nervous, excited, apprehensive. Of course, I hadn't read this letter at the time, but perhaps that exchange, which came about so naturally, illustrates your statement: "The fear of performing on that first day of class … is completely natural" (ibid.).

In my class, I have made it a practice to discuss philosophy. In our first philosophical discussion of the year, regarding the topic of bravery, I asked students if they thought there could be a person who was never afraid. Some students paused to consider this, but Binh shot his hand up quickly. He said yes. I asked him who was never afraid.

"You, teacher, you are never afraid!"

I laughed and said, "Me? I am often brave, but I still get afraid sometimes."

Binh looked shocked. "You? What are you afraid of, teacher?"

I paused, as my mind flooded with the many fears that haunt me, still vivid memories of violent, frightening times, scrambling to think which one of my many fears would be tame enough to share. (Paulo, what a perfect time that would have been to talk about my first-day fears!) I quickly decided to share my fear of hurricanes, a fear that began when my family got caught in a hurricane while camping. We hadn't received notice to evacuate until the storm was upon us. The story sparked a torrent of other storm fear stories, mostly related to the terrible storm we had had that year on June 2, which the children still called "the Friday storm."

More recently we have read aloud *Life Doesn't Frighten Me* by Maya Angelou (1996). It had been a gift to Fergus, a second-grader, in celebration of the end of his nearly three-year chemotherapy treatment. We discussed Maya Angelou's tough talk in the verses and the scary illustrations by Jean-Michel Basquiat. The students discussed the idea that Angelou couldn't really *not* be frightened by ghosts and big dogs and sounds in the hall because they *are* really scary things. They asked a lot of questions: Then why does she say they don't frighten her? Does she lie on purpose? Is she lying to us? To fool us? Or is she lying to herself? Is she trying to fool herself into feeling brave so she can face those scary things? Then they all thought of their scariest image and illustrated it for a *Life Doesn't Frighten Me* book of our own. At one point I wondered if this was too scary for the children. I have fixed your line— "In reality, facing a fear is the first step in turning it into courage" (Freire, 1998c, p. 48)—on a post-it and stuck that to the lesson I do on fear. It must be said.

You write about reading the class. I guess I jump the gun. Part of how I address my fear about the first day of school is to face it, as you suggest. I spend the week before the first day of school visiting my students' homes, meeting the students and their families. I can't wait for the first day of school, and so I go out and read the students in their neighborhoods, their homes, with their families. That way I know where my students are coming from, literally. I know who their people are. I know the names their families call them. I know what they are proud of and what worries them. I begin to trust these families. My students and their families begin to trust me.

I find it striking that some students are very much the same people at home with their families and in the classroom. Other students are like two different people. Seeing that contrast in some of them reminds me how hard I must work to begin to know them. Today, about six weeks into the school year, during a philosophy discussion, was the first time that I saw Belicia show her sharp, bright, argumentative edge. I'd been impressed by that side of her when she was squeezed on an old sofa between her mother and older brother the afternoon I visited them at the shelter, responding boldly to her brother's challenges. I felt so happy that day when I saw her assert herself this way, her feisty mother's daughter. I felt heartened that she would fight for her education, in the same way her mother had.

You wrote: "Only as learners recognize themselves democratically and see that their right to say 'I be' is respected will they become able to learn the dominant grammatical reasons why they should say 'I am'" (ibid., p. 49). Today, after a reading of *Let's Make Rabbits* (1982) by Leo Lionni, we were discussing what it means to be real, or not real, and alive, and whether all real things have shadows, and other ideas. Belicia said, "Chalk is real. A piece of chalk has a shadow, but chalk writing on the board, it doesn't have no shadow."

John, a native English speaker, began by pointing to Belicia's words on the chart paper and quoting, "It doesn't have no shadow." At first, I thought John was going to criticize her for using nonstandard English. I was still writing his words on the chart paper and thinking whether he would understand an explanation of the Spanish double negative, when they resolved it themselves. John continued, "That's a double negative, so it really means, 'It has a shadow.'" He wasn't commenting on the nonstandard English but rather on the precision of the language of her argument, in which they were both seriously engaged.

Belicia self-corrected in a heartbeat. "It doesn't have a shadow," she said firmly, triumphantly, making her point clearly. John nodded and said, "Then I agree with you."

You wrote: "The affective existence of countless children is rotten, almost crushed, like broken glass" (Freire, 1998c, p. 50). I could not read that line without thinking of Elonzo, a student in my class during my first year of teaching. I knew that there was a good deal of domestic violence in his home. In fact, a couple of weeks earlier, he had told me about a particularly violent rampage by his father that included smashing a mirror. Elonzo had lately been showing even less attention than usual, frequently disrupting the class. I had tried to be understanding, but I was losing patience. It was a warm day in the spring, and Elonzo had on a short-sleeved tee shirt. My aide noticed a cut on his arm that was red and swollen; it seemed infected. She brought him to the nurse, who examined it, then called his mother to take him to the doctor. The next day, Elonzo came in with several stitches in his arm.

Apparently shards of glass from the broken mirror had fallen into Elonzo's bed, where he had run to hide during the fight. As he quickly slid under the covers, a shard had been driven deep into the flesh of his arm. For weeks Elonzo bore this unspeakable pain of broken glass under his skin without complaint, until his short-sleeved shirt revealed the angry infection. The doctor had to cut open the wound, remove the glass, clean it, and stitch it closed. I had been distracted and irritated by Elonzo's disruptive behavior, when Elonzo's existence was shattered, like broken glass. And then I think, *This is not a ghetto.* Imagine if I were teaching in the neighborhoods of Trenton or Philadelphia, where I used to organize, or in Holyoke or Springfield, larger cities near here? How many more children are there whose affective existence is like broken glass?

"Teachers must not be afraid of tenderness, must not close themselves to the affective neediness of beings who are indeed kept from being" (ibid.). I am thinking of Raymundo, the angriest student I ever had. After surviving a traumatic standoff between his mother and the police, he was placed in a foster home that maintained his body but gave him not an ounce of love. I was pregnant that year, and as the months progressed, Raymundo and I developed a strong rapport. He inadvertently called me "Mommy" more than other students and frequently asked why we couldn't come to school on weekends. I finally stopped teaching a week after my due date passed. On that last day before I left for maternity leave, Raymundo wrote me a story. It was written in the present tense, "like I'm right there with you and a video camera," about what would happen when I would go into labor and have my baby. His story detailed how my husband would drive me to the hospital, how I would have pains and lie on a table and the baby would "pop out." The last line of the story was: "and then we all go home." I cried when he read it to me. I hugged him and asked how he was feeling. He said, "I'm happy, mad, and sad."

I had given Raymundo my love, and I was afraid it hadn't been enough. Thank God that Karen, my substitute teacher, a class parent who had been volunteering in the class all year, transformed her love into action. Raymundo had in fact been very angry at Karen when I left, pushing her out of my chair, shouting, "You're not Ms. Cowhey! Get out of here!" Karen was a foster parent. She got a phone call at the end of the school year, asking if she could take a boy matching Raymundo's description for placement. Karen couldn't, but she recruited a gay couple she was friends with, and asked if they'd be willing. They considered it carefully, then said that they would be his foster parents and would promise to keep him until he returned to his parents or became available for adoption, in which case they would adopt him and he would never have to go to another foster home again. Raymundo was placed in one more foster home for two weeks while Karen pushed their application for child-specific approval through the bureaucracy. Now, two years later, Raymundo is a very happy and well-loved boy with two dads and a stable home. Karen's tenderness and action allowed Raymundo to be.

When you write "We cannot teach content as if that were all there is" (Freire, 1998c, p. 51), I think, "Yes!" This is why I love teaching! We learn to make sense of the world, and to affect the world. This is what the content is *for.*

In struggle,
Mary

P.S. Paulo, I could write to you all day, but poor Sonia, we must think of her, too. I know she reads all your mail these days, and look how long this is already. I loved your sixth and seventh letters, too, and could go on and on about those as well. Well, perhaps Sonia could bear it if I go on just a *little* longer.

You point out that an education practice in which there is no coherent relationship between what the educators say and do is a disaster. I couldn't agree more. At my undergraduate college, an education professor *lectured* about the importance of cooperative learning. When I started teaching, I was saddened by the way many elementary classrooms replicate the model of individual teachers lecturing, occasionally forcing unwilling students into groups for brief activities. Between my graduate work at UMass, watching the collaboration of the professors in my program, and developing a team teaching model in my school, I feel like I've overcome at least that educational double standard. In my class, students *and* teachers struggle to work in cooperative groups.

We don't just teach how to write a persuasive letter. This week my colleague, Kim Gerould, wrote a letter to the editor about bilingual education that was run as an op-ed piece in our local newspaper, so we shared that in writing workshop. We don't just talk about environmentalism. We take extra trash bags on all of our walking field trips and collect litter as we go. I remember a saying from the African-American community that I organized in Philadelphia: "Yeah? I'm from Missouri." I quickly learned that Missouri is the "Show Me" state. Hip people who wouldn't take jive off nobody were ready and willing to challenge the contradiction between saying and doing. I learned that lesson pretty fast.

Last week I observed a lesson by a student teacher who was substituting for her cooperating teacher. I could sense her growing frustration, the increasing volume of her voice as she struggled to get students to listen to her. I thought of this seventh letter. I knew that the student teacher wanted to be heard by her students. She floundered between lawless permissiveness and manipulative authoritarianism. That is often so hard.

In our classroom as a whole, we struggle with the issue of management. We have thirty-one students, more than other classes in our school, but far fewer than classes in other cities. We have about seven students with attention deficit disorder and/or hyperactivity (one medicated) and/or severe emotional needs. Ours is a challenging group. After reading your letter, it struck me that some of our students were "interrupted in their right to speak, to have a voice, to say their critical discourse," and that we, as teachers, need to help them "defend that right, which after all, is also the right to act" (ibid., p. 65). I thought hard about this problem, about how we can manage ourselves, our space, our students under a framework of democratic radicalism. I met with Kim Gerould and Kathy Malynoski, my co-teachers, and we established a framework of expectations for the children: "The disposition to listen to others, not as a favor but as a duty, and to respect them" (ibid., p. 66). We decided on a detailed plan of changes and improvements. Kathy now calls it "the new regime." I'll let you know how it goes. For now, I dream of "a school in which we talk to and with the learners so that, hearing them, we can be heard by them as well" (ibid., p. 68).

Mary Ginley

Thirty-Nine First Days

*From the very first day of class, [teachers] must demonstrate to students
the importance of imagination for life. ... The imagination that
takes us to possible and impossible dreams is always necessary.*
—Paulo Freire, *Teachers as Cultural Workers: Letters
to Those Who Dare Teach* (1998c), p. 51.

August 24, 2007

Dear Paulo,

Sonia, my mentor, my teacher, my friend, says that "once you know, you can never not know again." Knowing is hard, but I suppose that not knowing is even worse. I mean, if I really became a teacher to make a difference, then I need to know how to do that and not just pretend that showing up and getting kids ready to pass state tests is good enough.

I'm a fifth-grade teacher, and I've been teaching for a long time. This is my thirty-ninth year in the classroom. Thirty-nine first days, thirty-nine classes of squirming kids who are excited to be back with their friends but, for the most part, unexcited about getting back to the grueling routine of getting up early, heading off to school before it's barely light, sitting in classrooms with fluorescent lighting dutifully reading what they're told to read, turning to page fifteen in the math book and figuring out what decimals are, and learning about the properties of matter and then heading home to homework and chores. It is so clear that most of them don't want to be here.

A teacher once told me that she spends the first day making sure that the children in front of her know exactly who is in charge and what her expectations are. I told her I spend the first day making sure that they want to come back for the second day, and the third and the fourth and all the rest of the days until they leave me at the end of the year.

It was fairly easy when I taught the little ones. They love school, and all it takes is a hug and a funny story and a team-building game and we're off and running. But with nine-, ten-, eleven-, and twelve-year-olds it's a bit different. They've "been there, done that." Some of them, like my soon-to-be thirteen-year-old fifth-grade student who couldn't get out of third grade until he read at grade level, have been there for a long time. They've done more "read this passage and choose the best answer to the following questions" in their short school career than anyone should do in a lifetime.

And so another year begins. Week one is (no surprise) as terrifying and exhausting as ever. Week one is the one when you get to school more than an hour early every day so you can get seriously organized because it's so nuts. Week one is the one where you crawl home every evening with every bone in your body aching and your throat sore from talking entirely too much. Week one is the one when you get memos from the office wanting assorted lists *now!*—bus lists, free lunch lists, schedules, lists of resource room kids, ESOL kids—lists (by the way) that they *have* in their computer and (I think) might easily access if they hit a few buttons. Don't ask me which buttons ... I'm not the computer expert.

This year's fifth-graders have arrived, twenty of them, fourteen boys and six girls. The girls are vastly outnumbered by (squirrelly) little boys who bounce around and play imaginary games with the animal crackers I give them for snack because no one brings a snack although everyone is starving by 10:30 A.M.—games that involve crushing certain animals and spreading crumbs around the rug.

Yep, it's one of those classes. Jason was expelled two years ago for breaking into the school with his older brother, stealing two laptop computers, and throwing them in the pond because "we were bored." He was only in third grade at the time. He's back.... His dad petitioned the school board to get him back in, and he really *does* hate this "friggin school" with the teachers who "suck." Tommy was the one who, when he was in fourth grade, wanted to see if he could get around the back of the pole on the landing on the staircase and got his head stuck behind the pole. It took three adults greasing his head and the pole and four adults looking on trying not to laugh to get him free. Tom cries at the drop of a hat and freaks out when we have fire drills (yep, I teach fifth grade). So far, I've caught him before his panic gets out of hand and calmed him down before he starts crying and screaming, but one of these days if I'm not vigilant, poor Tom, who is already famous for being a bit weird, is going to go over the edge. Vasiliy, Jack, Ralph, and Fernando are just little boys, the kind of kids who fall off their chairs on what seems to be a schedule and look at me and say, "Huh?" when I ask them a question. When they raise their hands, it's always to ask, "Is it almost time for lunch?" "How long is it till we go to gym?" or "Can I get a drink?"

Tired doesn't even begin to describe how I feel. And just like other years, I think, *I can't do this one more year. I am way too old for this.* But because I've been doing this so long, I know it will get better. I know we'll make it.

We'll make it because I know it isn't *their* job to meet my expectations but *my* job to meet theirs. We'll make it because I know that *I'm* the one who has to find out what they care about, what they worry about, what they wonder about, what they want to know, and help them find the answers to their questions. We'll make it because it is *my* job, not theirs, to show them how smart they are, to show them worlds they never knew existed, and to help them uncover the giftedness within themselves. Like Emily Dickinson, "I dwell in possibility; I open every door. ..."

It happens every year. As they discover how much they can care about a character in a book who's an outcast and a bit strange, they realize that they can care about the real people in their classroom who aren't "cool" and "in." As they figure out unique ways to solve math problems, they realize that they have the power to solve their own problems in unique ways, too. As they find ways to negotiate disputes peacefully in the classroom, they begin to find ways to do it at home and in the neighborhood. And as they begin to see themselves as intelligent, thinking, problem-solving people, they see their options for the future as unlimited. When I ask my kids at the beginning of the year what they want to do when they get out of school, many of them shrug and say, "I dunno … get a job, I guess." By the end of the year, they're talking about being scientists, engineers, teachers, and doctors. A few have decided they'll run for office to change stupid laws like state testing, and the others have promised to work on their campaign and vote for them.

I *know* the kids who are fighting over the limited number of pillows and the kids who look at you blankly when you ask if they brought in their homework and the kids who squirt hand sanitizer on desks and smear it around, and the kids who tell me they HATE the "friggin uniform" and they HATE school and that the teachers here SUCK. All of these kids will eventually decide that they LOVE this friggin school and LOVE this crazy class and don't want to leave. And we'll learn together and laugh together and read some great books and solve problems and, miracle of miracles, we'll become a community of learners.

Thank you, Paulo. If it weren't for you and people like Sonia, I wouldn't know how to get from "school sucks" to "how can I bear to say good-bye to this amazing group of children?" If it weren't for the two of you, I'd most likely be still trying to get them to do what *I* want, instead of trying to figure out what *they* want. If it weren't for the two of you, I might think it was enough to show up and cover the curriculum. Because of the two of you and because I've been teaching for thirty-nine years, I know how this story ends, how this school year will end if I can hang in there.

But, for now, at the beginning of the year, I'm just trying to get through each day. Right now, I hate this friggin school, and I'm not particularly crazy about this class, and frankly, school does suck. It's a good thing I know the end to this story because otherwise, right now, I'd be out there looking for another way to meet the mortgage payments. Instead, I'll leave my house each morning before dawn to meet this group of kids who, already, are among the most important people in my life.

With much gratitude,
Mary Ginley

Part 2: Fear/Courage

Don't let the fear of what is difficult paralyze you.
—Paulo Freire, *Teachers as Cultural Workers: Letters
to Those Who Dare Teach* (1998c), p. 27.

Courage is a topic that Paulo Freire wrote about often. To him, having courage did not mean being fearless, but rather facing one's fear with determination and humility. In *Teachers as Cultural Workers: Letters to Those Who Dare Teach* (1998c), he wrote about many fears: the fear of not comprehending a text, the fear of change, the fear of fighting for our rights, the fear of facing a class for the first time. This last fear especially resonated with some of my students who were just entering the profession, and reading Freire's words filled them with hope and reassurance. Several of their letters are included in this section.

In his "talking book" with Paulo Freire, Ira Shor eloquently summed up the power of fear: "When I speak with teachers, fear is like a damp presence hovering in the room" (Shor and Freire, 1987, p. 54). That "damp presence" was tangible in many of my students' letters to Paulo. Also included in this section are letters from teachers who named their fear of losing their job, or the challenge of facing unmotivated students, or the fear of not knowing enough, or not being able to put into practice all their values and hopes. In these situations, fear is not simply a feeling; it is real, concrete, and palpable. Yet these letters remind us that although fear may be a constant companion in education, courage is equally available to everyone as well.

◯∂

≈ *Sarah Hamlett* ≈

Teaching for the First Time

The problem is to act without being paralyzed by your fear.
—Paulo Freire, *A Pedagogy for Liberation: Dialogues on Transforming Education,* with Ira Shor (1987), p. 60.

November 19, 2002

Dear Paulo,

In your second letter, you talk about not letting "the fear of what is difficult paralyze you" (p. 27). This year, I have encountered many difficult things. First, the fear of teaching for the first time. Also, some of the readings for this graduate class have been difficult for me. But I think that I have faced them in a way that has allowed me to deal with them.

You talk about using available resources, and I think that it is important not to be afraid to ask for help, or to find help. In that same letter you say, "Studying is a demanding occupation, in the process of which we will encounter pain, pleasure, victory, defeat, doubt, and happiness" (p. 28). That can be said for a lot of things, including teaching and learning. Without the pain, the reward wouldn't be so sweet.

I also gained a lot from the fourth letter, "On the Indispensable Qualities of Progressive Teachers for Their Better Performance." I specifically appreciated the first sentences, where you stated that these are "qualities acquired gradually through practice" (p. 39). That reassured me that I am not expected to be the perfect teacher my first time.

Sarah Hamlett

◌

≈ *Angélica Ribeiro* ≈

Fear of Disappointing

*No matter what society we may be in, or what society we may
belong to, it is urgent that we fight with hope and fearlessness.*
—Paulo Freire, *Pedagogy of Indignation* (2004b), p. 122.

December 6, 2005
Dear Paulo,

Education in my country, Brazil, is not only a pedagogical problem but also a political problem. The discrepancy between a politician's salary and a teacher's salary is huge. The government in Brazil is always saying that they don't have money to invest in education or in minimizing poverty. Nevertheless, overpasses and tunnels are built. How can they build them if they have no money? It seems politicians have forgotten that they wouldn't be in the position they are in without education.

I have been teaching for eight years, and part of that experience was at a public Brazilian language institute. I remember crying sometimes because some students didn't care about my classes, even though I had spent so much time planning and thinking about the best way to teach the content. The workload, the bad working conditions, and the low salary also discouraged me. But what made me stop crying and go back to work the next day was the love I have for my profession and students. Besides love, the joy of living I carry with me made me overcome those brief moments of disappointment. Because of this love, I'm always trying to improve my teaching by studying, reading, and taking part in teacher training programs. Unfortunately, not every teacher does the same. And many of them do not even like their profession for the same reasons that made me cry. I feel sorry for them. I wish that they could see the beauty, importance, and pleasure, which overcome the low salary and bad working conditions, of being a teacher.

Although I love my students, I can't avoid feeling fear, especially during the first classes, when I'm still in the process of getting to know them. I believe this is a fear of somehow disappointing them. After reading in one of your letters that fear is normal and that we as humans have the right to feel it, I feel better now.

Thank you for your words.

Angélica Ribeiro

Lynn Sisco

More Questions than Answers

Having fear is a manifestation of being alive.
—Paulo Freire (with Ira Shor), *A Pedagogy for Liberation* (1987), p. 55.

December 12, 2005
Dear Paulo,

Your words are inspirational. Yet I feel defeated. I have not yet begun my teaching career, and I feel utterly overwhelmed. I grapple with the concept of praxis, and how I can take action against the injustices and inequities in our educational systems. I have many questions, but I have not yet found answers or solutions.

I am uncomfortable, unsure, and perplexed. Was that your intention all along? Were you encouraging teachers to reflect on their teaching and challenge themselves, even if it caused them some discomfort? Maybe I am supposed to feel a bit overwhelmed. Maybe that's the point—I mean, look at the subtitle of your book: "To Those Who Dare Teach." Are you daring me to take on this tremendous challenge of being a responsible, knowledgeable, and humble educator?

I wonder, would you laugh at me for being so nervous, so scared? I worry: what if I don't have all the answers? What if I do not help and empower each and every student? What if my efforts are not complex or creative enough to incite change?

For now, I will take each day as it comes, and try to be hopeful as I embark on this journey, as I begin my new career....

Sincerely,
Lynn Sisco

Nancy Costa

Lessons from Paulo

One of the most dreadful mistakes we can possibly make as we study, either as students or as teachers, is to retreat before the first obstacle we face.
—Paulo Freire, *Teachers as Cultural Workers: Letters to Those Who Dare Teach* (1998c), p. 28.

September 28, 2001

Dear Paulo Freire,

Even though I found parts of *Teachers as Cultural Worker: Letters to Those Who Dare Teach* difficult to read, I must tell you that it was inspirational. It is what teaching is supposed to be. You made it sound possible, attainable, something to strive for. You mention in your book that we should not fear what is difficult. Teaching is certainly difficult, very difficult if it is done to the extent that you describe. I particularly like the idea of teaching as a political act. I had never thought of it quite that way before. Education certainly does seem to be about power and control. You have opened my eyes to another way of viewing education. Teachers should be empowered, and your book helps one feel empowered.

Just as studying opens new horizons for students, so, too, does teaching open new horizons for teachers. As teachers share their knowledge with students and students question that knowledge and share what they know and have learned with their teachers, then teachers grow and learn and expand their knowledge. If a teacher can excite her students to want to learn more about a particular subject, then she has passed on her joy of learning to the students. It is that excitement that you write about so often in your book. It is the ability to question what you are taught and what you are not taught that is so important.

These are some lessons I learned from you:

That it is not possible to be a teacher without loving your students;

That it is not possible to be a teacher without loving teaching;

That reading and writing are intertwined and that both are needed to study and learn;

That writing takes practice;

That if you need help in understanding something you should seek help;

That you should not run away from things that are difficult;

That after you have read something, you should critique it, discuss it, challenge it, question it, and then you will truly understand it;

That teachers should assert themselves and view education as political;

That teachers should be loving, courageous, humble, tolerant, decisive, secure, honest, competent, patient and impatient, and have a joy for living;

That teachers need to fight for what they believe in;

That teachers should learn from teaching and learn from their students;

That teachers should be committed to social justice, liberty, and the individual rights of their students.

Now it is time to try to incorporate into my practice some of the principles you have written about. It will be challenging, but exciting. Thank you for the inspiration to try.

Sincerely,
Nancy Costa

⌣

⁓ *Dalia Mostafa* ⁓
Fighting for Democracy

*But fear is no abstraction, and neither is the "why" of fear an
abstraction. Fear is altogether concrete, and is caused by concrete
considerations—or considerations that seem concrete, so that, in the
absence of any demonstration to the contrary, they might as well be.*
—Paulo Freire, *Pedagogy of Hope: Reliving
Pedagogy of the Oppressed* (1994), p. 124.

May 9, 2001
Dear Paulo,

I do not really know how to start. Writing a letter to a person like you is much
more difficult than writing a letter to a friend or family member. I do not really
know how to address you, but I will try.

Reading your book created many contradictory feelings inside me. At some moments, I learned how to change and improve myself as a teacher. Reading other parts
of your book brought back memories about my previous teaching experience in my
country. Some of them are not very pleasant indeed. I am also a little mad at you
because you made me feel guilty that there are some things that I should have done
and dealt with in a different and better way as a teacher. But as you said, knowing
helps you grow. After reading your book I gained some knowledge, and I think I
will grow to be a better teacher.

There is something very interesting about your book. Although it was meant to
be about the Brazilian experience, I felt that there is this sense of universality to it.
It applies to almost every country everywhere, if not all of it, at least some parts. I
myself felt that it was talking more or less about Egypt.

For instance, I liked the idea of the importance of trying to make a connection
between materials being taught and students' backgrounds. It does not make any
sense to me that in my country they are teaching students a translated American
story about a boy whose father bought him a car as a graduation gift. This is being
taught throughout the country in some places where the students and their families
hardly have anything to eat. To me, teaching a story like that serves only one purpose:
to make students mad at themselves and the world around them.

You said that nobody receives democracy as a gift, and instead we have to fight for
it. Teachers should help their students to be critical thinkers in their reading of the
world around them. You also mentioned that it is important for the teacher to make
connections between what he says and what he does. When I was teaching I once tried
to make a change which I thought a lot of students would benefit from. I thought that

some of them would do better in English if I spent extra time with them away from the rest of the class. I decided to have them come to school an hour earlier to spend extra time with them and give them a jump start about what would be done in class that day so they could catch up with their peers. Two days later, the principal called me to his office and asked me to stop doing this because it is against the law and because I could be telling my students things against the government during this extra hour of class. Although it is a painful experience to write about, it shows that teachers can be very powerful in making change. Of course I had to give up what I had decided to do, because I knew that this could cost me my job. What do you think, Paulo? Now after reading your book I feel so ashamed of myself. I should have continued doing it anyway. Do you think I was not honest with the students because my words and the promise I made ended up different from what I did?

Thank you, Paulo. You made me feel bad about my past teaching experience but hopeful about my future.

Oh, one last thing. Would you be interested in coming to visit Egypt to help teachers there make changes? You would probably end up being exiled there, too, but maybe you would be able to do something before that happens.

A growing teacher,
Dalia Mostafa

Laila Di Silvio

Modeling Democratic Principles

As a democratic relationship, dialogue is the opportunity available to me to open up to the thinking of others, and thereby not wither away in isolation.
—Paulo Freire, *Pedagogy of Hope* (1994), p. 119.

February 10, 2000
Dear Paulo,

I am a preservice teacher who has been reading your letters and taking from them what I can. I am in the process of developing my own educational philosophy and thus have been experimenting with many ideas. I have a sense of why I am here and even of a mission, but I lack the words to convey my beliefs powerfully. Prior to my wanting to become a teacher I had always considered myself an educator. I feel that educating children is a community affair. I do not think that a classroom is, or ever should be, an isolated place. It is now a question of how I can best translate my international skills into an American context.

I love history and social studies. Partially that is because they are subjects I found fascinating growing up. I had teachers who were successful in bringing the world to me. But I love these subjects also because I think they are where democratic teaching can thrive. For me, this means sharing the knowledge we possess as teachers while also recognizing that our students have knowledge, too. It also means covering controversial topics that loom large in students' lives but are often pushed aside as nonacademic or secondary.

I need to admit that I am scared of conflict. This is one of the fears that you have encouraged me to look at. In devising my lesson plans I am trying not to run from conflict. I know that if I don't test the parameters of what I teach now, I will likely become increasingly complacent in my teaching. I try to explore why it is that I avoid it. I remind myself of whom I am trying to serve. Social studies education also must entail looking at human rights. What are the rights and privileges that we enjoy? What basic rights do we have limited or no access to? What about our brothers and sisters abroad? Do they enjoy these same rights? I feel it is my responsibility to encourage, promote, and even demand critical thinking among my students. We must start with our own realities and extend our perspectives ever wider.

Paulo, I am rambling. I think so much these days. Yet I am still unable to produce concise conceptions. I finally feel ready to begin my work in the classroom. I have been exposed to many theories and have some good ideas. But I need to try them out. It is time for me to generate my own knowledge. This process will happen next semester for me.

I see the beauty you say is found in ethical struggle. I believe that to be true. I feel as though I have spent much of my adult life fighting for social justice, but I have done little for my own country. This plagues me. I have had tremendous opportunity to visit, live, and work in several cultures and nations other than my own. I have taken much from those experiences. Recently I have also felt as though I am starting to give back to those communities. Yet it was time for me to start planting some roots in my own country. I would be doing a disservice if I were to leave my knowledge at another country's borders. I would also be failing myself if I left behind my community development. I am a political being who sees the world in a certain way. It is important that I recognize this and that I continue to live and eventually teach passionately.

Paulo, I must be honest: I don't love my democracy. I do, however, love the idea of a society that combats social injustice. I hope that my classroom can be such a place. I want to explore with my students how we can ensure individual rights: theirs and others. I do agree that modeling democratic principles starts in the classroom. I am worried about finding the balance between authoritarianism and permissiveness. Will I constantly evaluate my teacher/learner relationship? It is easy to agree with you in principle, but will I grow weary of fighting the system? I will likely be working in a school that adheres strictly to a content-based curriculum. I feel that working with such a framework in the center simply ensures that multicultural education stays relegated to the margins. Inclusive teaching becomes secondary to a mainstream curriculum that teaches only one history. I envision teaching thematically and without textbooks, so as not to fall into that trap. But it is a lot of work. Will I keep the energy that I feel now? Paulo, I hope so.

With faith,
Laila Di Silvio

☙

◦ *Tzu-Pei Kuo* ◦
Easy to Say, Not to Do

If we are progressives, and indeed open to the other, we must make an effort, humbly so, to narrow the distance between what we say and what we do as much as possible.
—Paulo Freire, *Pedagogy of Indignation* (2004b), p. 21.

November 30, 2004
Dear Dr. Freire,

I am writing this letter with a highly respectful mind, and humble attitude, as a student should. This is a traditional Chinese greeting when a student has to write a letter to his or her teacher. Even though I never had a chance to encounter you, I regard you as my teacher, because you have taught me through your words.

I didn't really like you at the very beginning because you broke my dream, the dream of reading a thin book. I thought it wouldn't take me too long to read *Teachers as Cultural Workers,* but it took me several days to check the dictionaries to understand your words. Unfortunately, I didn't really understand even after a long time. I just had a feeling that your theories were very similar to those of Confucius, so I thought there was nothing new I could learn from you.

I had to read your book because it was a class requirement. During that period of time, I was questioning the meaning of being a teacher. To be a teacher was always my last choice. When I was young, I regarded teachers as the controllers. Teachers dominated everything and forced me to compromise my ideas. When I started to teach, I tried to break these traditional boundaries. I tried to provide a free learning space for my students, but in the end I couldn't even free myself.

I read your letter about the fear of learning and teaching. I could not stop my tears. I finally realized that I have a fear in my mind, but I had never admitted it. I thought that it would be embarrassing if I admitted I have a fear of being a teacher. I always thought that teaching should be an easy job and anyone could be a teacher. I couldn't find the value in being a teacher. Your words helped me understand how much it takes to be a good teacher. For the first time in my life,

I am so proud of the job I am doing now. I believe that while it's easy to be called a teacher, it's not easy to act as a real, professional, and profound teacher. It's not easy to be a teacher who always notices students' needs. It's not easy to be a teacher who provides different ways for students to learn. The word *teacher* is easy to say, but not easy to do.

Thank you, Paulo, a teacher who has taught me a lot through your words.

Best wishes,
Tzu-Pei Kuo

⟨⟩

⟐ *Elizabeth Robinson* ⟐

Defying the Paralysis of Fear

> *Indeed, fear is a right, but one to which corresponds the duty of educating it, facing it and overcoming it.*
> —Paulo Freire, *Teachers as Cultural Workers: Letters to Those Who Dare Teach* (1998), p. 48.

November 28, 2004
Dear Paulo,

How I wish you were here to discuss the state of affairs in our world today! The United States is choosing leaders on the basis of their "gut convictions." The world is described as divided into liberators versus terrorists. "Liberal" and "intellectual" are increasingly thought of as terms for people who are not to be trusted. The United States sees itself as the world leader, and, unfortunately, our actions cannot be contained within the boundaries of our country. Our country has declared war against any nation that is not in agreement with hunting down and killing all "terrorists." With a public so scared for its own safety and so focused on the "War Against Terror," all other issues have become mere distractions.

Fear is a great motivator, and it seems that the government knows exactly how to use fear to its benefit. The same fear that the government has bred to garner support for its war and its war budget, it is using to run our schools. If schools do not comply with the "standards" and show significant improvement in students' test scores, the government will take over those schools, replacing all the faculty and administration. No one is allowed to rethink or rewrite the state and governmental standards; they must be followed exactly. What can teachers who are scared for their jobs, overworked, and underpaid do in this situation, Paulo? It seems that teachers themselves need liberation!

You have given us all the tools we need to find our own solutions. I draw inspiration from your Second Letter in *Teachers as Cultural Workers, Letters to Those Who Dare Teach*. You write: "The issue is not allowing that fear to paralyze us, not allowing that fear to persuade us to quit, to face a challenging situation without an effort, without a fight" (p. 27). We must gather strength and ideas from other educators and from students and figure out what must be done to improve the situation for all.

Finally, Paulo, I want to thank you. Your view of the world has opened my eyes to see that the tools of the trade lie within us. I know that it takes patience, constant analysis, and overall love to be an educator. I want to bring hope and strength to other educators so that the children we serve may realize that they, too, have within them the tools they need.

Thank you, Paulo!
Elizabeth Robinson

∽

⟅ Kathy McDonough ⟆

Teaching for Liberation

We are political militants because we are teachers.
—Paulo Freire, *Teachers as Cultural Workers: Letters to Those Who Dare Teach* (1998), p. 58.

Fall 2005
Dear Paulo,

I was in the audience once when you spoke at a college in New England. I was hardly familiar with your work then, years ago, having read only your essay "The Importance of the Act of Reading." But I knew I was in the presence of someone special, someone who understood the hopefulness of education, the seriousness of teaching, and the joy of learning. I slowly started collecting your books, planning to carve out time to read them. I noticed that I rarely found one at used book stores—I think people don't want to give them up. My habit is to buy more books than I can possibly finish; I can't resist. So yours, like many others, sat on my shelf.

Finally, and thankfully, I just read *Teachers as Cultural Workers: Letters to Those Who Dare Teach* for a class—it's a title with which I was unfamiliar. If I had known of it, how could I have resisted "For those who dare teach?" You understand the complexities of teaching. You understand that it is a daring profession. Daring, for we reveal ourselves as we teach, we take stances that are sometimes unpopular, and we affect the lives of all who spend time in our classrooms. You dared to start a movement in Brazil, empowering many through the act of acquiring literacy. You dare us now, through your legacy, to be self-aware and to teach to liberate.

It is easy in these times to become discouraged as a teacher. There are demands that we focus much of our energy preparing children to take high-stakes tests. Often, curricula are mandated throughout districts, writing instruction has become formulaic to prepare students to get high scores, and in some schools reading instruction is scripted. How do we meet the needs of our students when powers residing outside of our classrooms tell us what to teach? Recently, a colleague of mine spoke in a citywide seminar of teachers and made a comment about teaching as a subversive activity. She arrived at work the next morning to learn that the previous evening someone had made a telephone call to her principal reporting her as a troublemaker. She was warned not to step out of line. Whose lines are we to walk in? When lines are drawn in education, aren't we assuming only one way of knowing and thus continuing the marginalization of many of our students?

To take a stance as a critical educator takes strength and bravery. Your work reminds us of the emancipatory possibilities in education. You inspire us to be daring and to teach in ways that honor all of our students' identities, cultivate critical thinking, and pursue ongoing reflections about why we teach. Thank you for reminding me why teaching is a noble profession.

I look forward to getting to know you better as I take another of your books off my shelf and begin to read.

Warmly,
Kathy McDonough

Part 3: Pedagogy

> *It is fundamental for us to know that without certain qualities or virtues,*
> *such as a generous loving heart, respect for others, tolerance, humility, a joyful*
> *disposition, love of life, openness to what is new, a disposition to welcome*
> *change, perseverance in the struggle, a refusal of determinism, a spirit of*
> *hope, and openness to justice, progressive pedagogical practice is not possible.*
> *It is something that the merely scientific, technical mind cannot accomplish.*
> —Paulo Freire, *Pedagogy of Freedom* (1998a), p. 108.

From the beginning of his career, pedagogy was at the heart of Paulo Freire's work. Although he had not necessarily planned on being a teacher, he discovered teaching at an early age and stayed in the field, in one way or another, throughout his career. In a dialogue with Ira Shor, he said,

> By teaching, I discovered that I was able to teach and that I loved it. More and more I began to dream of being a teacher. I learned how to teach the more I loved teaching and studied it. (Shor and Freire, 1987, p. 27)

Nevertheless, Freire made it clear that teaching was not only about knowing and mastering particular methods. Teaching, for him, was a project of liberation, dialogue, and collaboration. He described "banking education" (Freire, 1970), or simply depositing knowledge into students' heads, as diametrically opposed to a liberating education, which is "not a manual of clever techniques, but is rather a critical perspective on school and society, learning for social transformation" (Shor and Freire, 1987, p. 13).

In this section, teachers and academics grapple with such issues as the "exhilarating and exhausting" nature of teaching and the problem of presenting a "stealth coup" as a concrete topic for study among working-class university students. From a teacher who struggles to convince her family that education is a dignified profession, to another who provides a testimony to teaching, they ask questions that strike at the very core of pedagogy: Do I have the courage to teach? Can methods from one context be used in another completely different context? How do I create an environment for learning that is both critical and joyful? Can education liberate?

Through their own autobiographies, they also illustrate the power of teaching to change individuals and society.

⤫

⟿ *Daniela Alvarez-Bradley* ⟿

On Being a Teacher

Indispensable to teachers' struggle is the knowledge, which they must forge within themselves and which we must forge within ourselves, of the dignity and importance of their task.
—Paulo Freire, *Teachers as Cultural Workers: Letters to Those Who Dare Teach* (1998c), p. 34.

December 4, 2001
Estimado Paulo,

It is with great reverence that I sit and write this letter to you. If I had not read your book, *Teachers as Cultural Worker: Letters to Those Who Dare Teach,* I would be writing this letter with great trepidation. But as I understand now, you must be very humble, or, as we say in Spanish, *humilde,* and therefore I write this letter as a colleague to articulate my admiration for your laudable life, and to explain the impact your words have had on me.

Your words resonated for me in many ways. As I endeavor to be a teacher, your emphasis on the role of the teacher in society particularly struck a chord with me. It took me a long time, and tremendous struggle, to get where I am now, and believe me, nothing has ever felt more right to me. But in my family, one that has worked very hard as immigrants to acquire the high-status positions they now possess, they do not view the teacher as having a significant role in society. They are culpable of maintaining the theory that teachers are, as you stated in your book, mere "coddlers" and babysitters. They do not, no matter how hard I try to convince them, understand that teaching involves academic rigor, intellectual insight, and curiosity, as well as a myriad of other attributes.

It has been hard for me to resist the temptation to follow the path my family had predetermined for me. Sometimes, I feel alone—without support. But after reading your books, I have found new inspiration and motivation to continue on this path and determine my own life. I was scared for a while, as I feared that if I failed, I would have to hang my head low and listen to the inevitable "I told you so … *te dije que enseñar no era para vos.*" But now I understand that being scared is just a natural part of life. I must now have the courage to face my fears, overcome these obstacles, and make my dreams become a reality.

By now you may be wondering what my dreams actually are. I want to be an English as a second language (ESL) teacher because I would like to help advance the disadvantaged minorities in the United States. Ironically, being from a family that immigrated to the United States has functioned as a catalyst toward these goals. Growing up viewing firsthand the inequitable distribution of power and resources, I knew that I wanted to help remedy this situation.

I understand my family's disappointment in my decisions. They worked hard and sacrificed so much to provide my brother and me with everything so that we would never have to endure their hardships. Although that is commendable—and I thank them for it dearly every time I see them—I wish to work now so that others will not have to sacrifice as they did. I want to create a democratic classroom environment where all students learn to respect each other for their individual qualities, regardless of their ethnic background or socioeconomic status. I want to be an advocate for the rights of my students and their families, because I believe, as you do, that every person has a right to a proper education and equitable living situations.

Your beautiful insights and realistic ideologies, sprinkled with just the right amount of idealism, have helped countless teachers and administrators understand the power they hold. I hope that one day, I will be able to apply the ideologies and practices that you preach and vigorously practiced throughout your life.

Thank you for all your hard work and relentless caring and devotion to the betterment of your country and to humankind.

Atentamente,
Daniela Alvarez Bradley

⚬⚬

= *Lisa Varandani* =

Saying Yes to Teaching

The educator must live and work impatiently patiently,
never surrendering entirely to either.
—Paulo Freire, *Teachers as Cultural Workers: Letters*
to Those Who Dare Teach (1998c), p. 44.

November 30, 2004
Dear Paulo,

I have to admit that at times while reading your book, I have wanted to throw my hands in the air and run from being a teacher. This was compounded by the fact that all of my teacher friends and professors say that they find your work inspiring, making me even surer that I am not cut out for this profession. What you may not have guessed from this statement is that I'm not new to teaching: I've been teaching and training teachers for a number of years. When I teach I give it my all. I try to make my lessons as learner-centered as possible, personalizing materials, using different groupings, sharing power in the classroom and curriculum, getting feedback and responding to it, and so on. This is what I know as good teaching, and admittedly, I find it to be both exhilarating and exhausting. This is all couched, of course, within the larger context of low pay and only moderate respect as a professional.

I guess that is why, rather than feeling inspired like my colleagues and classmates, at first I was overwhelmed and discouraged by your letters. I find teaching in the way that I have been doing it to be all-consuming, and adding any more responsibility onto my shoulders felt like too much. When I think about it carefully, in many ways, you seem to be advocating for the kind of teaching that I already do. In fact, I applaud your efforts to professionalize the field and find myself having the same struggle when training teachers. At closer look, you seem to be adding a greater political element, beyond the politics of the classroom, which up until now I had not included in my thinking about teaching. Suddenly, I felt I was being burdened by more than I could handle as a low-paid, overworked teacher.

I can't tell you exactly when the shift within me occurred. Perhaps it was during a class discussion in one of my graduate courses, perhaps it was somewhere within your poetic and inspired words. What I do know, however, is that I slowly started to rise to the challenge to live my life and my profession in an even more intentional way than I had before. How can I *not* advocate for my students in a greater political sense? How can I *not* teach them to do this for themselves? Teaching can be so isolating. Pockets of greatness taking place in individual classrooms, when not linked to the world at large, are not enough. I see now that we are doing a disservice to our students and the rest of the world if this is all we do. I can do nothing less than guide my students to be active, critical participants in their own lives and in the world and community around them.

Your call to action is a bold one. It almost scared me off. As a new graduate student who has just finally said *yes* to continuing in the profession of teaching, I thank you for that boldness.

Sincerely,
Lisa Varandani

⌒ *Hera Zinno* ⌒
Teaching Vows

To change the world through work, to "proclaim" the world, to express
it, and to express oneself are the unique qualities of human beings.
—Paulo Freire, *The Politics of Education: Culture,*
Power, and Liberation (1985), p. 21.

Fall 2004
Dear Paulo,

Your words and ideas have touched all of us, and they will help us to change the world. For those of us who dare to teach, we will vow to you, in your memory, the following oaths:

- We vow never to be "coddling mothers" to those we educate.
- We vow to make an effort to understand as fully as we can, our surroundings and the people we come into contact with and educate.
- We vow to remember that teachers are political agents, and always live by their beliefs.
- We vow to speak of love without fear and to be courageous enough to love.
- We vow to try a thousand times before giving up and to know the "universe" of the dreams of our students.
- We will remember that we are conditioned but not predetermined and by remembering this, we will carry on your name, your wisdom, your words, and your visions.
- As educators and as members of the human race, we vow to stick together and challenge the system, never to settle, never to accept the so-called norm, and to live in the "permanent tension" between patience and impatience.

Paulo, thank you for your wisdom, and for sharing it with us.

Yours truly,
Hera Zinno

∽

∽ *Carolina Rothkegel* ∽
The Courage to Teach

We can learn a great deal from the very students we teach.
For this to happen it is necessary that we transcend the
monotonous, arrogant, and elitist traditionalism where the
teacher knows all and the student does not know anything.
　　　　　—Paulo Freire, *The Politics of Education: Culture,*
　　　　　　　　　　　Power, and Liberation (1985), p. 177.

November 28, 2004
Dear Paulo,

I would like to introduce myself before starting this letter. Although I am young, I have been a teacher for many years in my country. My native language is Spanish, and I am from Chile. Currently, I am working on my master's in bilingual education at the University of Massachusetts. I work in the United States helping immigrants to acquire a basic knowledge of English so as to be able to survive in schools in this country. Most of my students are Spanish speakers from Central and South America; others are from Africa.

My experience as an immigrant in this country has been very important in shaping my professional practices. I feel involved in my students' feelings. They struggle to learn English, missing their families and trying to open their spaces into the new lives that most of them are just starting to be familiar with. As an educator I know that my students have a long journey ahead of them, and, based on my professional and cultural understanding of this country, I try to support them in their learning process as much as possible.

Throughout my studies I learned about you and your alternative pedagogy. I know that you have written many interesting books, but until now I was not familiar with them. The first book that I had the chance to read was *Teachers as Cultural Workers: Letters for Those Who Dare Teach*. I appreciate each one of those letters, and I identified with most of the messages in them. Your words and methods clearly can and should be used, with some adaptations, all over the world; they are more than just a set of techniques associated with students' learning or professional development. You made me reflect on the art of teaching. Throughout the reading I also understood how important it is to observe my students, their comments, feelings, and their curiosity, as well as their progress and their strategies for learning. Knowing these things will help me to shape my teaching, improving my interactions with students and, consequently, providing them with a more nurturing classroom experience.

Your pedagogy and your life experiences are an example for all educators. You did not show fear in expressing your beliefs. That fact has contributed to educators' understanding the importance of education in society. Your books benefit us all. I feel inspired by them, and I am sure that educators from everywhere can become better teachers because of you.

Before finishing my letter I would like to cite a paragraph from your "First Words: A Pedagogical Trap," in *Teachers as Cultural Workers,* since it inspires me and touched me as a teacher.

> The task of the teacher, who is also a learner, is both joyful and rigorous. It demands seriousness and scientific, physical, emotional, and affective preparation. It is a task that requires that those who commit themselves to teaching develop a certain love not only of others but also of the very process implied in teaching. It is impossible to teach without the courage to love, without the courage to try a thousand times before giving up. (P. 3)

These are your words, Paulo, and all that is left for me to say is: thank you for them.

Carolina Rothkegel

∽

⌁ Elaine Stinson ⌁

The Responsible Learner

> *[E]ducation is cultural action for freedom and therefore an act of knowing and not of memorization.*
> —Paulo Freire, *Cultural Action for Freedom* (1970), p. 1.

April 2000
Dear Paulo,

Remembering that the act of learning is an open-ended process and one that unfolds within its own context, both social and cultural, is challenging. As an educator who is bombarded with content to "cover," the act of discovery happens less often than I believe it should. Teachers have information to share, that is true. But the difficult part is finding the balance between state and district mandates while attempting to create a democratic community of learners, a place where teachers listen to their students and are listened to.

Many people see teaching as a process that involves disseminating the "important" information to students whose learning is then measured through a standardized test. In contrast, many of my colleagues understand that teaching is a process whereby learning evolves, or "unfolds," as you have written. Learning is about understanding facts, yet it is also about understanding *who* created the facts; learning also recognizes the personal references of the learner. The latter takes more time and care because it involves study of the material, the learners, and the teacher, and it is a more thorough process.

I think that your fifth letter in *Teachers as Cultural Workers: Letters to Those Who Dare Teach* (1998c) helped me to crystallize some earlier thoughts from your previous letters. The act of making meaning out of print involves understanding the context of the words, just as the act of studying my students is to understand their interactions within their environments. How then can I comprehend my students without knowing the context of their lives—in essence the context of how, why, and what they learn? If I present a topic to a group of students, perhaps one word, will they each have a different understanding of it? Studying my students makes perfect sense to me, and it places a *weighted* obligation on me as the educator. Once I learn something, am I not responsible for knowing it? I believe so. If our relationship with the student is based on how we respect the truth as we understand it, and in turn, reconcile that with our actions, then our relationship with our self is no less important. In essence, I am now responsible for reconciling my own actions in regard to studying my pupils. Now that I have understood the importance of such action, how can I ignore that, or push it aside as something I don't have time for while striving to improve as an educator?

The best environment for learning is based on being responsible for pedagogy, curricula, and for the practice of thoughtful reflection and subsequent action. How shall I prioritize this new understanding so it doesn't get lost in the demands of society, school boards, or time constraints? My hope is that it will become a natural process, just as anything intended and practiced does.

I have found an intriguing connection between many of your theories about teaching and the intentions of multicultural education. Multicultural education is based, in part, on the idea of valuing differences that exist in people, specifically their culture, and how culture affects learning; it is about respecting and learning how one constructs personal knowledge. Multicultural education promotes change, and it is a transformative process, requiring that teachers recognize the filters that each learner uses when processing knowledge and the filters they see through as educators. In "studying their pupils," as you encourage, teachers must do the same thing. Isn't that the context you refer to? Those who are multicultural educators must study their pupils and all that this implies and then allow that data to inform their practice. Seen in a broader light, those who dare teach, in this way, really are true multicultural educators.

Sincerely,
Elaine Stinson

⤢

⪪ *Ira Shor* ⪫

A "Stealth Coup" Threatens Us

Experiments cannot be transplanted; they must be reinvented.
—Paulo Freire, *Pedagogy in Process: Letters to Guinea-Bissau* (1978), p. 9.

August 2007
Dear Paulo,

On March 31, 1997, we ate together for the last time. That day was cold, wet, and windy, but your habitual warmth filled the table at a Greek restaurant in Manhattan. I couldn't know then that I'd never see you again. I miss the charm of your expressive face. I miss the way you spoke "this English" (as you put it), a hard language for you, into which you inserted Portuguese words and pronunciation, like the word *there* sometimes sounding like "dairy." I also miss your passion for knowledge and your graceful humility, which made you listen as long as possible to people before you felt comfortable speaking. Most of all, I miss the great gift of discussing politics and pedagogy with you.

At the Greek restaurant, I brought some good news about younger colleagues with whom I was studying working-class culture and pedagogy. Your eyes brightened with this news, because "social class" in the United States was a kind of thorn in your thinking. "Class" discourse, driven out of U.S. public life by anticommunism, has been recovering gradually since the 1960s and the more recent end of the Cold War. For you, "social class" was an uncertain topic because you wondered how North Americans would receive your Marxist analysis, unlike such conversations in Brazil and elsewhere. So you wanted to hear more, at our lunch, about the new project. We planned a meeting in the fall in Massachusetts where I'd bring some colleagues testing critical literacy with working-class students. But we never held that meeting because time ran out on you only a few weeks after we talked. If we could meet again, I'd bring along colleagues. And I'd ask you to do a second "talking book" with me because things have changed for the worse since our lunch more than ten years ago and since we published our first talking book in 1987, *A Pedagogy for Liberation*.

At this moment, I see a stealth coup d'état unfolding year by year in this country. Its ominous evolution is very different from the military takeover that exploded on you and Brazil in April 1964. Instead of a singular military attack on the state and society, this stealth coup follows three decades of "culture wars" and "conservative restoration," a series of campaigns to reverse the egalitarian gains of the 1960s. These successive moves against equality and economic justice continued in the 1990s and fed into a stand-off in the 2000 presidential election. That election was decided extraparliamentarily five clamorous weeks after the polls had closed. Finally, a conservative Supreme Court awarded victory to the candidate who had lost the popular vote.

After the capture of the executive branch by neoconservatives, what I call "the stealth coup" proceeded step by step through various instruments, some illegal (secret surveillance, torture of detainees, leaking classified information to sabotage critics, as in the "Scooter" Libby/Valerie Plame case), some legalistic (bypassing Congress with executive orders and with invented devices such as "presidential signing statements"), some deceptive (gross lying about WMDs and Al-Qaeda in Iraq, to justify war there), some juridical (a right-wing majority on the Supreme Court overturning precedents, restricting democratic rights), and some rhetorical (right-wing talk radio, tabloid news-papers, and cable TV keeping the conservative base mobilized and the liberal opposition defensive). The nonmilitary nuances of this power grab and the media cover-up of the story have helped screen it from public alarm or outrage. In such circumstances, I need to reflect with you on how to teach against this threatening trend.

If we could do so in a second talking book, I'd begin by reviewing your own coup experience: what was visible and knowable in the months leading up to April 1964? About the April coup, you said a few things in *A Pedagogy for Liberation*: "When rumors of a coup came up in early 1964, many people in Brazil preferred not to believe them. ... My feelings then were different. I felt a coup was possible, even though I leaned towards thinking that maybe it wouldn't happen ... because of the optimism of the people at that time" (pp. 61–62). You had popular movements for social justice challenging the elite, as did we here in the 1960s and 1970s. Faced with mass demands for democracy and equality, Brazil's elite called out the generals; ours did not, using instead its considerable institutional powers—in the government, the media, the economy, the school system, the police forces—to reassert command.

In the years following the Brazil coup, the generals were not merely unpopular but also unsuccessful in managing the economy. So, the military was obliged to accept a democratic opening that allowed you to return from exile in 1979, and for the Work-ers' Party to consolidate soon after that. Here in the States, the stealth coup has been successful as well as disastrous. Enormous wealth and power have been funneled to the corporate top of society, with billions transferred upward from working families and out of the public sector, and with the protest culture of the 1960s dispelled. But at least four major crises dog the conservative regime in Washington: the catastrophic war in Iraq with its 4000 U.S. dead and $600 billion cost; the abandonment of the poor of New Orleans after Hurricane Katrina; the economic decline from a burst housing bubble built on bad loans; and a predatory health care system as sick as the 47 million Americans who don't have health insurance.

How can critical practice pose the notion of a "stealth coup" as a problem for class-room study? How do I concretely present such an abstraction to my working-class students, who read the tabloids and watch cable? Agreeing with you about "banking pedagogy," I don't lecture in class and avoid the "white noise" of teacher-talk, what you called "the narration sickness" of teacherly discourse in the classroom. Instead of polemics or tranquilizing narratives, I prefer constructive problem-posing that front-loads student expression. However, the subject of a stealth coup d'état does not easily fit such problem-posing. It is not a generative theme circulating in stu-dent experience or language. Therefore, it lacks everyday concreteness. The notion of a stealth coup belongs to my abstractness, my social cognition, and my political discourse. Any theme or discourse so unilaterally the property of the teacher risks closing down dialogue and installing monologue.

About the politics of dialogue, you supported the teacher's right to present her or his positions to students. You said that one mystery of critical practice was for the teacher to affirm her or his politics without disconfirming the voices of the students. Because all pedagogies are political, including those that do not question the status quo, you argued that critical teachers had a right and a responsibility to place their values and perceptions into the ongoing discussion. I agree with these protocols for critical teaching. But, in practice, subject matters far from the everyday life and language of students present special complications; they seem to require more scaffolding to contextualize them for students. The more dense the scaffolding required from me to pose an abstract theme, the more I will address students in the declarative voice of explanation, hence the greater the risk of losing touch with the interrogative voice of questioning.

Another complication is that critical teachers now have a harder time questioning the status quo than twenty years ago, when the conservative restoration was less advanced than it is today. In this decade, education is generally more restricted and policed through surveillance, required syllabi, and mandated testing. Perhaps the best option, then, would be to pose the theme of the stealth coup through competing sources, with some texts confirming and some denying the antidemocratic trend. However, sources I could choose do not frame recent events in terms of a stealth coup, which is my own formulation. Perhaps then, it's sensible to shelve the concept of a stealth coup and teach from sources that do acknowledge the repressive drift in power relations. But those sources address the topic in academic or formal idioms familiar to me but foreign to my nonelite students, requiring my provision of a decoding scaffold for them. This reiterates a communications problem in critical practice for nonscholastic students, which we first discussed in *A Pedagogy for Liberation* in the chapter entitled "How Can Liberating Educators Overcome Language Differences with the Students?"

The puzzle of how to teach the stealth coup, then, is the first item I'd put on the agenda if we could do a new talking book. For a second item, I could report on my use of a theme that much interested you when we last saw each other—social class. I've made some headway, I think, using this theme, because the economic hardships of my students give "social class" generative roots in their lives. My students are far more stressed out now than they were in the 1980s. They work longer hours at low-wage jobs to pay increased tuition, higher textbook costs, runaway gas prices, and so on. They can't afford college unless they work many hours a week, because tuition and the cost of living are rising faster than their wages. Their many hours on the job interfere with their academic work, while their academic work interferes with their jobs; they are too busy with classes to earn all the money they need and too busy making money to earn all the good grades they need. This is a conundrum of the working class in college that leaves them short on cash as well as undereducated. (In this Brave New World, many of their teachers are also overworked and underpaid; my English Department has ninety adjuncts and only thirty-five full-timers).

Such conditions make many students (and teachers) cynical about the status quo, even if they don't question it critically or oppose it politically. My students have little free time to feel sorry for themselves or to attend protest meetings. Few imagine becoming opposition activists, democratic reformers, or critical thinkers. Such goals are luxuries in the low-rent district of the academy where we study and in the working-class neighborhoods where the students learn what to expect from life. Still, despite all the obstacles to critical inquiry, if I find ways to pose the status quo as a problem in words legible to their experiences and discourses, debates do occur and their habitual perceptions and social relations get questioned.

In questioning social class as a generative theme, I've been experimenting with data bases for problem-posing. I bring to class quantitative and visual materials regarding income differences, working conditions, concentrations of wealth, outsourcing of jobs, immigrant employment, industrial outputs, and race and gender relations in the job market, as well as data on the choices young people make in terms of college majors, postgraduate occupations, drugs, alcohol, smoking, sexual activity, abortion, places to live, recreation, crime, politics, and so forth. I bring in line graphs and bar graphs, information tables, pie charts, opinion surveys, geographical data maps, "then and now" studies, census extracts, and disaggregated population statistics for decoding, interpretation, and discussion.

I call this approach "stories in the numbers" because each data base tells a story in numerical terms about how we live (the generative contexts). I ask students to translate the numerical representations into written texts. We then debate how to read and write the data. I also pose questions of social interpretation: Is this situation being reported good or bad for society? Who benefits and who loses because of this condition? How did it get like this? How could it be changed? For example, I bring in a chart tracing the percentage of national wealth controlled by the top 1 percent over the last hundred years, asking students to write a paragraph decoding what the numbers say and explaining what were the best and worst years to be super-rich in the United States. Next I ask them to theorize what happened to make the best or worst years come and go, especially the long stretch of leaner years for the super-rich after World War II that changed into triumphant wealth for the elite after 1980. In another instance, I bring in a map chart encoding teenage pregnancy rates in different regions of the country. Students discover that the South has the highest rates. I ask them to theorize why that region has more teenage pregnancy than others. Their writing produces some hilarious theories (such as hot weather makes people want more sex) and some economic explanations (such as the South is poorer and poor girls are at higher risk for teenage pregnancy).

This "stories in the numbers" approach, then, is one way I reinvent your generative theme method. Of course, organized opposition in society on social class would be an enormous asset to my critical teaching, giving the classroom something larger to feed into and to feed from. You said in our talking book that education alone cannot be the "lever" for transforming society, a lesson you took away from the coup:

Yes, it is true that after 1964 I grew more aware of education's limits in the political transformation of society. But, nevertheless, through education, we can first understand power in society. We can throw light on the power relations made opaque by the dominant class. We can also prepare and participate in programs to change society. (Shor and Freire, 1987, pp. 31–32)

To understand power in society. To throw light on power relations. These are goals that guide my practice when I experiment in the hostile time and place I now inhabit.

What many of us gained from your work is a convergence of educational theory with democratic communications, a method for curricular practice with a philosophy of knowledge, an ethics of mutuality with a politics of social justice. I remember a question posed to you at various meetings in the States: "Paulo, is there hope?" You would always answer, "Yes." Hope to you was not mere wishing for good things to happen. Hope to you had legs that made the road by walking. Hope meant acting every day in whatever ways possible to make real our dreams for a more just, less violent world. Such hope is on my mind when I act, only more so since the birth of my son, now four, named for you, our Little Paulo.

Even in these threatening times, many hopes circulate amid a surprising amount of opposition. But my frustration is that opposition is divided into separate spheres of concern—global warming, antiwar, children's needs, school financing, immigrant rights, labor organizing, reproductive freedom, gay marriage, and so forth. The need for consolidated opposition is urgent. You were a figure who brought together isolated or divided groups. Wherever you spoke, you wanted your visit to be a pretext for solidarity and for reflection on what can be done. For this and more, you are still needed and very much missed.

Abrazos, Ira

⁓

⁓ Andrée Rose Catalfamo Fee ⁓
Can Popular Education Work in U.S. Educational Settings?

> *The educator's biggest problem is not to discuss whether education can or cannot accomplish, but to discuss where it can, how it can, with whom it can, when it can; it is to recognize the limits his or her practice imposes.*
> —Paulo Freire, *Daring to Dream: Toward a Pedagogy of the Unfinished* (2007), p. 64.

April 1997

Dear Paulo,

I came upon the format for communicating with you in the bargain bin at the Strand Book Store in New York. I had just attended a day-long conference at the Learning Alliance called "Can Education Create Social Change?" At the conference, a number of people spoke about the influence of popular education and of your work on their own teaching practices. It was an energy-charged time for me.

As I walked into the conference that morning, a man approached me. Timothy Leary–like in appearance, he introduced himself and immediately started asking me questions about who I was and where I had come from. I had the feeling of being interrogated, although in a nice, sort of laid-back way. After I told him that I was a student of adult literacy education at Penn State, he leaned in closer and whispered to me confidentially, "You know, I have this friend. He writes a lot of books about education. You should check him out sometime." And with that, he reached into his ancient knapsack and pulled out a copy of your *Letters to Cristina*. I nodded in agreement with the man and told him that I had studied your work to some degree, but that I hadn't read this particular book, your newest at the time. He said, "Well, you can hold on to this book during the conference. I'll need it back in a little while, though."

I read the first part of *Letters to Cristina* while waiting for the morning's activity to begin. A combination of your retrospective history and theoretical musings, the book is based on your correspondence with your niece, Cristina. When that correspondence first began, Cristina was a child, and her letters to her "Uncle Paulo" were full of questions about your life in Geneva, where you were in exile. Later, as Cristina grew up and began to pursue a career, she encountered your writings in academic situations. So Cristina asked, "I would like for you to write me letters about your life, your childhood, and little by little, about the trajectory that led you to become the educator you are now."

Needless to say, I was captivated not only by the book's contents but also by its creative style. However, my hippie friend was eager to retrieve his copy, and at the end of the morning sessions I had to relinquish it.

Later in the day, my boyfriend and I walked into Greenwich Village, eager to shop at the Strand Book Store. Almost immediately I made my way to the bargain bin, where I can somehow always find good academic books at a 50 percent discount. I was flipping through the stacks of books, when *poof!* There appeared a copy of *Letters to Cristina*! I figured it was fate, and placed the book onto my stack for purchase.

I have to be honest: I am a little bit jealous of Cristina. Imagine, having Paulo Freire for an uncle! Imagine being able to write to you with all my questions about education, life, culture, and more. It was while wishing I could have a correspondence with you that I thought, well, why can't I? So I started constructing a "dialogue" with you. And maybe one day I'll get to meet you. If I do, I'll already have my questions prepared.

So, Paulo, here's my question for you: Can popular education work in U.S. educational settings? In *Issues in Freirian Pedagogy*, Tom Heaney ended a rather lengthy discussion of your ideas with the following critique:

Participatory and democratic pedagogical practices might be adapted to American schools, but the critique of social and economic oppression linked with collective action for social change creates dissonance, destroying the neutrality of the schools and unmasking their complicity in maintaining the economic and political imbalance of the social order. Historically, liberatory programs for literacy have been sustained by the government only during the brief time following a revolution, as in Nicaragua or Guinea Bissau—a time when the possibilities for change are real and the political apparatus for accomplishing those changes is at hand. The pedagogy of Paulo Freire has limited potential outside such chaotic and transitional periods in a nation's history. (Heaney, 1995, para. 31)

I wonder what you might think about the notion that your work is applicable and useful only in societies that are in a state of revolution or postrevolution? Frankly, I agree that the U.S. government is not likely to fund educational initiatives that create cracks in the status quo. Collins (in Welton, 1995) noted that although teachers who want to use your methods to break out of the paradigm of banking education do exist, they are also fearful of "risky pedagogical currents which challenge status quo arrangements," adding that teachers who try to use problem posing and other techniques that you advocate do not get support for their ventures from administrators. Thus there seems to exist a sigh of disappointment among many progressive educators who are inspired by your theories yet see them as not useful, or even downright dangerous, in their classrooms. In fact, I had one adult educator tell me that your theories were "passé" and irrelevant.

I do not think that is the case. At the heart of your pedagogy is the idea of "problem-posing education." To me, it is important for people everywhere to gain critical thinking skills, regardless of their geography or cultural background. Understanding the workings of one's society, should that understanding lead either to an agreement with or a struggle against the status quo, is vital for every person. Your pedagogical notions of dialogue and praxis encourage learners to think deeply about the cultural contexts in which they live, and to talk about what they observe with the instructor and other students. Certainly, in the case of adult literacy students, if the low-literate began, through the process of problem-posing education, to understand their world, would they not be better able to become agents of change for themselves, their families, and their communities? With the recent U.S. welfare reforms and other measures designed to remove the poor from public assistance, it would seem to be beneficial for people living in poverty to learn critical thinking skills in order to become more "self-sufficient." Not only can problem-posing education be used with adult literacy students but it can, and should, be used with students at any level of academic achievement, for we can all benefit from strengthening our critical thinking skills, and we all constantly need to re-evaluate the culture and our place within it.

No, Freirian pedagogy isn't passé. In fact, I think it may be just what we need right now.

With all my admiration,
Andrée Rose Catalfamo Fee

∽∾

⊱ Carlos REC McBride ⊰

Pedagogy of Love

Transformation has to be accomplished by those who dream about the reinvention of society, the recreation or reconstruction of society.
—Paulo Freire, *A Pedagogy for Liberation: Dialogues on Transforming Education*, with Ira Shor (1987), p. 36.

There's a war going on outside, no man is safe from…
—("Survival of The Fittest," *Prodigy Mobb Deep: Shook Ones*, April 1995)

August 31, 2007
Dear Paulo,

I am writing to thank you for the work, the words, the love, that you have contributed toward education and liberation, primarily for those who are less privileged. Paulo, now I am committed to fighting the injustices that continue to oppress my people. There are many of us who are doing the work, but not enough, as I am sure you know. I am committed to doing work that will manifest three generations ahead. When I read your work, I feel as though you are speaking directly to me, letting me know that I made the right decision in my life to want to make change. Before this, my life had been full of death and pain.

Death. I was a young thirteen-year-old when my best friend, Kirk, passed away. I had a job working at a fast food restaurant when I first heard that Kirk was gone. Apparently, he and another friend had been walking along a concrete wall that ran parallel to a highway, and he fell down a sewer pipe. He ended up with a concussion and after some time in the hospital passed away. The passing of Kirk hit home really hard. I remember the funeral home filled past capacity with family and friends. Tracey, my other best friend, and I cried endlessly at Kirk's closed casket. That seemed like one of the longest days of my life.

That would not be the first time I would encounter the passing of a close one. In fact, it became such a regular event that by the time I was twenty and my mother had passed, my emotional expression was somewhat subdued. It seemed as though I had grown immune to the pain, even though deep down inside I was crushed.

Death was not uncommon in my neighborhood. The summers were hot, drawn out, and full of rage. My community was poor and desperate. Opportunities were scarce and summer youth found no outlets in federally cut programs, so the corner fire hydrants were common swimming holes for many. We lived each night as if it were our last, going hard into the early hours of the morning with hangovers and landing from our previous drug trip. There were many of us in the streets, having to become men without knowing a childhood. For the most part, the majority of us came from single-parent households. The small minority who had two parents never saw them much because they were always working low-paying jobs.

We were a generation that was one hit away from watching our peers struggle with heroin and one rock closer to an epidemic of crack cocaine. We were young soldiers wanting to become generals in a game that promised us two things, death or prison. We were aimlessly traveling through life without a purpose, painting articulate murals of multicolored sorrow for the last victims claimed by street violence. We were hardened by the adversities that we faced as young adults. With little room for emotional growth, love was not fostered, and the only time we were allowed to show our emotions was during a funeral. Otherwise, if you were caught shedding tears for anything else, it was seen as a sign of weakness.

The school system failed us. There we were, in the first weeks of school in what should have been an exciting time for a "new year," but instead we were getting together drinking, smoking, and figuring out where we would go to hang out. By the time the average student was graduating, many of us had already gone to jail, been killed, or became parents. Our lives were in turmoil.

Life. After dropping out of school, I was on the express lane to becoming another statistic of an urban fatality. It was not until the birth of my first child, Desiree, that I realized that something in my life had to change. I was only twenty but felt as though I had lived three times the years, and still, as a parent I had no idea what direction I was headed. Nothing in my life during that time was stable. As much as I dreamed of having a family, I knew that at that time in my life, I was not ready.

It took a great many unfortunate circumstances finally to wake me up to the reality of needing to succeed in my life. After dropping out of school and receiving my G.E.D., I worked a number of manual labor jobs until I found myself faced with a difficult situation in life. I needed to make a drastic choice and abandon the precarious lifestyle I led and sincerely focus on finding a solution to become a better provider for my daughter.

I was introduced to a new organization called the Learning Tree, an organization that fostered the development of young teens who had taken the wrong path in their lives. Working a factory job at the time, I went straight to the Tree after a long twelve-hour shift. I took basic writing courses and applied to the James Baldwin Scholarship program at Hampshire College in Massachusetts, a partnership program the Learning Tree had set up.

I was accepted into Hampshire College as a Baldwin Scholar, and my future would begin to take a slow turn in a direction that I could never have imagined…

It took me some time, and all the willpower I could possibly muster, to grasp the idea of being in a structured learning environment after so many years of being out of school. The intimidation and frustration of being an older student and the feeling of being inadequate pushed me to broaden my perception of being a "student of the academy." I feared and loathed the thought of becoming someone else as a result of my new education. I represented a rawness that was only learned and cultivated through the socialization process of growing up in the streets.

It wasn't until after the completion of my bachelor's degree that I finally woke up to what I was supposed to be doing with my life. Juggling miscellaneous jobs, I ended up teaching in a high school called Legacy in New York City. It was a small high school that served young folks who had been failed by their prior schooling. Legacy High School was their "last chance" school. I had little to no facilitation skills and could not produce a coherent outline for what I would teach. I relied on the only thing that I knew, and the only thing that was important to me in terms of the contribution I could make to the work in the classroom—and that was the sharing of my own experiences and the ability to listen to young folks' personal experiences.

That, Mr. Freire, was a life-changing point for me. My relationship with the young folks was profound, a relationship that could only be fostered through the authenticity of personal exchange and support. We shared the understanding that there is no hierarchy in oppression, only an ugly beauty of living a life that promises very little to those who have no guidance, mentorship, and, most important, strangers to love. This experience propelled me to return to school and commit myself to the world of education and the opportunity to sharpen my skills so that I could be reborn and acquire the necessary tools I needed to champion my people.

Rebirth. Many folks find God and feel as if they have been reborn. I feel as if I have been reborn through love (God in the rawest form). Not the love for material things, or the love that is innate, but the love that is manifested through the understanding of one's awareness of one's purpose in life. I feel that I have been given a second chance to share my experiences with those who are living in the same world that I was in during my younger years. Teaching to learn, to learn more about myself through the experiences of others, is what I have come to embrace. To share what I know so that those who are in need can then turn around and do the same for others. To be a contributor toward the fight against the social injustices that prevent our young folks from excelling and realizing their potential.

The generation at hand, Paulo, is in dire straits. There is a state of emergency in urban education. Our kids are dying daily and getting caught up in false dreams that are disguised as the "American Dream." Along with like-minded educators, teachers, mentors, friends, students, and scholars, from Massachusetts to New York to Washington, D.C., to Chicago and California and beyond, I have solidified myself in the fight for social justice through education by way of consistently being true to myself, to my history, and my position in a quiet revolution that is making a big noise across the country.

I want to thank you, Paulo, for helping me believe that I can become a proponent of social justice in education. I write this letter to you to reach out and assure you that your work has changed me in a very big way. I have found my calling, and I am driven by an intoxicating passion to help liberate those who are lost, while challenging the status quo that continues to repress the growth of young scholars and intellectuals. I have an obligation, Paulo, to impact the potential of youth and the way youth think about themselves. I write to you on behalf of the family and friends I have lost along the way, for those who will probably never learn how to free themselves from the oppressed conditions we live in, for those who are fighting the same wars as I am, and, most important, for the young revolutionaries who will continue to practice the pedagogy of love.

With gratitude, love, and respect,
Carlos REC McBride

∽◦∾

⌒ Elizabeth Rendón ⌒

Testimony to Teaching

> *Whether the teacher is authoritarian, undisciplined, competent, incompetent, serious, irresponsible, involved, a lover of people and life, cold, angry with the world, bureaucratic, excessively rational, or whatever else, he/she will not pass through the classroom without leaving his or her mark on the students.*
> —Paulo Freire, *Pedagogy of Freedom* (1998a), p. 64.

November 2005
Dear Paulo,

I went into teaching without a degree in education. From the very beginning, I enrolled in courses that were designed to help me become a licensed educator. It was in those courses that I first heard of you and your work. I had not read your work, but I had heard about your ideals, and they inspired me to become an advocate for my students who, I felt, were often misunderstood.

Now, as a doctoral student, I am actually reading your work for the first time. I must say that at first I found your writing hard to understand, but the more I read, the more I understood your thoughts and beliefs. I am awed by the way you put good teaching into words. Practices and concepts that are taught in teacher training schools are oftentimes unattached to the students' real life experiences, leaving an incomplete understanding of what real teaching means. In *Teachers as Cultural Workers*, you provide clear and concise reasons as to why we need to provide quality education to our students. Your "letters" are not like other textbooks that list teacher practices; they are words with feelings that allow educators to deeply understand the impact we have on students.

In one of your letters you talk about testimonies, which are a critical part of teaching. Through these testimonies, teachers are better able not only to reach but also to relate to our students. Your belief in constant commitment and dedication to defending students from the unjust situations that society yields is more than just an ideal. I can see how imperative it is for me to fight against the inequalities embedded in our community. Also, I now have a drive to empower students to continue this battle for social justice.

Paulo, I want to thank you for your work. Now that I have read what you are all about, I can tell you that I honestly admire you for standing up for the rights of all children. Many educators follow the mandates of the district we work in, and tend to forget the real meaning of the act of teaching.

Thank you. You are truly an inspiration!

Sincerely,
Elizabeth Rendón

Part 4: Praxis

Critical reflection on practice is a requirement of the relationship
between theory and practice. Otherwise theory becomes
simply "blah, blah, blah," and practice, pure activism.
—Paulo Freire, *Pedagogy of Freedom: Ethics,*
Democracy, and Civic Courage (1998a), p. 30.

Praxis, a term intimately connected with Paulo Freire, is part of what makes his work both enormously meaningful and important to teachers, community workers, and academics. For Freire, learning needs to consist of both reflection *and* action, not of simply one or the other. This means that learning and working—whether through reading, writing, doing science or art, farming, or teaching in international settings—are fundamentally human activities that have a transformative potential.

Teachers, teacher educators, and other academics all struggle with striking the right balance between theory and practice. Many teachers frequently complain that their education courses do not prepare them adequately for the classroom because they fail to provide enough practical knowledge, while professors often lament the paucity of theory in everyday teaching. Even community workers and others whose work seemingly may not call for much theorizing are challenged by this tension. It can safely be said that the most persistent dilemma in teaching and learning is how to translate theory into action without minimizing the significance of either.

The letters that follow explore the issue of praxis as it relates to various contexts: an art classroom, the preparation of teachers for urban schools, working with troubled youths in community settings, and others. Despite tremendous differences in context, they all share a view of teaching as moving beyond the boundaries of teaching as talk and transmission.

⚭

⚭ *Jacqueline Pinn* ⚭

A Good Vision, Not an Easy One

I am more and more convinced that educational praxis, while
avoiding the trap of puritanical moralism, cannot avoid the
task of becoming a clear witness to decency and purity.
—Paulo Freire, *Pedagogy of Freedom* (1998a), p. 38.

November 28, 1999
Dear Paulo,

As with all endings, beginnings emerge. And so it is that I have completed my first encounter with your thoughts. My head is full, my belly is full. I haven't digested it all yet. But, then again, you would not want me to regurgitate it back to you, would you? No. You would want me to digest it. Chew on it. Savor it. And begin to incorporate the theories, the dialogue into my very being. That would be what you would want, no? Or, perhaps there is nothing you want from me at all but that I understand the ground I walk on, the place from whence I engage others. Oppressed or oppressor? Until I read this work, I would never have assigned the question to me, a black woman. But, somehow I do now. And it is not altogether a comfortable feeling, this question of where I stand in all of this. I feel as though I now exist with this dirty little secret: I have been guilty of oppression, of cultural invasion, of addressing oppressed people as if I have all the answers, as if, in some way, I am their salvation. How prideful, eh? What would you say, my friend? (Can I call you friend? I'll have to take that risk.)

Having read your work, may I tell you what I am conscious of that hadn't occurred to me before? First, I am now aware that no one holds all the answers. Hadn't I ever thought that thought before? Of course, but now I understand it in a different way. To assume that the young people with whom I work have a cultural identity that is in any way deficient is to function with them as their oppressor, not to assist them in their liberation. It is to carry on a tradition of noblesse oblige that is the antithesis of evolution and identity development. It creates separation rather than unity. It is scary to consider that I have been, despite my good words, a part of the problem, rather than a part of the solution.

Becoming a part of the solution would, necessarily, require a shift from controlling the transference of information (being a banker) to starting with people where they are, reflecting on questions that initiate critical dialogue between individuals, and taking actions based on the outcomes of those conversations. Praxis versus practice.

Becoming a part of the solution would, invariably, mean being more vocal about existing forms of oppression—even when I am a beneficiary of such forms of oppression—or perhaps especially when I am a beneficiary of such forms of oppression. But, then, if true revolution and change can emerge only from the oppressed and not from the oppressors, where, Paulo, do I fit? I am oppressed and I oppress others.

More than anything, I want to keep digesting your thoughts because they are potent medicine, indeed. What you have written about is the inclusion of voices among the least accessed peoples of our societies. By including these voices, we further our human cause and create not a new cycle of oppression and domination but, rather, a new (or in many instances old, very old) paradigm of equality. It is a good vision, not an easy one.

Jacqueline Pinn

∽

☞ Toni Hochstadt ☜

Teaching as Advocacy

All educational practice implies a theoretical stance on
the educator's part.... It could not be otherwise.
—Paulo Freire, The Politics of Education: Culture,
Power, and Liberation (1985), p. 43.

Fall 2000

Dear Paulo Freire,

I have spent three years working with youth in crisis in both an urban residential program and a wilderness residential/reprieve program. When I began this work I was full of good intentions. I had done a fair bit of traveling and moving around, both in my native North America and in Western Europe and East Africa. I thought I was worldly and that this was a strong quality.

The first thing I discovered on the job was *fear*. I was unprepared for the aggressive and often angry fronts the youth presented as a grasp for power in, and over, their lives. I dealt with this fear initially by being frozen. Then I shook myself, swallowed my pride, and spoke with my coworkers about what I had been experiencing. Gradually I came to trust my supervisor enough to reveal my fears to him as well. I found support to examine the source of my fears and summoned courage to face them. Often it came down to "How bad can this get? Am I going to be hit? I can survive that." In imagining the worst and facing it, I had freed myself from the earlier paralysis.

The next thing I discovered was that the youth I worked with were trying to live simultaneously as adults and as small children. They lived outside of their families for various reasons, and that made possible greater freedom of movement, resulting in, among other things, sexual relationships, prostitution, pimping, drug use, drug addiction, car thefts, assaults (as both victims and perpetrators), and burglary. These same individuals, at times, could be found with a stuffed animal in their arms, drinking hot chocolate and watching cartoons on the television. Some demonstrated developmental behaviors they had yet to satisfy, such as repeatedly calling a staff person, for no other reason than to get the response, "Yes, I am here."

Judgmental attitudes had no positive impact on these youth, so an open heart and an open mind were key. Support was needed when facing pregnancy, an abortion, an AIDS test, a rape, an overdose, a jail sentence. Accepting their situation was the first step, listening was the next, and giving honest and realistic responses and feedback was the final step in giving support.

For many, going to school was a struggle, as it represented another "must" imposed on their lives. Additionally, peer pressure in the schools steered them away from excelling. The message they seemed to deliver was "I am here because I have to be in order to stay out of jail, but you can't make me enjoy it or work at it." I never did have the opportunity to work with them in the school, although I did observe on occasion. My message to them was to pursue their dreams, as living a life takes a lot of effort, so you might as well "go for the gold."

What I discovered was the value of imagination. It took originality and creativity to reach these youth. It took risks of candidness to connect with them. It took resolve to see past their facades and begin to know the potential development of the person inside the tough exterior. These youth were survivors, but they had the opportunity to become more than that, if they could just find a secure connection from which to build. Each of us working with them wanted to provide a link to that greater potential. It took dedication and imagination to discover how and when to deliver a message that they so clearly needed to receive. I learned the value of storytelling, as it is used to carry messages in traditions of oral literature. I learned the significance of timing. I learned to be patient.

We worked as teams to identify issues, face them, and simultaneously provide care. We all came to know the value of providing food, at all hours of the day or night, as basic nurturing. We supported one another in accepting strengths with weaknesses and we appreciated the cohesion that came as a result of being in a group rather than individuals working toward the same goals.

In reading your letters, I have found encouragement, reminders, and the occasional "kick in the pants" as I consider myself in the role of educator. The greatest frustration I faced in my work with youth was with the government that oversaw their lives. The job of advocacy came late in my experience, but it gives me an idea of what it means to be an activist in my job as teacher and role model.

Thank you for sharing yourself with us.

Sincerely,
Toni Hochstadt

☜ *Kerri Warfield* ☞

Questioning, Teaching, and Growing

*It is my belief that today the progressive kind of teacher needs
to watch out as never before for the clever uses of the dominant
ideology of our time, especially its insidious capacity for spreading
the idea that it is possible for education to be neutral.*
—Paulo Freire, *Pedagogy of Freedom* (1998a), pp. 89–90.

July 2007

Dear Paulo Freire,

The first time I read your book *Teachers as Cultural Workers: Letters to Those Who Dare Teach* (1998c) was six years ago, when I was beginning my master's program in multicultural education at the University of Massachusetts, Amherst. At that time I had taught for only about two years, and I was searching for answers, strategies, basically anything that would help my practice as an educator: in other words, I was hungry. This is my second letter to you, and although I do not remember the exact words, thoughts, or questions addressed in my first letter, I do know that it reflected my appetite to learn more and also my anxiety as a novice teacher. With this second letter, I am looking at your work through different lenses. These lenses have fortunately become neither clouded nor dulled; in fact, they are sharper from experience and a desire to be a progressive teacher, a message that struck me from the first time I read your book.

There are still many questions I have about teaching. I have found out firsthand that being a "cultural worker" takes endless amounts of energy and comes with many frustrations. At the same time, it is so worthwhile and fulfilling. To quote your words, "with responsibility, scientific preparation, and a taste for teaching, with seriousness and a testimony to the struggle against injustice, we can also contribute to the gradual transformation of learners into strong presences in the world" (p. 33). I believe this statement illustrates our importance as educators.

As I went through each letter, I gravitated toward issues that I have personally tackled and questioned as an educator, particularly as a middle-school art teacher, my chosen area. For example, your second letter, "Don't Let the Fear of What Is Difficult Paralyze You," addresses the fear in learning and teaching. I have felt this fear as a student and as a teacher. Insecurity creates mental blocks. In art class, I often have students who stare at a blank piece of paper or hurry through a project because the discipline to create something worthwhile has not yet developed. I find that self-discipline is a hard thing to teach. What I have tried to do in my classroom is to model projects for my students, give them a variety of ideas to start with, and encourage them to ask questions in order to spark their creativity. I also praise accomplishments (even the small ones), give constructive criticism, and try to create projects that they can relate to.

In your first letter, you mentioned that education needs to make sense to the learner; they need to see how it can be used in their lives. I struggle sometimes with finding these connections, but I do strive for them. What has really made a difference to my teaching is that I fear less, that I am not afraid to address concerns regarding my students, and I am not afraid to try projects that may fail. I believe that my confidence, in turn, makes my students more confident.

Your letter on the indispensable qualities of progressive teachers was both uplifting and discouraging. Let me explain. I found truth in your description of progressive teachers, people who show humility, lovingness, courage, tolerance, and patience, and who promote the joy of living. My discouragement comes from my belief that there are still not enough teachers in our school systems today who have many of those qualities. I wish I were wrong, but too often students and parents complain that certain teachers show aggression, ambivalence, lack of trust in students' abilities, and, in general, they make it clear that they hate their jobs. Is it our job as colleagues to intervene? How does an administration and staff correct this problem? We have workshops, training programs, and so on, that address similar issues every year, but permanent implementation seems to be a problem. More money and funds would help, but I think it is more a question of moving from a traditional school to a more democratic one, as you mention in the foreword to your book *Teachers as Cultural Workers*. Will we ever get there as individuals and as a nation?

Your work is about the connections that exist in education and those that should exist. For example, you believe that there should be relationships among education, culture, and identity in order to create a functionally democratic school. I believe that too, but the idea can feel so big. Were you ever discouraged? Did the injustices of your life motivate you to work harder, to be stronger? How do we move past "no" and "can't," "not now" and "if only"?

Thank you, Paulo Freire, for motivating me to ask these questions again, for we cannot grow as educators if we don't continue learning, re-examining, and questioning our educational paths.

Sincerely,
Kerri Warfield

⟨∞⟩

≈ *Deb Habib* ≈

Seeds of Solidarity
Cultivating Hope with Hammers, Shovels, and Ideas

> [My] hope is necessary, but it is not enough. Alone, it does not
> win. But without it, my struggle will be weak and wobbly. We
> need critical hope the way a fish needs unpolluted water.
> —Paulo Freire, *Pedagogy of Hope: Reliving*
> *Pedagogy of the Oppressed* (1994), p. 8.

January 16, 2007
Dear Paulo,

I would like to tell you about the place I live. I start here because the place and community that I call home is where I interpret and practice your teachings as I learned them, carried forth with wisdom and grace by my mentor, Sonia Nieto.

I live with my family in the North Quabbin, a working-class and poor region made up of nine towns in central Massachusetts. Until the early 1900s, this area was a vital agricultural region. An 18-mile-long, 5-mile-wide valley with the Swift River running through was rich with rural life, vegetable production, orchards, and livestock. In 1938 this valley, with its four communities and the most fertile agricultural land in the area, was flooded to create the Quabbin Reservoir in order to supply Boston, 80 miles east, with drinking water. The creation of this reservoir eradicated most of the agricultural food production potential of the region and literally drowned the rural economy, causing great upheaval of families and lives. Subsequently, mills and tool companies in the region's two main towns, Orange and Athol, and neighboring towns supported the local economies through the 1960s. Then these mills started to close because of globalization. The vibrancy of the region radically diminished, leaving economic despair in its place. The people have been oppressed, and at the same time there is an incredible resiliency and authenticity found here. People know the value of hard work and understand creative survival.

We moved here ten years ago for a few reasons. It was a place where we could afford to purchase land to fulfill our creative vision and dreams, and we saw great need but also the potential for transformation. In these past ten years, since my study of your approach to pedagogy, I've learned a lot about what makes a community, about asking questions and about listening, about grassroots change.

My husband, Ricky, and I initiated Seeds of Solidarity Farm and Education Center from our commitment to liberation from a cycle of ecological oppression in a society that has become increasingly disconnected from the source of our sustenance and basic needs—food, energy, and shelter—while inequitably consuming much more than our share of the world's resources. The mission of Seeds of Solidarity is to provide people of all ages with the inspiration and practical tools to grow food and use renewable energy in their communities. We conceived the name Seeds of Solidarity from a sign we made for our first garden more than twenty years ago: "This land is planted in solidarity with those around the world helping to feed the people." Growing food as an act of solidarity and nourishment for the people continues to guide our lives and work. In the ten years since initiating Seeds of Solidarity, hammers, shovels, and ideas have come together almost daily, resulting in energy-efficient buildings, four productive greenhouses, solar-electric systems, a patchwork of fertile vegetable and garlic fields, and several vehicles powered by vegetable-based fuels.

I learned a great deal from your writings about the power of asking questions. Our mission and resulting programs for local teenagers, schools, interns, universities, and community organizations are informed by questions: Where do our energy and our food currently come from, and at what true cost or benefit, locally and globally, in the short and long term? As an organization, how do we best inspire and educate people diverse in age and background to consume less energy, make less waste, and grow and eat more local, healthful food? I aspire to be the kind of educator who listens to the heart of each young person I encounter in the youth programs we run, and meld this with the context of the world in which we live. How do I help them make sense of current social and environmental issues in order to envision and cultivate a positive future? When I tire of asking hard questions and wondering if it matters, the voices of the young people are energy, salve. Ray, a biracial African American young man is now an accomplished musician who was a member of our first SOL (Seeds of Leadership) Garden program for local teenagers in 1999. He wrote:

> I entered the program somewhat of a confused adolescent. I always felt I needed to stand out and usually that meant I was getting in trouble. SOL Garden marked the first time I realized people would listen to me as a person with ideas. I had to work with everyone to make a goal happen, to see everyone putting in their thoughts and input and listening to what I had to say. Finally my creative side was accepted and I found an outlet. I've adapted a bit of the SOL Garden philosophy—get out there, talk to people, don't force feed it, just educate and let people make up their own minds. The same thing can be said of my music. I just do my thing and let the people decide.

I am excited when a young person makes meaning of what they learn here, integrates it into their own lives, and then shares that gift of their own realization and transformation. Kacie, a young white working-class woman, joined our SOL Garden program when she was fifteen. The next year she became a youth mentor, and now five years later, she reflects:

> Because of SOL Garden, I think about my health, what I eat, how I live my life. I think about the world and how I have a choice to be an active citizen. I think about small things I can do to make a difference and I think about big ideas that could change the world.

In addition to our programs for young people, something very special has evolved out of a vision cocreated by neighbors that embodies a powerful web of community and solidarity. In 1998, soon after moving to this community, my husband, Ricky, was sitting under a tree, surrounded by mounds of freshly harvested garlic from our farm. A neighbor who makes his living as a woodworker and furniture maker stopped by to say hello. Ricky lamented the fact that this premium garlic would likely be sold at wholesale prices to buyers who might not know that it was grown on a beautiful hillside in Orange, Massachusetts. The woodworker shared his frustration that there are also many talented artists in the North Quabbin region who must travel miles from their home to find venues and fairs for their work. The conversation turned toward a discussion of agriculture and arts in our community. As the heat of that August afternoon grew, so did the passion in the conversation. Words exchanged turned into a vision of an event that would celebrate the agricultural and artistic richness and potential of the region. Two weeks after the vision was born, six of us broke bread over dinner and put twenty dollars each into an envelope marked "festival funds," and set a date for the First Annual North Quabbin Garlic and Arts Festival. Nine years later, the festival has grown into a very exciting phenomenon bringing thousands of people to the farm of our neighbor, who actually hosts the event on her land. The festival has boosted the cultural and economic vitality of our community while bringing people together across class, race, age, and political orientation. I've learned from organizing this festival that celebration is a critical component of education and community building.

I continue to guide our nonprofit organization, develop programs, and teach, with critical thinking and social action central to my practice. Yet I am also shifting, seeking to deepen my own approach to social and political engagement by strengthening my inner self through meditation and contemplation so that I can teach, learn, and act from a wiser and more centered core—and sustain being an educator in challenging times in the years to come. Yes, there is a lot "to do" in a world often consumed and [mis]guided by power. While we want Seeds of Solidarity to continue to serve as a learning place for social and environmental change, we also want our young students, young interns, and visitors to witness a farm, workplace, and lifestyle where time for reflection and rest is valued—so that they are inspired to carry on this work rather than run in the other direction. We ask ourselves and others what it means to practice sustainability and social activism in being as much as in action. What are some precepts for living lightly in a heavy world?

In addition to growing food, using renewable energy, and educating others in these practices toward self-sufficiency, self-determination, and social change, we aspire to nourish body, mind, and spirit by creating community with neighbors; balancing news intake with positive action; prioritizing love, play, family, and friends; pursuing livelihood with integrity; and pacing ourselves so that we can sustain the long road ahead.

A quotation from Subcomandante Marcos of the Zapatista land reform movement in Chiapas, Mexico, eloquently sums my hope for our community and for humanity at large:

That for everyone there be, always, bread to illuminate the table, education to feed ignorance, health to surprise death, land to harvest a future, a roof to shelter hope, and work to make hands dignified.

Thank you for your teachings, Paulo. They provide the guidance and inspiration to work deeply in my community and aspire toward justice, beauty, and liberation.

Deb Habib

∽

⁓ *Wendy Seger* ⁓

Context Matters

As an educator, I need to constantly 'read,' better and better, the reading of the world that the oppressed populations I work with make of their immediate context, and of the broader one of which theirs is a part.
—Paulo Freire, *Pedagogy of Indignation* (2004b), p. 63.

October 7, 2007
Dear Mr. Freire,
Context is always important in understanding one another, so here is a snapshot of mine. I started as an elementary school teacher in Kansas. My undergraduate degree in education is from Bethel College, a small Mennonite school in North Newton. There, one of the important components of education was a biweekly convocation designed to inform students' social conscience. We were challenged to think of our life's work in the context of service in response to our faith. The first time I learned of your work was in the early 1980s through my spouse, Lyle, who was studying at Saint Paul School of Theology in Kansas City, Missouri, a United Methodist seminary. Your writings were part of the Saint Paul curriculum, challenging the seminarians to understand ministry in the context of a social gospel. Being a liberation theologian meant struggling for systemic change for those who are oppressing as well as those who are oppressed.

You can imagine how I was drawn to the introduction to *Teachers as Cultural Workers*, as the author, Joe Kincheloe, describes how his undergraduate studies were also at a United Methodist school. It was in that context that he was first introduced to liberation theology, a social theology from Latin America that had the potential to "change the moribund mainstream Protestant religious institutions of the United States" (p. xiii). However, I was bewildered as I read about the painful rejection of Mr. Kincheloe's writing by a professor who would accuse him, first, of plagiarism, rather than explore his thinking through discussion. I offer my spouse's embracing of your work in contrast to the rigid viewpoints that can still be perpetuated in the organized church.

Our lives became more focused on issues of justice after Lyle's graduation from Saint Paul. Together, and apart, we began to carve out careers in a context of service. It was not without sacrifice. The influential writings of Latin American theologians led Lyle to Nicaragua twice during the 1980s. As a way to be in solidarity with the people and make a statement against the U.S. policy of support for the Contras, the participants consented to travel into the war zones where the fighting had taken its worst toll. Anxiety, like an unwelcome guest, was an unforgettable presence in the homes of those who waited for the delegation's safe return.

A few months after the second Nicaraguan trip, we accepted the opportunity to serve as missionaries in Montevideo, Uruguay. Uncomfortable with the title of *misionero*, we knew that we would be changed more than those we were sent to serve. And that is what occurred. We were vulnerable to frustrations and humiliations similar to those that immigrants encounter in the States. Permanently imprinted on our minds was the experience of being second-language learners. We remember the courage it took to master simple acts of living: making a phone call, purchasing medicine, shopping for *alimentos* (food staples), and communicating with our daughters' teachers. Yet, we were sustained by the care of those who supported us both there and back in the States. We returned to Kansas after almost three years in Uruguay.

For the next decade, our lives continued to remain connected with the Latino communities where we served as pastor and teacher. It wasn't until our move to New England that I would hear the regular mention of your name. As a graduate student at the University of Massachusetts, I found my way into the courses of Sonia Nieto, where I once again would reflect upon my role as a teacher of students of a nondominant culture. For four years I worked to understand how the identity of my students could not be separated from the language they spoke. I was obliged to consider their language and culture in cocreating the kind of academic environment that is needed for equity in education. Once again, as in Uruguay, I was transformed through the candid reflection of my identity as a participant in a dominant culture placed in an urban context. At times, it was reaffirming; at other times, discomforting. That is where my present connection with you begins.

I still struggle with being white and serving Latino and other children of color. I am keenly aware of the overwhelming number of white, monolingual teachers serving urban schools. I understand that multicultural education embraces access to good practices and basic literacy across the content areas. I've written reflections about the naive lack of awareness of cultural differences and simplistic attitudes or solutions concerning race and culture. And yet, after all the work, I am still left with my membership in an Anglo Caucasian European group of early immigrants who are now preoccupied with securing the gates of entry into our country with an infallible lock of control. How do I reconcile being white?

In the foreword to your letters, Donald Macedo and Ana Maria Araújo Freire speak of moving from being a paternalistic, pseudo-critical educator to one willing to look at one's work as the political project that it must be. My work must involve "dismantling the oppressive structures and mechanisms" (p. xvii) that create the inequity by using the cultural capital I can assume due to my class privilege. How do I make my cultural capital available? Am I part of the solution through language? My work in literacy has led me to reveal the nuances of academic language while upholding the dialects and home languages of the children. I become their learning partner in discovering how academic language can help them reach their goals, whether it be to change unfair administrative policies (such as having no recess) or convince a family member to quit smoking.

It was in your words about the attributes of teachers that I find the *heart* of becoming accepted. Tears well up whenever I read:

> Indispensable qualities to the progressive teacher are qualities acquired gradually through practice. I shall start with *humility*, which here by no means carries the connotation of a lack of self-respect, of resignation, or of cowardice. On the contrary, humility requires courage, self-confidence, self-respect, and respect for others. Humility helps us to understand this obvious truth: No one knows it all; no one is ignorant of everything. ... [B]ut to humility, with which teachers perform and relate to their students, another quality needs to be added: *lovingness*, without which their work would lose its meaning. And here, I mean lovingness not only toward the students, but also toward the very process of teaching. (P. 74)

I believe we share an understanding of the teaching heart. You would understand why it is amazing that, each year, we learn to embrace the child most difficult to love. You know the sacrifice we make in our family relationships because of our choice to spend large amounts of leisure time in study and planning for lessons that include the concerns and passions of our students. You understand how the joys, worries, and anxieties of our teaching context rest right below our consciousness. Through your words, I find affirmation and tolerance of my context if I commit to the continued nurture of these qualities.

This is a time of unseen accountability in schools. Laws governing the educational landscape have put urban schools in a state of crisis as educators struggle to build the capacity of every child to meet high-stakes testing requirements. As a result, there has been an emergence of many "prepackaged educational materials" in urban schools that do indeed speak of authoritarianism's "total lack of faith in the possibility that teachers can know and can create" (p. 15) or listen to the voices of their students in designing the curriculum. My letter to you comes while making an important personal decision about my future work. The school in which I previously worked accepted a model that is not open to inquiry into practice. There was little space given to consider the situation, "recognizing what is taking place in context, as well as how and why it is taking place" (p. 14). How important is the context of learning? Should those for whom the curriculum is intended inform our praxis? Is it possible that, allowing the context to inform our practice, the quality of the endeavor might be improved?

My answer to the questions above is *yes*; the context is vital to the success of the endeavor if the learning is to be meaningful and enduring. It is for this reason I draw upon your words about courage to take a step into a new position. I am committed to an initiative that values the process of inquiry and supports the creation of learning communities within each school context to inform their practice. I agree with you when you write,

> As teachers, we deal with people, with children, with adolescents, and adults. We participate in their development. We may help them or set them back in their search. We are intrinsically connected to them in their process of discovery ... with seriousness and testimony to the struggle against injustice; we can also contribute to the gradual transformation of learners into strong presences in the world. (P. 62)

I have begun a journey with several schools willing to take on the challenge of making changes in their practice. Through a focus on literacy, the schools become involved in whole school reform, reflecting the goals of the community of learners and the staff. There are risks. Any successful change of practice requires change in philosophy of even the most seasoned educators. There is always the threat of resistance in place of cooperation. However, you offer encouragement to those willing to take on this journey:

> We forge a school-adventure, a school that marches on, that is not afraid of the risks, and rejects immobility. It is a school that thinks, that participates, that creates, that speaks, that loves, that guesses, that passionately embraces and says yes to life. It is not a school that quiets down and quits. (P. 83)

Mr. Freire, thank you for your writing, your gift of language, and your passion for learning, creating a legacy for those of us who seek to make a difference in the lives of others. We desire to arise each day to meaningful work. We want to be remembered not for the great units we've taught, or the awards we were given, but where we placed ourselves. We want to be remembered for being kind, stubborn, gentle, assertive, and relevant. We also want time to be with our families and celebrate our work. It is good to have others like you to show us the way, keep us balanced in our faithfulness and critical reason, and push us to try the difficult. May we demonstrate our honor for your work by hearing your voice as we help others find theirs.

My warmest regards,
Wendy Seger

꧁

⁓ Adriana Morehouse ⁓
Daily Acts of Praxis

> *The climate of respect that is born of just, serious, humble, and generous relationships, in which both the authority of the teacher and the freedom of the students are ethically grounded, is what converts pedagogical space into authentic educational experience.*
> —Paulo Freire, *Pedagogy of Freedom* (1998a), p. 86.

October 2000

Dear Paulo,

As I reread your letters, I find myself thinking about your ideas again and again. This doesn't happen just after I read them, but even hours and days later. Every time I read them, I find them different. I don't know up to what point there are one or many truths in what you write. I think that there are different truths for each person who reads them. I have to confess that although I enjoy your writing and it stimulates my intellect, it gives me a headache to read your letters. I don't know if it's because I am reading them in English or because you do not write "democratically." Even though your ideas are for everyone, not everyone can understand your writing.

In your writing, you frequently mention fear. As you say, fear is a human response, and when we admit that we feel fear, we become more human. I agree with you on this. Nevertheless, I believe I have a right to "my fears" in private. I am not willing to share them with my students; they belong to me, and it is my job and not theirs to confront my fears. It is not that I want them to see me as perfect. However, I do not want to impose another burden on them.

Paulo, it seems to me that there is a contradiction in your writing. On the one hand, you admit the "humanity" of teachers, yet on the other, you give us a task that is almost superhuman. You give us such a daunting responsibility that it generates in me the fear that you write so much about. You insinuate that teachers must be political agents. I don't know specifically what you mean. When you explain it in such a global and idealistic way, it seems so far from my daily life that it seems unreachable. I need to define this in terms that are concrete for me, that make sense for me and my daily personal and professional life. I wonder if the small daily acts in which I engage count for you, and if you would accept that I am a political agent in my own way?

I end this letter with profound gratitude because you remind me of the need always to reflect and evaluate my actions, my profession, and my life. Sometimes in the daily grind of life, I've put these things on the back burner. I am grateful for all you have taught me, but especially for helping me look inside myself.

Your admirer,
Adriana Morehouse

ᐧᐧ

⊱ *Tom Wilson* ⊰

Learning Moments
Raging a Bit, and with Hope

> *I am younger at seventy-five than when I was forty! I hope*
> *that in another ten years I am younger still than today....*
> —Paulo Freire, *Daring to Dream* (2007), p. 85.

September 6, 2007
Dear Paulo,

While you have been traveling for the last ten years, you have never really left. In this time my thinking about you has been hardly linear. Rather, there are a plethora of images, a rich kaleidoscope of learning experiences that give expression to the influence you had and continue to have upon me. To give some sense of order to these patterns, I have taken the letters of your first name, one by one, as a rather loose organizational move. I first offer a gerund or two to signify ongoing action, then follow with an event or events that illustrate the action, or as you were wont to say, "concretize the experience." I believe these remembrances, these learning moments, while subject to the vagaries of time, are faithful accounts of the events they describe. They are forever with me. I also pose a few questions for you that I should have but never asked.

PAULO: Partying (with Passion)

Partying. You joined with Myles Horton at Loyola Marymount University, Los Angeles, to put the final touches on *We Make the Road by Walking: Conversations on Education and Social Change* (1990). After meeting with you, Myles returned to the university's guesthouse in which you and he were staying. You had to attend another meeting. While waiting for your return, Myles breaks out the rum (I think rum) and pours drinks around. After a while, you show up. Myles says, "Paulo, come on in, we're getting drunk, have a drink or two." You replied, "Yes, yes, maybe more than two, don't worry though, I'll catch up." You did, and the stories flowed, as did the rum.

After this cocktail hour, we all moved on to Pacific Palisades for further libations and dinner in honor of Myles's eightieth birthday. I asked you who had influenced your own thinking, on whose shoulders do you stand? As I recall, not in any particular order you responded, "Marx, Gramsci, Fromm, Freud, Maslow, Fanon, and of course, your John Dewey." (Maslow, I thought to myself, in what way? I still regret not asking this question). The Dewey connection had a longer shelf life and remained with me. For the 2003 American Educational Research Association conference I organized a symposium entitled "Paulo Freire and John Dewey: Soul Mates or Kiss'n Cousins?" It was a standing-room, overflow-into-the hall kind of a session. I wish you could have been there.

Passion. You always expressed strong emotional attachment for food and good drink. I often cite your writing in *The Politics of Education* (1985)—excuse my paraphrase, for I don't have the book in front of me—of not trusting anyone who does not like to eat or drink, and you are not talking just about fruit juices. Your passion menu also included friendship, love, justice, fairness, and lest I forget, the spirit and vitality of Brazil exemplified in no small manner by samba and equally important, Brazil's games in World Cup *futbol.*

P*A*ULO: *Attending*

Always listening to what people had to say, rarely nodding in agreement or disagreement, just understanding. I first met you at the University of Massachusetts, Amherst (1984 or 1985), where you were giving a series of seminars organized by Peter Park. I wanted to invite you to come to the University of California, Irvine, to meet with a group of some forty-five high school teachers (history, English, arts, foreign language) who were due to attend a ten-week intensive summer institute entitled "Ethics, Aesthetics and Critical Reasoning across the Humanities Curriculum" funded by NEH, the National Endowment for the Humanities (we were under the radar, since William Bennett, the conservative guru, had just become the director of NEH). On the first day of the Amherst meeting, Peter asked me to meet with the two of you in the foyer of the auditorium where Paulo was scheduled to speak. Talk about nervousness—I had read *Pedagogy* when it first came out in English, yet here I was to meet the author in the flesh. Peter introduced me, you smiled, put your arm around my shoulder, and as we walked down the aisle toward the podium, you asked if I would join you, Elsa, and Peter for dinner, and if I liked Chinese. Talk about attention. Paulo, if you had asked if I liked cockroach, I would have said yes. You and Elsa did come to Irvine to meet with the teachers. This initial meeting resulted in our fourteen-year friendship; you also came on at least four other occasions. During the first time, my codirector sent a message to all humanities faculty, particularly the UCI Critical Theory Institute, saying, in essence, "You must come and hear this guy." Jacques Derrida was a perennial visiting professor to the institute. Did you know him, did he know you, do you know if he knew of your work?

PAULO: <u>U</u>ndercutting, <u>U</u>nflinching, <u>U</u>npacking, <u>U</u>nrelenting, <u>U</u>nveiling

Paulo, I call these the *March of the Uns.* For me, they characterize your approach to fairness, democracy, and justice. They are constant reminders that rarely leave me alone, but rather give hope and comfort as they impact my own—to borrow your words—"ontological vocation." It is impossible to give up. I am now one year older than you were when you left on your trip, yet how can one not continue to face the oppression that confronts us as long as one is able to do so? With this task in mind, here are a few things that continue to have your imprint:

Continuing to develop the Paulo Freire Democratic Project (PFDP) within the School of Education at Chapman University. Do you recall the Omaha, Nebraska, Pedagogy of the Oppressed Conference with Augusto Boal? I asked if I could use your name for the project. You said of course, and we shook hands to seal the agreement.

Establishing the only bust of you in the world (we think, other than the "Swedish chair") on the Chapman Campus. Nita was actively engaged in the process and gave the keynote address when the bust was unveiled as part of the university awarding you posthumously the honorary doctorate in 1998.

Working to establish La Escuela Freire: Academy for Culture, Leadership, and Civic Engagement, a secondary charter school for downtown Santa Ana, California. As you probably recall, Santa Ana is largely Hispanic/Mexican, with high immigrant and poor populations.

Editing *Memories of Paulo* along with Peter Park and Anaida Colón-Muñiz (manuscript in preparation)—a collection of remembrances from individuals who had personal contact with you regardless of the length of time. It is not focused on your works but on you and who you are, although the distinction between the two is hardly pure. Nita will write the introduction, Peter McLaren the afterward.

Working with a number of educational institutions including schools, universities, and county school districts on critical pedagogy and participatory action research.

Teaching all courses, regardless of subject content, critically. All of these endeavors will remain hopefully true to the *March of the Uns*, to the power of an undercutting, unflinching, unpacking, unrelenting, and unveiling pedagogy of the oppressed.

PAULO: Loving

Such a powerful word in all of its meanings! Previously I mentioned Eric Fromm as one who influenced your thought. In his *The Art of Loving* (1989) (have you read this?), he writes that love is both personal and social: "There is no division of labor between love for one's own and love for strangers.... [To] take this insight seriously means indeed a rather drastic change in one's social relations from the customary ones" (pp. 116–17). Love plays out in "the small details of daily life" as well as in the economic system wherein "the *principle* underlying capitalistic society and the *principle* of love are incompatible" (pp. 118–19). I don't think you would disagree with Fromm's analysis, nor would he find argument with the thought in your *Teachers as Cultural Workers* (1998c) of an "armed love of those convinced of the right and the duty to fight, to denounce, and to announce" (p. 41).

At the personal level, I felt this emotion as we drove to Pacific Palisades for Myles's birthday party. Remember, we were in my 1971 Camaro (I still have it). If I am not mistaken it was the first time you came to the States after Elsa's death. We talked about love, birth, death, and sorrow—you about her, and me about my son

David who died in an auto accident when he was twenty years old. Tears were shed, compassion shared, love expressed, and comfort found in that old Chevy.

I don't know how many times after a meeting or a talk or just a conversation during dinner, I regretted not having a tape recorder. One incident in particular stands out. It was in Irvine, California, at Raul Magaña's house. You deconstructed (if that word does it justice) the word *sexuality* and how you came to recognize yourself as a sexual being. No true love could exist between two individuals without authentic, nondomineering, tender sexual relations. After thirty-four years of marriage, I can relate.

PAUL*O*: *Obligating (and other *O*s)*

Here my thoughts run in phrases, rather than organized passages, sort of a free-form discourse: *obligation* as moral duty, not externally driven but coming from and characterized by the heart (love/emotion/passion), the head (tough minded, rigorous thought, realistic in nature), the hands (the doing, the action, the movement to prevent intellectual "blah"), to *overcome* oppression in the name of democracy, fairness, and justice, doing right because it is the right thing to do, a promise to the self in concert with other selves, *obliterate* all traces of oppression as an *ontological* vocation, the *ought* (not to commit the fallacy of confusing what *ought* to be with what is), *outrage* as captured in your *Pedagogy of Indignation* (2004b), "being *open* to the new, to the different, to innovation, to doubt" (p. 12). As I ramble here, I am listening to the American band Rage Against the Machine wherein the Machine can be, drawing from its website, anything from overpowering others to the "overall international state capitalistic machine that makes one just a mindless cog and not to think critically and never confront the system" (http://www.musicfanclubs.org/rage/biographical.htm). Talk about the educative power of music!

Paulo, in all of these remembrances I have not attempted to lay out what I specifically learned from you. Rather, the totality of your life and teachings has relentlessly permeated my sense of self. I have reached an age older than you when you died. When I get discouraged, tired, and in the middle of the night contemplate truly retiring, I think of you and my obligation to myself and your memory. Then as the sun comes up, I get out of bed, rage a bit and with hope, become once again engaged to confront that gray, smothering ozone of oppression that still bears upon us all.

I do miss you.

Tom

cs

≈ *Sara L. Young* ≈

The Challenges of Aligning Cultural Integrity with Social Justice

> *"[In] the face of changes in understandings, in behaviors, in tastes, and in light of the negation of previously respected values, we must neither simply become resigned, nor rebel in a purely emotional manner.*
> —Paulo Freire, *Pedagogy of Indignation* (2004b), p. 6.

October 15, 2000

Dear Paulo,

I must begin by thanking you. Thank you for your ideas, your theories created from practice, your passion and energy, and your courage to write and practice what you believe to be right; thank you for taking the time to express your truths in written form so that we may also share them.

On cultural identity, you write in one of your letters, "Only as learners recognize themselves democratically and see that their right to say 'I be' is respected will they be able to learn the dominant grammatical reasons why they should say 'I am'" (Freire, 1998c, p. 49). This is a crucial point that many teachers miss in their effort to correct the speech of their students in the United States, Brazil, and other countries. In the United States, the media typically uses the conventions of "standard" English. It is not that students don't know or have never heard the "correct way" of speaking. Rather, they are speaking and forming a language that they feel comfortable using that reflects their cultural identity. I agree wholeheartedly with your conviction that students will not learn the standard grammar until they feel that their own grammar is respected.

In the sixth and seventh letters in *Teachers as Cultural Workers: Letters to Those Who Dare Teach* (1998c), you mention that education is political: "We are political militants because we are teachers" (p. 58). I agree: we are trying to change the world, we are revolutionaries or political militants, if you prefer. As you caution, we must not attempt to "deposit" information or our liberal ideology into our students. We must allow them to create their own vision out of their own knowledge and experience of the world. We should expose them to different ideas, multiple perspectives, and critical questions, but in the end it is they who must decide. They will not make our change, they must make their own change.

I struggle with reconciling these two messages. In order to truly have social justice I believe we must eliminate institutionalized racism, sexism, heterosexism, classism, and Nativism, among other forms of oppression. This is political, economic, and social change, and I believe it is 100 percent necessary in order to truly make change. Yet at times, honoring the cultural beliefs or knowledge of my students impinges on social justice for all people, and that presents a dilemma for me. For example, in the community where I teach, the Catholic Church and many parents, among others, preach that homosexuality is wrong; therefore that is what many of my students believe to be true. This belief interferes with my political quest for social justice and the ability for all families in the community to feel safe and valued regardless of sexual orientation. However, this belief is part of some of my students' cultural identity. How do I respect and honor these students' cultural identity/values/beliefs when it interferes with the other part of my job, which, according to you, implies "our involvement in and dedication to overcoming social injustice" (ibid.)? I refuse to collude with oppression, yet I also want to respect the culture of my students and their families. That is my current struggle. Please offer any words of wisdom.

Respectfully yours,
Sara L. Young

∽

⌐ *Amadee Meyer* ⌐

Changing the World a Little Bit

We are transformative beings and not beings for accommodation.
—Paulo Freire, *Pedagogy of the Heart* (2004), p. 36.

Fall 2004
Dear Paulo,

I am a twenty-three-year-old American. In the past few years, my view of the world has changed drastically. I've had the opportunity to do a great deal of traveling and meet a diversity of people, and these experiences have caused me to pay more attention to what is going on—in my community, in my country, and in the world. When I look at the world, I'm not happy about the ways things are. I'm not satisfied with the ways that humans treat each other. I'm not satisfied with the ways we ignore issues that don't directly affect us. I'm not satisfied with where my country is going.

Being so unsatisfied, before I read your work I was discouraged. I wanted to be an active participant in my society. I wanted, as so many young people do, to change the world. But I didn't know how to do it in a way that would make a difference, and at the same time allow me to enjoy life's pleasures. You've opened my eyes to the fact that as a teacher I really can make a difference in a meaningful and lasting way. I've wanted to become a teacher since I was an elementary school student because I so admired those who taught me. I see now the positive effect they had on my thinking. They changed the world a little bit when they taught me, and I will change the world a little bit when I teach my students.

When I am at home, in the United States, I am sure that to promote democratic participation is to improve people's lives. I want all my students to understand that we live in a very complex, nuanced world. Nothing is black and white, and attempts to fit people, events, or issues into categories of right and wrong, or good and bad, invariably leave out part of the story. I want my students to respect the ideas of others but know that everyone has a bias, a history, a worldview that causes them to hold one idea or another. I want my students to be honest about their own biases, seek to uncover them, and see the world without the veil they create. I want my students to learn the histories of oppressed groups, understand that equality has not been achieved, and work to end institutional practices that alienate one group or another. I could go on and on. These are my goals for my students, but I realize that they are also my personal goals. I need to continue to learn all of these things.

But someday, I would also like to teach abroad, and while I am sure of my convictions at home, I don't know how to justify them in a place where there is no pretense of democracy. How can I bring my ideas about critical thinking and critical literacy to a place where conformity is encouraged and respected? I'm scared, because I know my ideas would be met with opposition. As an outsider, I would lack legitimacy. I don't want to come in as a paternalistic, colonizing educator. That practice has gotten Americans into trouble all over the world. But halfway around the world there are countries where people believe everything their government-controlled media tells them, where people participate in activities that reduce the quality of their lives. They live in a system that was created to eradicate inequality, but it swarms with hypocrisy and fails in that mission. It's not my country. Does that mean I can't introduce a new way of thinking there? Does that mean I shouldn't try to change things? How can I teach critical literacy within the context of culturally responsive pedagogy to learners of a culture that does not respect critical thinking?

I hope that I can answer these questions so that I can become a better teacher to students everywhere. How will I answer them without you here to guide me? I will read what you've written, and I will rethink it, and rewrite it, and re-create it to develop my own pedagogy. And I will hope, that someday when I am gone, someone will read what I have written, and rewrite it again, to create a new picture of the world.

Amadee Meyer

∽

⸙ *Patty Bode* ⸙

Radicalizing the Reading of the World through Art

> To change the world through work, to "proclaim" the world, to express
> it, and to express oneself are the unique qualities of human beings.
> —Paulo Freire, *The Politics of Education: Culture,*
> *Power, and Liberation* (1985), p. 21.

September 25, 2007
Dear Paulo,

As I write this letter to you, I am overwhelmed by the contradictions between the role of art as an avenue of hopeful transformation in schools and the severe reduction of arts programs in schools. Your words in *Pedagogy of the Oppressed*, published almost forty years ago, ring true to the struggles in U.S. public schools today. The restrictions placed on teachers by the government's legislation in *No Child Left Behind* have deeply affected the creativity of teachers and students in K–12 classrooms. As the arts are diminished or obliterated in public schools by a focus on education as conformity, I seek your perspective on what it means to become more fully human by cultivating creativity and supporting the restoration of humanity in youth and their teachers. Currently, I see a wave of activity in U.S. schools that runs parallel to your description of a few men and women denying the majority their right to be human. You explain:

> [T]he oppressor consciousness tends to transform everything surrounding it into an object of its domination. The earth, property, production, the creations of people, people themselves, time—everything is reduced to the status of the objects at its disposal. (Freire, 2000, p. 40)

Examining our schools through this lens, the teachers, students, administrators, and even the time they spend together, are being reduced to objects or statistics and measured against the state's rigid definition of success.

Teachers' intellectual prowess is ignored by state policies that insist on prepackaged, scripted curriculum. In the process of conforming to such restrictions the creative spirit of classroom communities is diminished. The primary means of this domination is prescription that stagnates growth and creativity. You write:

> [O]ne of the basic elements of the relationship between oppressor and oppressed is prescription. Every prescription represents the imposition of one individual's choice upon another, transforming the consciousness of the person prescribed to into one that conforms with the prescriber's consciousness. Thus, the behavior of the oppressed is

a prescribed behavior, following as it does the guidelines of the oppressor. (Ibid., pp. 28–29)

And because the oppressed have adopted the guidelines of the oppressor, they become fearful of freedom.

The specter of oppression casts a wide shadow over pedagogical practices in many U.S. schools today, where teachers are conforming to prescribed methods devoid of praxis. Teachers who have used vibrant engagement in their teaching practices such as welcoming community members into classrooms, bringing students into neighborhoods to conduct interviews, participating in field work at cultural institutions, and developing artistic strategies for uncovering ideas are now reporting a restriction on their pedagogy. In many cases, reflection on practice has been replaced by a fixation on test scores. Local participation in problem-posing education, and community development of curriculum, have been usurped by conforming to so-called accountability measures in the form of standardized tests. This cyclical fear of loss of control is perpetuated, ironically, by giving up control to conform to a prescribed curriculum. The fear of freedom is reinforced by the threat—and in many cases the reality—of state government take-over of schools. This abuse of dominance has resulted in the sweeping alienation of students and teachers in many areas of discourse across school curricula at all grade levels.

In many schools, art programs have been obliterated. In cases where art programs remain, they are stretched thin and compete with test preparation programs for students' and teachers' time and attention. These conditions are most prevalent in districts filled with students whose voices have already been hushed by other social structures such as economic instability, poor housing conditions, and access to health care. In such places, the creative spirit of youth is overshadowed by these conditions.

In the project for teachers and students to become more fully human, the critical spirit must be nourished. The struggles and resilience of students' lives and teachers' resistance to conformity can be expressed through creative curricula that offer students the possibility of questioning knowledge and cultivating critical reflection. When students create paintings, drawings, sculpture, video, and photography, they intertwine their questioning and their academic achievement with cultural expression. When teachers create classrooms in which such artforms can be explored, they push the boundaries of what counts as knowledge while deliberately expanding students' skill.

I see the role of the art teacher as an emancipatory one. Teachers provide the necessary support for students to engage in an education that is not restricted to "reading the word"—but includes reading the context, and reading the world. Since your first printing of *Pedagogy of the Oppressed* in 1970, the expressions and contexts of *the word* and *the world* have been increasingly mediated by visual imagery in the form of web-based media, video, the expansion of television, digital exchange of photo/video, printed image, and also traditional visual arts. These expansions of visual ways in which we read the world have far-reaching implications for art teachers and their students. Problem-posing art education calls for a commitment to promoting the role of art as a construction site of critical knowledge and reflective practice. With the evidence of visual forms pervading cultural discourse, and a growing population constructing knowledge based on image-saturated media more than print-based experiences, the study of art becomes a matter of citizenship and social justice.

Visual media and visual imagery hold great promise as means for critically reflecting on the context of one's world. Simultaneously, the oppressor uses the power of visual imagery, and as you have described, it is in the interest of the oppressor to keep people in a "state of submersion, impotent in the face of oppressive reality" (ibid., p. 34). Visual culture can be used to "submerge human beings' consciousness" (ibid., p. 33) and to domesticate the oppressed. Visual media may be a tool for the oppressive reality that "absorbs those within it" (ibid.). As they engage in reflection and praxis with their students, critical art educators expose the tension of visual culture, a tension that simultaneously can lead to engaged praxis and to increased power for the oppressor.

I have seen this engaged praxis come in many forms. First-grade students investigate the original meaning of an ancient sculpture from South Asia, and compare it with contemporary sculptures they see in their city or town in the United States while reflecting on the role of enduring material forms in a community, and how such sculptures help them read their world. Teen poets develop video expressions of their spoken words and combine that video with interviews of elders in their families and neighborhoods to reflect on a spectrum of ways of reading their world. Seventh-grade painters document the plight of homeless people in their neighborhoods by creating murals to exhibit in town halls, public libraries, and courthouses, calling attention to the disparities in society and motivating government officials to respond. Third-graders visit a shopping mall and examine how the design of the buildings, the displays, and the signs prey on children's concepts of consumerism. They design an alternative marketplace that emphasizes community responsibility.

These examples and many more demonstrate the ways in which art teachers show true solidarity with the students who may be striving to read their world and inviting others to do so with them. You have noted that the oppressed must struggle for liberation with those who show true solidarity, that they must acquire critical awareness of oppression through the praxis of struggle. I am keenly aware that educators of all disciplines who teach students of all ages are poised to demonstrate solidarity. Yet the arts in schools hold a unique opportunity to make the struggle visible and to offer opportunities for praxis.

I have spoken to art teachers who view their role as that of nonconformist leaders. While I was interviewing art teachers about their vision for art teacher preparation programs and their influence on art teaching in schools, one art teacher told me:

> Art education is about nonconformity—taking risks and being different and letting the kids feel like this is a really important place that they can make a difference in the world. You don't have to be like everybody else. [Art education] is a political stand. It's a progressive stand. You don't have to believe what everybody else believes or you don't have to look like what everybody else looks like. Art to me is one place where the kids could get that—and I certainly don't see that happening as a focus or result of the [state's curriculum] frameworks.

Another art teacher emphasized the role of art education in schools as a means to broaden students' reading of the world:

> What would it look like to teach student teachers about art being a non-conformist enterprise? Through art making in schools, students are expressing anger, fears, political statements. There are plenty of artists right here [in this community] to bring into the curriculum. Art making is non-conformist and art teaching should be non-conformist.

Removing art teachers and eliminating artistic opportunities from schools are deliberate acts to create more conformity. When the teacher's role is reduced to an automaton that dispenses scripts, the possibility for teachers' and students' creative expression is suffocated. Such prescription creates multiple layers of oppression so that not only are the students turned into "containers," into "receptacles" to be "filled," but the teachers are also depositories of the state (ibid., p. 53). Banking education stops inventiveness. It does not allow for restless, hopeful questioning of the cause of oppression. To transform is to create, and banking education dehumanizes by choking out creativity. Access to the arts in schools is a matter of democratic necessity.

Now that I am teaching students who will become art teachers, I rely on your vision more than ever to help sustain the creativity of these future art teachers and their forthcoming generations of students. I am more conscious of my role as a teacher-student as my students are questioning the practices of the schools they enter. When they name their world by citing practices with which they disagree, I ask them to investigate the root causes of those practices. When they become excited about ideas that they hope their young artists will grasp, I urge them to explore their students' curiosity. When they engage their students in a study of a painting, a video, a sculpture, or a television commercial, I listen for the critical reading of the world through that study. When they are feeling rebellious about school structures, I encourage a stance of courageous fighting balanced with tolerance.

Your footprints in the landscape of education and your handprints on countless teachers have left enduring marks of change. Your influence on my teaching is far-reaching and includes my work in K–12 art classrooms, community art settings, and now art teacher preparation programs in college classrooms. As a teacher who was taught and mentored by a teacher who was taught and mentored by you, I count myself fortunate to be a "second-generation Freirean." My goal is to proceed humbly as a teacher-student with genuine praxis in art education.

I have come to realize that the role of an art teacher is to radicalize the reading of the world. You have explained: "Radicalization, nourished by a critical spirit, is always creative" (ibid., p. 19). With your inspiration, arts programs, art teachers, and art students can thrive with such a critical spirit. I hope to live teaching-as-learning with humility. I strive to model a love of teaching. I thank you every day.

With love and hope,
Patty Bode

❦

❧ *Michelle Fine* ❧

Chatting across Texts, Geography, and Time

In reality, we do not have children who drop out of school for
no reason at all, as if they just decide not to stay. What we do
have are conditions in schools that either prevent them from
coming to school or prevent them from staying in school.
—Paulo Freire, *Teachers as Cultural Workers: Letters*
to Those Who Dare Teach (1998c), p. 6.

September 1996
Dear Paulo:

I write eagerly, but struggling, trying to imagine how we can best communicate, in writing, when so much of you (and even a bit of me) is about our hands, our pauses, twinkles in eyes, smiles, grimaces, translations across dialects, and leaps from passion to words. I hope we can talk across the borders of language, geography, and paper, and still retain that which makes you magic; that which makes me smile. Do you think we can fax and FedEx delight and outrage? I'll try to start us in this conversation, speaking to my worrisome thoughts on critical consciousness gone awry in the 1990s.

I write, like all of us, multiply positioned. As mother of Caleb, a newborn, trusting, smiling; Sam, a delighted, inquiring nine-year-old, filled with wonder, fledgling politics, and still unscathed trust; and Demetrius, a 19-year-old adolescent still peeling the emotional shackles of foster care off his body and mind, revealing a gorgeous, smart young man who has seen too much, growing into love. I write, too, as a researcher with urban adolescents who have been long deadened by social and school structures and practices, and yet remain alive with the possibilities of dropping out, fleeing, and voicing critique. Ultimately most reproduce their poverties through often courageous acts of resistance. And I write as educational theorist and activist seesawing between a deep desire for what could be, and an equally deep despair, for what is.

I read Myles Horton revealing much the same to you, and the end of his life, in *We Make the Road by Walking*.[1] He was searching for what he saw as "pockets" of radical possibility. I want us to shift metaphors and imagine, instead, that we are searching for connected raindrops of radical consciousness, sprinkled globally. If we can imagine that, I want you to help me invent pedagogical strategies, organizing tactics, that inspire a refreshing, collective shower. That is, I ask you, Paulo, for no less than a rain dance.

Your work has enabled so many of us to imagine "what could be": democratic classrooms, engaging pedagogics, schools as sites of provoking *conscientização*. Puddles of possibilities ripple across the U.S., and the world, indebted to you for intellectual vision and for political commitments. Schools, neighborhoods of adults and children, community-based organizations breathe your legacy.

And yet ... in daily praxis, within most schools, especially those educating the most impoverished students, we confront the next generation of theoretical and political Freirian contradictions: the gaping space between "what is" and "what could be." These spaces are filled with oppressive structures and relations of what presumes to be a "public" education. These bureaucracies are committed, at once, to stealing dignity and to disciplining the bodies and minds of students, teachers, and parents. There are few bad guys—but deeply perverse politics, well-suited institutions, and people doing their jobs.

In my work, I collect narratives of young children and teens growing old while young, in poverty, sacrificed bodily, intellectually, emotionally, and spiritually for global capitalism, emboldened sexism, and modem racism. Five-year-olds in some neighborhoods know better than I their chances of surviving the gunshots outside their windows.

In these communities, critical consciousness nevertheless flourishes. But it has been dispersed, institutionally exported, and contorted. Witness the loathing and fragmented urban diaspora of adolescent passion and outrage. We hear it in humor, drugs, and rap; in depression, desire, and crushed spirits; in painful violence and in the sweet making of innocent babies filled with hope, and likely to find little. Inside this diaspora lay the buried mana of critical consciousness. Bubbling in individuals, exiled from institutions, often ripping the insides of communities. One might hopefully say, it awaits creative "sense making"; that is, critical consciousness work.

In *Education for Critical Consciousness* you invite readers into your hope—"the more accurately men grasp true causality, the more critical their understanding of reality will be." You continue, "Once man perceives a challenge, understands it, and recognizes the possibilities of response, he acts. The nature of that action corresponds to the nature of his understanding. Critical understanding leads to critical action."[2]

I excuse you, "the man," assuming you know and share my concerns for the symbols and meanings of language and exclusions. But more fundamentally, we are now surrounded by a series of ironies related to the critical insights you assume will provoke action. Indeed, in the United States, fantasies and mythologies of merit, mobility, and justice have been deservedly debunked, and replaced by cynicism and critical thoughts, proliferating among children, adolescents, and young adults. But these thoughts, rich in analysis and critique, are detouring into flight, outrage, and Othering of equally oppressed, though differently raced, classed, or gendered Others. It is this dispersion and the perversion of critical consciousness that I'm worried about these days. Critique may lead to action, or to individualism, despair, self-blame, or racist violence. Let me try to explain.

On Dispersion. To capture the notion of critical dispersion, I introduce some data, collected almost a decade ago, indicating that urban students who embodied and voiced the most dramatic forms of critical consciousness were the most likely to drop out of high school. In the early 1980s, in a small study of low-income urban students, I found urban dropouts to be among the most sophisticated adolescent narrators of critique, possibility, and focused outrage. Depleted by institutions that had deadened their spirits and flattened their passions, they simply left.[3] Suspect of the relation of schooling and the economy, schooling and their cultures, schooling and their spirits, some retreated, some "acted out," most questioned in silence. Almost all exiled prior to graduation.

At seventeen, seeking transformation and embodying resistance, they were riveting. Four years later, by age twenty-one, they were defeated. Bathing in despair, their critique of economic and social arrangements had boomeranged, converted into regrets and self-blame. They were, by young adulthood, self-impaled on the knife of social reproduction that had been camouflaged as resistance. As unskilled and undereducated young adults, they couldn't mobilize, for self or collective. The strength of their earlier social critique had collapsed. They were now young adults—surrounded by debts, obligations, children, and regrets.

Like these students-cum-dropouts, across the United States, and in urban schools in particular, I hear public school teachers who also carry critique, resist oppressive pedagogics and curricula, and try to transform their workplace bureaucracies. Over time, I've learned that they too are those most likely to flee public schools early in their careers, or at least close their doors because their schools were suffocating them intellectually and spiritually. Bureaucratic structures force a silencing of possibility and an exiling of critique. Teachers' spirits are broken not so much by students, but by the oppressive conditions of their labor that privilege bureaucratic rationality over community; fragmentation over connection; substitutability over relationality.

Bureaucracy has no room for critical consciousness, from children or adults. Its tacit job is to surround and contain critique, and so the voicing of critical consciousness provokes institutional exporting of children's and adults' bodies and spirits. Silencing is not simply a feature of this institutional life—it is the defining feature.

So, now, back to consciousness and action, but with a focus on us. Haven't we accumulated enough evidence of the "public" genocide of voice and critical consciousness in schools to move us into action? Haven't we learned enough to force us to press relentlessly for a democratic public sphere and to speak out against bureaucratic "efficiency" smothering public life? Haven't we witnessed for too long the dispersion and destruction of critical consciousness turned against self and Other?

On *perversion*. There is another twist in which I worry critical consciousness, these days, is going substantially awry. You may be unwilling to concede it sufficiently critical, but bear with me. This is "critical consciousness" perverted through Othering, exclusion and race hatred expressed most recently by poor, working-class, and middle-class whites.[4] Indeed, in many public school communities that are predominantly low income, African American, and Latino, we see what Cornel West has called "the crushing of spirits."[5] Sometimes, expression of individualized outrage. But from white working-class communities we can hear a different kind of liveliness. A "critical" energy brews a felt, critical consciousness, which is performed often through

Othering, that is racial/ethnic assault. White Identity formation is being organized oppositionally, sustained as a binary conflict, sauteed in hatred.

Indeed, as you say, understanding leads to action. This time it's segregation, racism, and violence, state sponsored and community narrated violence toward immigrants, Affirmative Action, teen mothers, women on welfare. We may claim their consciousness is insufficiently critical, or misdirected. But they wouldn't. Critique surfaces from economic dislocation, loss of community, xenophobic and racist fears of invasion, and violence. Their critical consciousness, unlike dropouts and fleeing teachers, surfaces collectively and loud. Little self-blame, few regrets, get in the way of these actions.

We might argue that these white folks, like the Irish who refused to allow lesbians and gays to march in the St. Patrick's Day parade, suffer from class oppression dislocated/projected onto a raced or sexualized Other. Even if that were the case,[6] do we have the pedagogies that incite, for those so near the "bottom" and still looking "down" for the "origin" of social problems, a systemic analysis of power? How do we assure that critical consciousness does not drift downward, or outward, into victim blaming? How can we reveal the dialectics of capital, race, gender, and the state that prompt despair and exit rather than voice and organizing, that deflect pain and outrage away from the state and elites, and onto the bodies of Others? And how can we stir this talk in public, not just in radical pockets or safe havens?

As I reread you, I resonate to your notion of a "militant democracy." You advocate "a democracy which does not fear the people, which suppresses privilege, which can plan without becoming rigid, which defends itself without hate, which is nourished by a critical spirit rather than irrationality" (*Pedagogy of the Oppressed,* p. 58). But I worry that class privilege has been so thoroughly laminated around and embodied by people and institutions, that even compelling collective critique drips back onto "the people" or deflects spontaneously onto anointed Others. Pockets of radical possibilities, at best, create safe spaces (ghettos?) for analysis. Meanwhile, broad-based institutional violence persists, skillfully accommodating (or annihilating) pockets of radical resistance.

Hegemony and oppression tear with many rips, leaving tattered communities, adults, and children. Yet, as I have tried to argue, hegemony is not total. Crumbs of critical consciousness sprinkle throughout adolescents' intellectual, cultural, and emotional lives, embroidered with gender, race, class, politics, biographies, languages, geographies, sexualities…. When I'm engaged in an adolescent's interview, or reading her writings, reviewing his photographs, or listening to their music, I hear how keenly they know that something is terribly wrong. Adolescents know they can't trust the institutions they are supposed to trust, nor can they hope to make these institutions better. While shadows and legacies of feminist, civil rights, and other liberation movements lace commentary narrated by adolescents, they need our help converting self-blame to social analysis; individual access to institutional transformation; personal pain to collective outrage. Listen to a poem written by a young African American teen, Tanzania Roach, about schooling, educators, and social researchers—about us.

Don't Hurt Me Anymore

Don't follow me
like a rapist stalks his prey
Don't quiet the words I have to say
like a rapist covers the mouth of his victim to hold back what she must say
Don't rip savagely apart my dreams
as a rapist rips the clothes off his victim don't throw me down when I try
    to get up like a rapist throws his victim down when she tries to escape
Don't beat me when I struggle to learn and survive
    Don't pin my thoughts down
like a rapist pins the arms of his victim on the cold concrete
Don't heave your hateful thoughts down on me
like a rapist thrusts his body into his screaming victim
don't force me to say what you want like a rapist forces his victim
to perform debasing sexual acts
Don't leave me crying without a shred of confidence to go
    on without a shred of dignity to continue living
Don't make me second guess myself
when I know I have the right to speak
You've left me with the hate I never asked for
Rapist. Racist. They look almost the same.
Rapist. Racist. They are the same.

Our responsibility, as theorists, activists, teachers, and worriers is to listen to Tanzania; to wedge open these plural critical consciousnesses; educate against the dispersion of social critique and the retreat to self-blame; resist the projection of "something's wrong" onto raced or sexualized Others. And, if that's not enough, we need to link these diffuse puddles of radical possibility—Horton's pockets—into what Chantal Mouffe calls "chains of equivalence."

Bear with me a moment longer. Can you imagine any of this happening within the bureaucratic institutions of hierarchy, power, and containment that currently constitute public schools?

You were Brazil's commissioner of education, and so I lay at your feet questions you have fed me over the years. I have taken seriously your vision, and have traveled with you between theory, politics, research, and praxis. Now I ask you to take seriously the fruits of your intellectual and political commitments.

Paulo, on late nights, in the rain, when I'm depressed about urban schooling and yet thrilled by the questions of children and adolescents, when the possibilities of rippling social movements are, at once, seemingly endless and impossible to envision, you've gotten me through. Now I relish our chatting in texts, across pages and geography. I look forward to having you inside my mind again, blending your words with mine, struggling together through the grandchildren questions of Freirian theory and praxis.

My fondest thoughts and thanks,
Michelle Fine, Professor CUNY/Graduate Center

This letter was previously published in *Mentoring the Mentor: A Critical Dialogue with Paulo Freire,* Paulo Freire, James A. Fraser, Donaldo Macedo, Tanya McKinnon, and William T. Stokes, eds. (Peter Lang, New York, 1997).

Notes

1. Freire, Paulo, and Myles Horton, *We Make the Road by Walking: Conversations on Education and Social Change,* edited by Brenda Bell, John Gaventa, and John Peters (Philadelphia: Temple University Press, 1990).

2. Freire, Paulo, *Education for Critical Consciousness* (New York: Seabury, 1973), p. 44.

3. Fine, Michelle, *Framing Dropouts* (Albany, NY: State University of New York Press, 1990).

4. See Weis, Lois, *Working Class without Work* (Albany, NY: State University of New York Press, 1991); and Weis, Powell, and Wong, eds., *Off-White: Essays on Race, Power, and Culture* (New York: Routledge, 1996).

5. See, for example, West, Cornel, *Keeping Faith: Philosophy and Race in America* (New York: Routledge, 1993).

6. I don't quite believe that it is, because elite whites may feel the same but don't have to say it, because their working-class brothers and sisters will do the dirty narrative work for them.

~ *Jason G. Irizarry* ~

Questions and Quandaries from the Academic Borderlands

> *Thus, to have an effect, I cannot live on the margins of the system.*
> *I have to be in it. Naturally, this generates a certain ambiguity.*
> —Paulo Freire, *The Politics of Education: Culture,*
> *Power, and Liberation* (1985), p. 178.

Spring 2006
Dear Paulo,

   Saludos, mi amigo. Although we "met" only several years ago, I feel as if I have known you my whole life. You penned my story before I had the awareness and the vocabulary to do so. You crafted, through your words and actions, a script for my possible role in life prior to my introduction into the world. While the grand narrative regarding the aspirations and outcomes for poor, urban, Latino youth is well entrenched in society, your work offered a counternarrative—additional possibilities for my life, new ways to play the cards that I was dealt, a way to make meaning of, and contribute to, the struggle for social justice. It created a space, however small, that would allow me not to follow my father's footsteps into "state employment" as an inmate in the prison industrial complex. Despite the continuing forces of social reproduction, your work made it possible for me to participate in and promote social justice from a slightly different type of institution—academe. It is from within this context that I share the following experiences and questions.

Upon graduating from high school, I attended college through an affirmative action program aimed at creating opportunities for economically disadvantaged students to attain a higher education. My encounters with racist and classist faculty, staff, and students were frequent, further fueling my desire to achieve what they thought was impossible for someone like me. I was on a mission. My plan was to take what I learned and go back to my community to teach so that more members of my community would have options and a sense of agency in shaping their life's trajectory. Upon graduation, I returned to the school district in which I was educated to work as a middle-school teacher. I was tired of everyone defining success for urban youth by how far, ideologically and physically, they could remove themselves from their home community. I would go back and make a difference. I entered with knowledge of what Lisa Delpit (1995) has called the "codes of power," even though I didn't know to call them that at the time. I could now speak the languages of the oppressed *and* the oppressor. I had a decent command of how to use the proverbial "master's tools" (Lorde, 1984) and getting hired as a teacher gave me access to the master's house. Let the destruction begin. I'd show them. I'd be different. I wouldn't be satisfied with students regurgitating ambiguous facts for some test. We'd follow in your footsteps and reframe teaching and learning. We'd learn to "read the words" as a way to "read the world." We'd throw the banking method out the window once and for all.

To my dismay, the reality of my middle-school classroom was far different. I was overwhelmed by how poorly schools had served my students. The majority of them were performing more than two years below grade level, and several were functionally illiterate. Neither college nor my own experience growing up in this community had prepared me adequately for this work. I inherited a classroom that had been ransacked by returning teachers, left barren, devoid of paper, chalk, and anything else of value. We had two computers in the back of the classroom that had no keys on the keyboard. Worst of all, I had no books to use and was restricted from using the school copy machine for fear that it would break down as a result of making copies for academic work and become unavailable for the administration. Every possible impediment that could hinder student personal and professional growth was thrown at my students, almost all of whom, not coincidentally, were poor Latinos and African Americans.

Each day their beautiful faces stared at me, waiting for me to tell them it would get better if they worked hard, that they would be able to pursue higher education, obtain desirable jobs, and live out their dreams. While we worked very hard together, we were all embedded in a system that was in many ways designed to produce failure—theirs and mine. My voice was often overwhelmed by messages, overt and subliminal, from both the school and society at large that their lot in life was already predetermined. It didn't matter how hard they worked; most of them would never make it. According to city statistics and trends in educational attainment, more than half of them would not complete high school, and they were almost five times more likely to enter the prison system than a city or state college or university.

Since then, I have struggled with where—the space in which and the position from which—I should take up this work. As an employee of the school system, I was taking money from the same institution that was oppressing my students. Given what I perceive as the rigidity of critical theory, where one is positioned either as a member of the oppressed or as the oppressor, it was difficult not to feel at times as if I was on the wrong side. Although ideologically as well as in my actions I had different objectives, I still struggled with transforming the system from the inside.

As a teenager and young adult, I believed I was the poster-child for oppression. I was Latino, poor, and living in a housing project with thousands of other people confronting similar issues. However, as I grew into adulthood, this was an identity I could no longer comfortably claim. Even though teachers are grossly underpaid for their work and despite the fact that I began to repay student loans, as a city employee I was solidly middle income. (I deliberately don't use the term *middle class* because it implies certain values that I did not share.) Years of immersion into standard English and interacting with peers of varied backgrounds eroded both the Spanish and New York accents that I had, leaving me only with a strong sense of ethnic and geographic identity and without my *mancha de plátano* (a characteristic that purportedly makes one easily identifiable as a Puerto Rican). Coupled with a closely cropped haircut and the privileges afforded people with light skin, I was rarely a target of individual discrimination. My brother summed it up best when, during one of our conversations, he said, "Jay, now we have to reject your hood card." I was no longer perceived by many as a full member of the community that nurtured and enabled me to take advantage of educational opportunities. In the minds of many, I had crossed over. I looked like "the man," could sound like "the man," and was employed by "the man." Where did I fit in? Am I both oppressed and oppressor? Is there a gray area between the two where those of us who have played and continue to play "the game" can work to change the rules? How do you change oppressive institutions from within?

My frustration and inability to reconcile my multiple identities led me out of the public school classroom to graduate school to continue my education. Congruent with the mold of a first-generation college graduate, I thought that more formal schooling would help me find answers to some of my questions. I also believed that obtaining another degree would allow me to penetrate higher levels of the educational system. People in power would be more likely to listen to me as I represented the voices of my students because my educational credentials would afford me a certain level of legitimacy. I might even be able to assume a position of power and then really be able to change the system so that it worked for all people and not just the privileged few. In this sense, I viewed academic degrees like currency that would buy me access to opportunities for change. Yet the higher I climbed up the academic ladder, the more resistance I experienced in my efforts to promote social justice and educational equity.

Once I completed my master's degree I took a job at an institution of higher education as the director of a program aimed at increasing the recruitment and retention of teachers of color. I thought that I might be able to draw from my experiences as a teacher and the knowledge I had gained through schooling to help prepare teachers to work effectively in conditions similar to those that I encountered. For six years I worked with members of an urban community to create a cadre of committed teachers of color who came from the community in which they were going to teach. In addition to their traditional teacher preparation, we studied your work and tried to implement approaches to teaching and learning that drew from it. While there have been many students who have been impacted by these teachers, almost a decade later our success is more easily measured by narratives and stories of the accomplishments of a few individuals than by any substantive changes in the schools to which urban students of color are committed. The majority of Latino and African American students who live in this community still don't complete high school. They are still at the mercy of politicians and policy-makers who seem more concerned with measuring and publicizing educational inequities than remedying them.

My desire to effect greater positive change led me back to school. This time I set my sights on doctoral study—the ultimate seal of academic approval. At the same time, earning a doctorate, and all of my preceding academic pursuits, for that matter, simultaneously represented for me an act of resistance. It was the way that I made sense of my experiences, the way I reconciled my "school kid" and "street kid" identities (Flores-González, 2002). With the precise combination of family and community support, hard work, and good fortune, I achieved my goal. I now had the skills, knowledge, and credentials to effect change from within the institution.

Although my education will continue, my pursuit of additional degrees is over. As I try to settle into my new role as a teacher educator and researcher, I still find myself in an ambiguous place, an academic borderland, with a million more questions than answers. This borderland lies between, overlaps with, and connects the ivory tower and the oppressed communities with, and for whom, I work. It is the space where the oppressed challenge their oppressors, where the oppressors allow themselves to be taught by the oppressed. It's also often a lonely place from which people retreat, searching for the comfort of spaces where labels fit well and roles are more clearly defined. It's a place where hybridity reigns and identities are negotiated and constantly renegotiated. It's a constant reminder of why I do this work.

As I live out this borderland pedagogy, trying to put your theory into practice while working within and simultaneously transcending the academy, I feel an immense sense of responsibility to be more than a cog in the wheel. Like many academics engaged in the struggle for liberation, I grapple to make meaning of all of the daily tasks in which I engage to bring about the change called for in your work. For example, as I engage in scholarship as a form of revolutionary resistance, I know that the overwhelming majority of my written work will never be consumed by the community that I hope to serve through my efforts. In fact, it probably won't be read by many of my colleagues who have access to it, either. As many institutions of higher education try to narrow what counts as valuable outlets for one's work, I have chosen to submit my work to publications where I think it will have the most impact, and I am willing to accept whatever consequences accompany my decision. However, given that the average journal article is read by a very limited number of individuals, I still question the value of my decision to take up the struggle from the academy. As I read through *Pedagogy of the Oppressed* (1970), I wonder if you ever felt the same. I struggled with the language in the text, and I had to work diligently to gain full understanding of many of the concepts you present. That process continues. And even after reading the text several times, I still find myself stuck trying to unpack various passages.

Although I have great admiration for your work, I question who it was written for. At times it seems to me as if your work represents a border-crossing opportunity. That is, because of the complexity of the language, the cost of the text, and so on, it is often presented to members of oppressed communities through a liaison, a border crosser, someone from the community with access to the language and codes used in the books, to work with the consumers of the text to deconstruct its meaning. In many ways, as a result of your personal experiences moving from the middle class to experiencing poverty and political exclusion firsthand as a member of a lower socioeconomic class, you were an involuntary border crosser. You journeyed through academic institutions refining your skills, bolstering your credentials, and using your platform to address the plight of oppressed peoples.

I have tried to follow in your footsteps, but I often find myself mired in self-doubt about where and how I have chosen to contribute to the struggle, feeling, on multiple levels, like an imposter in the academy. While I am in the academy, I am not "of the academy." As a person of color committed to social justice and educational equity, I do not represent the average faculty member. Most of my colleagues have highly educated parents, have traveled the world, and have had a multitude of experiences afforded people with financial means. Conversely, neither of my parents has an undergraduate degree, and I just recently obtained a passport. My goal in the academy—to use the many resources that come through this institution to support work in the communities that most need it—also differs from most of my colleagues. My constituents are not only the students who pay my salary through tuition to the institution, but they are also students from oppressed communities embedded in a system that subordinates and disenfranchises them. In order to serve both groups and to access the resources and funds of knowledge in both communities to work for social justice, I have to exist in and constantly move between the two, spending much of my time in a borderland. My hunch is that if I look closely, I'll see you there.

Sincerely,
Jason G. Irizarry

Part 5: Conscientização

[C]onscientization is a painful birth.
—Paulo Freire, *The Ladoc "keyhole" Series*, (n.d.), p. 10.

For Paulo Freire, *conscientização* was a significant component of learning, as well as a way of being in the world. It was more than a mere psychological experience, however. Unlike the "consciousness-raising" movement popularized in the United States and other Western countries in the 1960s, Paulo did not see the process of *conscientização* as a personal, individual pursuit. To him, it was, above all, a social process that went beyond the mere seizing of consciousness. In fact, in order to distinguish it from a mere *awareness*, in one of his early writings, Freire wrote: "I am more and more convinced that the word should really be used in the Brazilian form, *conscientização*, and spelled that way" (pp. 3–4). For Freire, it represented what he called a "historical commitment" (p. 5), and because of this, without praxis, *conscientização* could not exist. It is, Freire wrote, "a critical insertion into history in order to create it, to mold it" (ibid.).

The letters that follow describe the *conscientização* of teachers and academics in a variety of contexts. They describe both personal encounters with Freire and encounters with his work, and they explore how his ideas became a catalyst for a change in the thoughts and praxis of their own lives.

~ *Stacie Tate* ~

Pieces of the Puzzle

Consciousness about the world, which implies consciousness about myself in the world, with it and with others, which also implies our ability to realize the world, to understand it, is not limited to a rationalistic experience. This consciousness is a totality—reason, feelings, emotions, desires; my body, conscious of the world and myself, seizes the world toward which it has an intention.
—Paulo Freire, *Pedagogy of the Heart* (2004a), p. 94.

August 30, 2007

Dear Paulo:

I discovered you late in my academic career. How is this possible, you ask? There are not a lot of schools of education that make your readings a part of their curriculum. I find this amazing if we are talking about systemic social change and humanist and libertarian pedagogy. Why wouldn't every school use your work? In fact, even when I was in graduate school, you were not a part of the curriculum. It was only because of my graduate advisor, who introduced me to you, that I became aware of you. I have been a faithful follower ever since.

You have provided several missing pieces of the puzzle. Yes, I realize that this sounds a little clichéd, but it is the only way I can describe what it means to find the answers to my questions, to realize that someone else believes what you believe, that the struggle for liberation is a common struggle and that there is a body of work that actually begins to demonstrate what freedom means for the world. The first book of yours that I read was *Pedagogy of the Oppressed*. I still have the pink and green bookmarks in the pages. I had to stop because it seemed like I had bookmarked or underlined almost every page, having a conversation with you as I read, writing questions such as "are the oppressors conscious of what they're doing?" and "why is Freire not studied more?" After reading this first book, I knew I wanted more. I knew that when people asked about my "theoretical framework," I could proudly say your name. But what did this all mean? I found the missing pieces, I put those pieces into the puzzle, but would I destroy it and put it back in the box, or would I frame it?

Framing your theories for others has been my goal. The frame that I speak of is your belief in the dialogic conversation. I remember you saying how important it is that students be able to transform their lived experiences into knowledge, to be able to use this knowledge to frame their own worlds in order to participate in their own learning process. This is the frame that I speak of—one that encourages curiosity and encounters a new body of knowledge, that gives a voice to the marginalized. The pieces and frame to my puzzle began with being able to connect my own practice to your theories.

Your work introduced me to the notion that before there can be any epistemological formation of theory and practice, there has to be a connection to humanity. You said that there has to be a curiosity and an intellectual conversation, but more important, a connection to others. My curiosity began as a teacher in Detroit. I always felt that my pedagogical practices embodied the ideas of intellectual curiosity. My practices were different from those of most of my fellow teachers, however, in that I continually asked students to challenge and question what they experienced in the classroom and in the world. There was also a humanizing side to my teaching practice that let students know that my job as a teacher went beyond the classroom. I began to realize that my practice helped students become successful at deconstructing the world around them, as well as letting them know that they were more than just a statistic. This dialogic conversation started before I knew that there was a word for what I was doing in my classroom. I had no way to talk about it, no way to begin to add to the vast puzzle of this theoretical idea. I began to see the connections. I recognized the "dialogic conversation" that advocates for educators to understand the value of theory and practice, but I wasn't quite sure what this meant for me and my students. For example, the banking concept: how do we understand and challenge banking education within a society that "methodizes reality"?

The banking concept is alive and well in this country and our schools. There are so many of us (I include myself in this because at the beginning of my teaching career I'm not sure I truly understood what problem-posing meant) who long for control, control of ourselves and control of others. We really have a habit of this in the United States. When we are asked to give up control, a lot of us don't quite know how that is done. How do we give up the mythical society that the media, literature, and politics ask us to believe in? You would be shocked at what we are asked to believe these days in the United States. We have an invented enemy, a war that's killing hundreds of thousands, and no one quite knows why. Even worse, to question this war means that we are traitors to our country. In spite of this, some of us are attempting to incorporate problem-posing education into our schools and society. All of this seems to go back to the fact that we must realize our relationship to the world, what it means to be human and that the struggle for humanity is a "conquest and not a gift." I have to remind myself about this. When I see injustice, or better yet, when I experience it, I have to remember your words. I wish it didn't have to be a conquest. It just seems that humanization should be a gift, a gift that is given and received freely. Nevertheless, until this is a reality, I will remain a part of the conquest for freedom.

I've learned from your teachings that we should embrace the challenge of self-actualization. We have to realize who we are within the context of the world before we can change it. That challenge enables us to create pedagogical practices that engage and provide students with, as bell hooks says, "ways of knowing that enhance their capacity to live fully and deeply." We move beyond the boundaries of compartmentalized bits of knowledge and narrowed perspectives so that teaching becomes a career that engages not only the student but also the teacher. In understanding ourselves, we move toward the practice of freedom, a practice of critical pedagogy. With critical pedagogy, teachers are able to rejuvenate their practice by connecting who they are to the lives of their students. This is what I have learned from you.

Critical pedagogy would use concrete values such as solidarity, social responsibility, creativity, and discipline in the service of the common good. You also contend that critical pedagogy moves away from traditional teaching approaches that emphasize acquisition of mechanical skills. You showed me that critical pedagogy should be viewed "as one of the major vehicles by which oppressed people are able to participate in the socio-historical transformation of their society" (Freire and Macedo, 1987, p. 157). You showed me that students are not just empty vessels awaiting the knowledge of formal education, but that they must create dialogue and problem-pose in order to become critical thinkers.

So what has all of this meant for me? How have I put together the pieces of the puzzle and how have I framed it? I've framed my pedagogy as "living by the soul," meaning an expressive communication system that fosters self-pride and transformation. I consider this communication system to be something deeply innate within educators who practice critical literacy and critical pedagogy. While curriculum is important, I believe that learning occurs when teachers are able to cultivate their students' purpose in this world. Teachers who "live by the soul" know the importance of cultivating their students' belief in themselves and their ability to change their lives as well as the world. My philosophy is developed not just by readings, but it is experienced when teachers live by those readings.

Today we see how society wants people of color, and in particular students of color, to operate within a system that allows them to lose their souls, to gain the notion that who they are and what they bring to society and classrooms can be discarded. Just as you state, I believe that societal assumptions about students of color dismiss the strengths they bring. I agree with your argument that there is a need not only to address the problems of students but also to recognize their strengths. In so doing, we change the view of urban schools because we bring a lens that sees the strengths, not the deficits, of urban students.

I also realize that there are several ways in which one lives by one's soul. Sometimes the soul lives by the rules of others and sometimes it is about forming a new discourse so that it can be transformed. What I hope to achieve with my own research is to offer moments that represent a hopeful and transformative ideology. I want to examine critical literacy and critical pedagogy as they are practiced within classrooms. One of the pieces to my own puzzle problematizes how critical engagement and practice can lead to student achievement within urban classrooms. My own take on your work is that at the core of critical literacy and critical pedagogy is the soul.

But even with all of this, nothing completes the puzzle without acknowledging your teachings on love, love of ourselves and of others, love of life and a passion for life. I believe that it is your passion that makes your work so meaningful to so many. Many of us feel this passion as we read your work. We know that the only way for change to happen is to think passionately, believe passionately, and work passionately with and for the oppressed.

I'm so glad to have this chance to write and tell you what your work has meant to me, but most of all how I am committed to continuing your legacy. Your words are not in vain.

In Solidarity,
Stacie Tate

☙

❧ Ramón Vega de Jesús ❧
The Fire of Conscientization Still Burns

> That's what conscientization is: a seizing of reality; and for that
> very reason, for the very utopian strain that permeates it, we can
> call it a reshaping of reality. Conscientization demythologizes.
> —Paulo Freire, *The Ladoc "keyhole" Series.* (n.d.), p. 6.

September 8, 2007
Querido Paulo,

Seems like it was yesterday. So many years, so many events, so many *conscientizaciones* have come to fruition in so many people, in me, since I met you so many years ago at La Universidad de Puerto Rico, Río Piedras Campus. The day I met you, my best friend Roberto (Tito) Otero Fontánez and I had a chance encounter on campus, and he convinced me to attend your presentation. You were about to address a group of women. I had no idea you were in town, and I was just beginning to read about your work. To think that I almost did not attend because I had a class coming up (in hindsight a great decision to cut that class) and an impatient girlfriend waiting for a ride home. To think I almost did not meet you that day. That day changed my life. I remember that day as if it were yesterday, but the truth is that as many as thirty years have passed since then. ¡Ay Paulo, *si estuvieras aquí,* if only you were here!

So much has happened! So much to tell! I wish you were here so I could share with you all that has happened because of you, and converse with you about important moments of my life. It would be great for us to dialogue upon what your teachings led me to accomplish with the students who sat in my classrooms in Holyoke, Massachusetts, and in Hartford, Connecticut. I would love to be able to invite you to the courses I now teach at California State University, Stanislaus.

My *conscientización* began the day I met you, and it continues to be a lifelong process. Because of you, I now tell my students to spearhead their own conscientization process, to begin their encounter with *Pedagogy of the Oppressed*, to plant the seeds toward a badly needed *Pedagogy of Hope* that can only come from a reflection of their place in their community, not just of their immediate surroundings, but rather a global community.

When I met you I was a preservice teacher, a kid with more questions than answers but with fire enough in my brain, a fire that you kindled and that continues to burn to this day, a fire that is needed now more than ever in the face of prescriptive industrial educational models like No Child Left Behind. Your ideas are alive, but the law of the land is light years in the opposite direction of your teachings. It is time to overturn this failed industrial banking educational model that focuses on accountability and thought control in an imagined homogeneous community of learners that has never existed, negating everything we know about learning. The following quotation by Althusser holds the essence of what I am trying to convey and what I believe you have fought against:

> The role of the repressive State apparatus, insofar as it is a repressive apparatus, consists essentially in securing by force (physical or otherwise) the political conditions of the reproduction of relations of production which are in the last resort relations of exploitation. Not only does the State apparatus contribute generously to its own reproduction (the capitalist State contains political dynasties, military dynasties, etc.), but also and above all, the State apparatus secures by repression (from the most brutal physical force, via mere administrative commands and interdictions, to open and tacit censorship) the political conditions for the action of the Ideological State Apparatuses. (Althusser, 1971, p. 101)

One way of accomplishing this is by gate-keeping the venues to self-actualization, creating the tier system we have now in which critical thinking is not fostered but a submissive attitude is, a world that perpetuates the haves and have-nots.

These are certainly Orwellian times in which we live. Paulo, your idea of conscientization is the opposite of what Althusser described. It is an endeavor to break free of that mold and tear down barriers that stand between an individual and self-actualization so that one can understand one's position locally and globally and then begin to take action. To quote you,

> Education either functions as an instrument ... to facilitate integration of the younger generation into ... the present system and bring about conformity or it becomes the practice of freedom, the means by which men and women deal critically and creatively with reality and discover how to participate in the transformation of their world. (Freire, 2002, pp. 36–38)

You talked about teaching in ways that I could not fully comprehend at the time, but you planted a seed that only partially germinated with my involvement in *De*

Orilla a Orilla [*From Shore to Shore*], also known as *Orillas* (Brown, Figueroa, and Sayers, 1997; Brown, Cummins, Figueroa, and Sayers, 1998), a multilingual global learning networking organization that facilitates sister classes for educators concerned with language and culture. *Orillas* started in 1985, and I joined in 1989. My sister class at the time was from Oxnard (Channel Island), California. We exchanged cultural packets and communicated in chat rooms in real time.*

Paulo, you talked about la *educación bancaria*, banking education, warning against making the students passive recipients of information handed down from their teachers. You talked about your approach to *alfabetización* (literacy) and the importance of first finding an area of interest germane to the students, not an imposed literacy curriculum, but rather one of intrinsic motivation as the medium for both conscientization and literacy to develop. You referred to the group in Spanish as *nosotras*, the female version of "we" in Spanish. My friend Tito Otero and I were sitting toward the front of the amphitheater, and we had not noticed that there were only three males in the room. I kept thinking, "Why is he referring to us as females? Is it an error in translation from Portuguese to Spanish?" A few minutes into your dialogue, you explained to the confused crowd that you used the term *nosotras* rather than *nosotros* because the majority of the group were women. I learned by your modeling to dare to respect women in a male chauvinist society.

My head was spinning by the end of what was supposed to be a presentation but developed into an amazing dialogue. Many would have said that a dialogical approach with such a large group was impossible, but "impossible" did not seem to be part of your vocabulary or philosophy. When you modeled it that day, I learned that a dialogical Socratic approach was possible even with large groups. At the end of the dialogue, many approached you, and Tito Otero and I followed suit. Tito asked you, "*¿Entonces, cuál es el rol del maestro?*" (What, then, is the teacher's role?) You paused as you stroked your beard and then answered, "*El rol del maestro [pausa] es su suicidio como clase.*" (The role of the teacher [pause] is his or her suicide as a class.) The fire in my brain was now a bonfire, as I could not immediately grasp your answer. Later in my development as a teacher, I came to understand the egalitarian search to coconstruct meaning and the conscientization process. When the teacher and student learn together, to paraphrase you, the student becomes the teacher and the teacher the student. The teacher-student hierarchy is broken in order to bring about an egalitarian search for meaning and understanding.

So much time has passed, but your words resonate in my mind today. Every class I come to know and facilitate is based on the tenets that you shared with us that day and in subsequent times. During your visit to Puerto Rico, you also stood in solidarity with the squatters in *Villa Sin Miedo* (Town Without Fear), and we learned about social activism through your modeling.

Although I had several sister/collaborative classes through the *De Orilla a Orilla* computer network, the sister class from Oxnard (Channel Islands) California marked us all forever. It is the best example of conscientization and sociopolitical activism in my entire career as a teacher. The students from Channel Islands organized themselves as a group called Students for Cultural and Linguistic Diversity

(SCALD), and my students from Hartford, Connecticut, identified themselves as *Rompiendo Barreras* (Tearing Down Barriers) and they supported each other as California confronted Proposition 187, a proposal stripping all illegal immigrants of health care benefits regardless of age, and later Proposition 227, an initiative to eliminate bilingual education in California. You met my sister class and their teacher, Bill Terrazas, at the 1993 California Association for Bilingual Education (CABE) conference in California. If you were here today I would love to invite you to sit in my office to show you a photo I treasure of you and my sister class at the CABE conference. Great memories!

Out of the experiences mediated through *Orillas* and my work with Puerto Rican circular migrant students came the idea for my research and doctoral dissertation (Vega de Jesús, 2004). My objective was to enable a consciousness-building dialogue that delved into the constructs and coconstructs of students regarding their perceptions of cultural and national identity. Paulo, I really wish you could have read this work and met these students. Some of them took part in *Orillas* and were members of the *Rompiendo Barreras* project that I mentioned before.

After being a teacher, a school counselor, and a school administrator, I am now an educational psychologist and a professor of teacher education in the California State University, Stanislaus, campus. I now serve the agricultural communities of California Central Valley. I now pass on these experiences and what I learned and keep on learning from you to *la nueva cosecha,* the new crop, of upcoming teachers. My goal is to continue to instill consciousness-building in them so that they pass it on to their students, creating a far-reaching domino effect. I also teach graduate students, and it is so refreshing to see that most of them are versed in your approach to learning and conscientization. Now when they ask what is the role of the teacher, I start by answering that someone wiser than I once told me that "the role of the teacher is his or her suicide as a [social] class." Your legacy is alive in them! Thank you for lighting up my fire! I miss you dearly.

Siempre en la lucha,
Ramón Vega de Jesús

Note

*The sister class partnership involves teachers in bilingual, foreign language, and English as a second language programs (elementary and secondary level) from around the world. It also involves educators working with refugees and immigrants and educators who wish their students to benefit from a rich cross-cultural learning context. The webpage for the project is www.orillas.org/welcomee.html

⟡

⁓ *John Raible* ⁓

Lessons in Humility
Understanding Teaching as Struggle and as Service

> *I like being human because I know that my passing through the world is not predetermined, preestablished. That my destiny is not a given but something that needs to be constructed and for which I must assume responsibility. I like being human because I am involved with others in making history out of possibility, not simply resigned to fatalistic stagnation.*
> —Paulo Freire, *Pedagogy of Freedom* (1998a), p. 54.

Fall 2006

Dear Paulo,

I wish I could thank you personally for leaving us with a shining collection of works that brim with inspirational ideas. Please know that I find, in my perennial rereading of your thoughts, the inspiration that helps me stay motivated in the ongoing struggle for social justice. I do intentionally—although not lightly—use the word struggle, because that is how I continue to understand the work I do as a teacher and educational researcher in the field of multicultural education.

I first came across your ideas as a pre-service teacher who was overflowing with youthful idealism and optimism. Around 1980, as a young person seeking a meaningful direction in life, one through which I could make some sort of contribution to the ongoing struggle for social justice, freedom, and peace, I found my way into education courses. During these formative years, I was naturally drawn to the progressive ideas of radical educators from the 1960s and 1970s. I first encountered your words when my professor, Sonia Nieto, invited us to read *Pedagogy of the Oppressed* as one of the two texts used in her class. I was immediately hooked on your notion of *conscientização* and I felt energized by the possibilities of a problem-posing education. The more I read, the clearer it became how teaching offered a role through which I could wed the democratic values I'd been raised with to my nascent political concerns and my love for young people. The ideas contained in your books spoke to me in what sounded like a strange yet recognizable dialect of a mother tongue I already knew.

Now, more than a quarter century since I first encountered *Pedagogy,* I look back and realize how profound your influence has been in my life. As someone who tries to link issues of educational reform with struggles for social justice, I have always tried to stand professionally with one foot inside public schools and the other planted firmly in the community. As a teacher, I have sought opportunities to collaborate with others (i.e., other teachers, paraprofessionals, administrators, parents, and students) to facilitate change from within. At the same time, I have made sure to seek ways to contribute to local struggles in the communities in which I have lived and taught. From my first job teaching in the rural Navajo Nation to urban Compton, California, and on to the college town of Ithaca, New York, I have always sought allies—both within schools and in the larger community—from whom I could learn and with whom I could forge strong bonds of solidarity, in order to work on education issues and advocate for school reform.

I see this balanced, inside-outside *praxis* as an expression of my understanding of your approach to education. I am mindful of my dual role as teacher-student and of the ways my students are at the same time my teachers. I admire your foresight in taking education to the people, through culture circles, and not sitting back and waiting for people to come to you via formal educational institutions. Your example of popular education reminds me that education and schooling are not synonymous. In his essay on what he describes as impoverished views of educational reform, David Berliner (2006) recently calculated that for every hour children spend in school, five are spent with their families and in their neighborhoods. Thus, many—if not most—of the important lessons in anyone's education are learned *outside* the confining walls of school buildings.

From my perspective, the 1:5 ratio of in-school time to out-of-school time is actually a blessing in disguise. I continue to be haunted by the gloomy recognition that, in far too many cases, school often functions, to paraphrase Malcolm X, as a "part of the problem rather than as part of the solution" to ongoing struggles for freedom and democracy. Even though I studied the origins of public schooling as I prepared to become a teacher, it is still easy to forget the not-so-benign ways in which schools historically have worked to "deculturalize" students, to use the term popularized by Joel Spring (2007), and to function as cogs in the social engineering schemes established by self-appointed elites. It's high time that someone reminded teacher educators and educational researchers what many teachers on the frontlines know intuitively: that schools are not only working effectively, but they are actually doing precisely what they were designed to do, namely, to maintain and reinforce social stratification, primarily along lines of race and class. This recognition has been confirmed for me not only by the work of radical school critics, but also through my professional experience teaching in different communities across the United States.

My early experiences living and working on the Navajo reservation as a novice teacher, followed by my five-year stint in an elementary school in inner-city Los Angeles, gave me firsthand insight into the related dynamics of entrenched poverty and what you have called the "banking" model of education, particularly as it operates in schools designed for non-elite children. By contrast, my more recent experience teaching in a well-funded school district in a college town that prides itself on the quality of its schools gave me further insight into the limitations imposed by schooling. Eight years spent teaching in Ithaca, New York, showed me in no uncertain terms that even among the relatively more privileged elites, children suffer under predictable ways of doing school. For example, even the well-dressed and well-fed children of the professoriate are labeled, sorted, and tracked, their natural exuberance too often pathologized and disciplined. Meanwhile, their youthful spirits dull under content-laden curricula driven by the standardization craze. Students with varying degrees of socioeconomic means and status are victimized under rigid mandates handed down by bureaucrats who live and work far removed from ordinary classrooms, let alone from students' home communities in working class and impoverished neighborhoods on the proverbial wrong side of the tracks. From my perspective borne of years' worth of practical experience in diverse public schools, school reform efforts, including *No Child Left Behind,* can be best understood as political distractions from the real struggle. As we enter the twenty-first century, I see our task as attempting to regain lost turf and refocus our work by connecting it more closely to the struggles of local communities. In my view, educators must resist segregating social conditions and processes of stratification—between classes, races, (sub)cultures, even generations—and raise awareness of schools' complicity in these processes.

One related question I wish I could ask you concerns the genuine possibilities for forging deeper relationships based on mutual respect and caring between students and teachers. As I revisit your ideas, I am struck by the potential (and necessity) for teachers to develop dispositions of humility. I appreciate the way your approach offers a way to circumvent the inadvertent arrogance that often accompanies the power and authority of the teaching role. In order to encounter differences effectively, your approach requires that we who would teach humble ourselves, in effect, to meet our students halfway. This parallels Sonia Nieto's (2004) multicultural perspective on differences, since it encourages teachers to affirm students holistically and to honor their heritages, no matter how impoverished and underprivileged they may appear to teachers from outside the students' home communities. Nieto's multicultural perspective recommends that, rather than view our students' backgrounds as problems to be remedied, we can instead understand them as providing rich resources from which teaching might draw and through which learning might be contextualized.

It seems to me that your ideas similarly invite teachers to come off our high horses of educated privilege and assumed authority to better meet students on their own turf, more as partners in the educative process and less as passive recipients of our charity and good intentions. In schools in the United States, this issue takes on added complexity and urgency when the teachers and students do not share racial, cultural, or class backgrounds. As a teacher educator and researcher working in the highly stratified U.S. context, I am particularly concerned about the added arrogance that is borne of racism, as it is rooted in a system based literally on notions of racial superiority. In light of persistent racism, my own work focuses on how we (educators, students, and families) might more effectively develop cross-cultural and interracial alliances, in schools and within and between communities.

In my view, genuine multicultural relationships are virtually impossible unless those imbued with more power and privilege somehow manage to transform their unintentional arrogance. If we are unable to do so, I fear that we will never be able to join students in their own "life-worlds," to use a phrase coined by Barab and Roth (2006). In your experience, what conditions lead (or push) teachers into this necessary process of what Nieto (1995) has referred to as "arrogance reduction"? For me, the reminder to strive for humility comes from cultivating a view of teaching as an act of service. As such, teaching involves a degree of personal sacrifice, such as putting up with less than ideal conditions for teaching and learning and maintaining optimism and commitment despite negative forces such as mediocrity, conformity, political repression, and widespread fear.

A related question has to do with the conflicting roles of teachers. I agree that teachers are also and always students, and that in a problem-posing pedagogy, students are also teachers. But since, in North American public schools, adults who choose to work as teachers are hired to play regulatory roles as well as educative ones (recognizing that we must act continually to enforce and reinforce the rules of school and that we are bound by district, state, and national regulations governing our profession), in your estimation, how reasonable is it to expect teachers to develop a critical praxis in solidarity with our students? As a popular educator who worked mainly outside of schools, have you seen *conscientização* take place inside schools? It strikes me as unlikely, because in the rare instances when teachers are able to go through their own processes of *conscientização*, as arguably they must before they can facilitate such a process with students, the recognition of contradictions may become so uncomfortable that they feel compelled to flee the schoolroom altogether. I worry that as long as teachers feel they are working in settings that belong to someone else, they will disconnect from their own sense of agency and remain unable or unwilling to engage students in a process of empowerment.

Finally, what are your thoughts about the future of public schooling in our increasingly global society? I recall your collegial public conversations in years past with Ivan Illich (1970), another visionary whose attempts to push our thinking about schools I deeply appreciate. I would like to know your latest thoughts on the basic disagreement between your ideas and his principled antipathy for not only schooling but for the notion of education itself. While many developing nations strive to implement Western industrialized models of school-based education even as progressive educators here critique them, I concede that it is unfair to ask people to go without the relative privileges that accrue from schooling. In other words, it seems unreasonable to throw the baby out with the bath water, to use a crass idiom. Just because schools are currently under the tight grip of those who would deny teachers academic freedom and professional courtesies such as creative license and flexibility, does *not* mean that we can simply abandon schools altogether and wait for something better to come along. As long as students are compelled by the state to attend, schools can and must be seen and experienced by students and teachers alike as sites for struggle and productive resistance.

One final thought: While I imagine that you spoke much differently when you were with your students in the culture circles, from my current vantage point as an academic I can appreciate the model you offer for addressing, through your writing, a larger and multigenerational community of educators. By choosing to write in the language of the academy, you made it not only possible, but more likely, that your cumulative body of work will live on in libraries and universities worldwide (barring the intentional destruction of such repositories or the violence of book-burning). When revolutionary philosophies fall out of favor or are temporarily forced underground, it is comforting—and necessary—for the ideas encoded in your books to be accessible to activist intellectuals now and in the future. I think we already have proof that your ideas will stand the test of time. I know that I am not alone in feeling this. To cite two fellow admirers who, like me, value your substantive contributions to the foundations of critical education,

> Deweyean education focused on problem solving, goal-seeking projects, and the courage to be experimental, while Freire developed critical problem-posing pedagogies and Illich offered oppositional conceptions of education and alternatives to oppressive institutions. It is exactly this sort of critical spirit and vision, which calls for the reconstruction of education along with society, that can help produce more radicalized pedagogies, tools for social and ecological justice, and utopian possibilities for a better world. (Kahn and Kellner, 2006, p. 33)

In closing, please know that you, Paulo, are not remembered as a teacher of mathematics, science, or even philosophy, or some other "discipline," but as a visionary who gave us a new way to pass on the gift of education to people to whom historically it had been denied. As an educator, you embodied a compassionate and committed concern for the reality of people's daily lives and struggles. Although you do not usually speak of it as such, I appreciate the deep spirituality that resonates throughout your work. This aspect of your body of work often goes unmentioned. Perhaps it is just as well not to call too much attention to it.

I am mindful of the awesome responsibility I inherit as an educator. I take comfort knowing that I am never alone, in that we who teach comprise collectively multiple links in a chain of empowerment that stretches backward in time, but more important, forward into the unseen future. If I am to serve humbly as one small link alongside countless others, your ideas, dear Paulo, are the iron through which that chain is wrought, and made ever more strong and tenacious. I do hope you know that and feel it in your heart.

With tremendous esteem and affection—*obrigado,*
John Raible

∞

Ernest Morrell
Teaching Became a Revolution

*If, in reality, I am not in the world simply to adapt to it, but rather to
transform it, and if it is not possible to change the world without a certain
dream or vision for it, I must make use of every possibility there is not only
to speak about my utopia, but also to engage in practices consistent with it.*
—Paulo Freire, *Pedagogy of Indignation*, 2004b, p. 7

October 7, 2007

Dearest Paulo,

I met you when I was just a child, a new teacher looking for language to explain what I could only feel but not say. I lived a lifetime in every day and with
every child, teaching in a nameless forgotten place, ridiculed by the world, in the
underbelly of a society sated on the pleasures of the coin and the bomb. There,
in Oakland, California, twenty-four years old, with the weight of the world on
my shoulders, I had no answers, only yearnings for peace, only the dreams of the
children, only the cold classroom with no windows and no heat, only the passion
for the words.

And then I met you and passion became focus, action became praxis, and the
challenges became the curriculum became the pedagogy became the reason and the
pathway. Children became comrades and the city became the classroom. Worlds
became texts and texts became the conversation with the world and those who held
it at bay for their own selfish interests.

Teaching became a revolution.

I learned to read by reading you and I learned to talk to myself as I learned to
teach as dialogue. And my life changed in the space of a paragraph as I reached
for the dictionary and learned a new language and in unlearning the vocabulary of
empire I became human, even to myself, and I understood what I had to do.

We are the narratives we allow ourselves to believe, and we are the words and
ideas that we create. Meaning is negotiated in the conversations between our acts
and the world in which they occur.

Pedagogy of the Oppressed became, for me, both a window and a mirror. For in it I
could see myself and my struggles with a history of dehumanization, and through it
I could see the possibilities for transforming my own identity while I helped those
who were also in search of themselves and an alternative to the options they had
been presented. And so I introduced my students to you and they introduced me to
a life I could only have imagined, and together we have lived and loved and written
and cried and made things happen that no one thought possible.

The curriculum is in the streets, in the cities, in the so-called despicable places. The pedagogy is love and rage and courage and discipline and humanity. To teach is to demand excellence; to teach is to invite the young to inscribe their verses into the drama of existence.

Students change the teachers who change the world. Teachers, through challenging the students, change the students who change the world. What place on earth is more exciting than a classroom where learning happens!

Paulo, I thank you for teaching me how to read and write, for giving language to life. For focusing my love, and for being my comrade in this struggle we call justice.

Ernest Morrell

~

≈ *Diana Caballero* ≈

A New Way to Read the World

Transformation has to be accomplished by those who dream about the reinvention of society, the recreation or reconstruction of society.
—Paulo Freire, *A Pedagogy for Liberation*, by Ira Shor and Paulo Freire (1987), p. 36.

August 10, 2007
Estimado y apreciado Paulo,

I need a new way to make sense of the world, a new way to read the world. How often I have said these words since our entry as a world community into the twenty-first century. This eternal optimist who was guided by your words and experience for over thirty-five years has permitted the cynic to take over ... well, almost. I say *almost* because my fervent belief in equality and social change continues—against tremendous odds—to make me a believer. But the stories from the field, the painful present stories from the field, demonstrate that the 1990s were merely a dress rehearsal for what we are experiencing today in the world of the classroom, the schools, the communities of color, and the immigrant communities that continue to struggle to seek a better life.

You have said that we cannot dwell on the history of meanness, of cruelty, or of injustice. I go back to your words and reflections to guide me through the morass and disarray that define the world of schools our children attend and that—even given our decades-long determined fight for social justice—continue to oppress and disempower them. Children of linguistically and culturally diverse backgrounds continue to be stripped of their language, culture, and identity, and their chances for survival are getting dimmer. Your words, your reflections, how you addressed the world guided me when I started my journey as a bilingual educator in New York City. I will rely on them as I continue my journey and once again become the optimist I have always been, or better yet, the critical optimist you have said we must be. When I begin to lose hope that we can really make fundamental change, I go back to your words. To do so, I must revisit ... and reflect...

When I started teaching over thirty-five years ago in a second-grade classroom of a New York City public school, I was motivated by a passionate belief in equality and social change. My commitment to educational change stemmed from my personal background as a working-class Puerto Rican growing up in the South Bronx in the 1950s. As a product of the New York City public school system, I learned quickly, but painfully, that to be accepted and to succeed meant giving up my language, culture, and identity. Along with thousands of others, I experienced a tracking system of inequality and humiliation where most did not—and still do not—survive. I made a commitment that the children I taught would not experience what many children, particularly Puerto Rican and Latino children, experienced in the schools when I grew up.

My family and the spirit and strength of the decade of the 1960s, a period characterized by a strong belief in equal educational opportunity, inspired me to finish my education at the City College of New York and enter the classroom in 1970. I was guided by a strong belief that public education needed to change if it was to meet the needs of the poor and working class in general, and the growing black and Latino communities in particular. I also became actively involved in the political and social movements of the times.

My first few weeks as a teacher in a public school classroom with primarily Puerto Rican and Dominican children and several children from El Salvador, Cuba, and Nicaragua, all recent arrivals to the United States, would lay the foundation for what I would be doing for the next three decades, whether it was in a public school classroom or a university classroom, as a teacher, professor, and as a community activist involved in the civil rights struggles of my community. Since then, my personal, professional, and political lives have always been integrated. And today, I am at a crucial crossroad.

Paulo, you gave me the philosophical framework for what I was doing in my classroom. I didn't know it then, but in my classroom, I began to embrace and create a pedagogy that was transformative, linguistically and culturally responsive, democratic, equitable, liberatory, humane, and reflective. It was also trial and error, but at that time, I had no name for my practice. I only knew that the times called for this way of doing school, "in the space in which the educational experience is lived" (Freire, 1996, p. 123). I just did what I thought was right for the children and their families because it was also a space where we were teaching the poor and the politically disenfranchised to read the world and change it.

You helped me to name my practice and to begin to take ownership of it. Because of my own experiences in the political movements of the 1960s and early 1970s, I knew that the dream of a different society for the next generations had to find its way to my classroom and, years later, to the university classrooms in which I would teach. Digging through the pages of *Pedagogy of the Oppressed* (1970) in English and Spanish, I tried to decipher and interpret its essence, trying to make meaning from such meaningful and complex concepts as *conscientização, praxis, hegemony, dialogical, dialectical, generative words, banking education, critical pedagogy, parallel pedagogies.* What once had been a difficult language became an accessible and personal one because of the practice in which it is grounded and the authenticity from which it is derived. I began to understand why teaching is a subversive and political act. As I heard about your literacy work in Brazil, about your struggles, about your imprisonment and exile, about creating liberating classrooms and spaces, I knew that I, too, had to create or re-create school in a different vision. Your writings reaffirmed and validated what I and other enlightened teachers were attempting to do.

The current political climate, however, requires an accelerated political agenda for parents, teachers, students, and the community. Some of us have been schooled in the ideology of resistance, but we have also seen our efforts blocked by the present right wing, conservative forces. And our current enemy has a face unlike any we have seen before. With the rise of conservative thinking and the implementation of a conservative educational agenda, our kids, particularly children of color and immigrant children, continue to drop out of school in increasing and criminal numbers. School is not the space where children can dream of creating a new world because they are being pushed out.

Somehow my feelings of hopelessness, at this point, seem so insignificant and unimportant in light of the truly difficult situations that many in our world and in the United States are experiencing today. When one thinks about what Brazilian society has endured and what many nations in Africa are experiencing today; about the death and destruction in an unjust war in Iraq; or how in the United States most poor children and children of color have no decent housing or health care; how immigrant families are being separated because of a right wing immigration policy; racism, police brutality, and AIDS are still present in our communities and how the victims of Hurricane Katrina were left to die because they were primarily African American: when one thinks about these realities, there is no time for hopelessness. In *Letters to Cristina* (1996) you take us through distinct and difficult facets of Brazilian society and you do so by telling your story. You also make clear your faith in the Brazilian people, an absolute faith in your people. When this exists, needless to say, there is hope. In *Pedagogy of Hope* (1994), you once again share your wisdom. You say that we "cannot ignore hopelessness as a concrete entity, nor turn a blind eye to the historic, economic, and social reasons that explain that hopelessness" (p. 8), but instead, you speak about critical hope and an education in hope. As you say, hope alone will not transform the world, but without it, changing the world is an illusion.

Once again, Paulo, you have illuminated my journey. I want to continue to help teachers to help our children make sense of the world—the world of the twenty-first century—but I need a new way to read the world and perhaps new ways to help teachers dare to teach. I always ask my students, future teachers, what their goals are for their students five, ten, twenty years from now. I always ask them if they want their students to create a better world. It is still my quest to learn how to prepare our students—future world citizens—to participate in the remaking of our world, genuinely dedicated in theory and practice, to the principles of democracy, social justice, and human rights. With these goals, there is no room for hopelessness.

Muita obrigada, Paulo, for refusing to let hope be extinguished…

Diana Caballero

∽

⸙ *Sawsan Abbadi* ⸙

Of Rage and Hope

And as far as making the world, our world, a better place goes,
there is no need to distinguish between modest or extravagant
actions. Anything that can be done with competence, loyalty, clarity,
perseverance, anything that strengthens the fight against the
powers of non-love, selfishness, and evil, is equally important.
—Paulo Freire, *Teachers as Cultural Workers: Letters*
to Those Who Dare Teach (1998c), p. 51.

December 3, 2002
Dear Paulo,

Beginning last summer, I started my journey through your work, which emerged out of a lifetime of struggle, passion, and commitment. Your profound faith and trust in the ability of ordinary people to become critical citizens and your effort to teach them not merely that they can read the words and be literate, but also *that they are literate* by being able to read the world, is a great humane mission. You have helped them set free their figuratively captive and disempowered body and soul because "we all have the privilege and the duty to fight for the right to be ourselves, to opt, to decide, and to unveil truths" (ibid., p. 15). You helped them recognize and identify with their intricate intertwined roles of critical agents and responsible citizens capable of transcending the local border to the global ones. As a result, they too have become teachers, learners, historians, and performers in the world. They have become, and will continue to be, the agents of action in the past, the present, and the future.

You write: "Every human being, no matter how 'ignorant' or submerged in the culture of silence he or she may be, is capable of looking critically at the world in a dialogical encounter with others" (Freire, 1998b, p. 14). You have taught them how to overcome their miserable conditions, the turmoil, and the oppression imposed on them by generating a nonviolent, non-neutral action composed of rage and hope. You have offered them the tools to uplift their submerged entities from the culture of silence to bud, bloom, and blossom within a new light, the light of knowledge, democracy, thought, and action by fighting because, as you remind us, "no one receives democracy as a gift" (Freire, 1998c, p. 89). Though you are invisible now, I can still shake your hand and say, "Thank you, thank you for all you have done!"

I was in constant touch with you when writing and editing a paper I wrote on critical pedagogy. I felt enthusiastic that many branches of knowledge, such as health, economy, and technology, are trying to implement the essence of your critical philosophy. You are the father and the inspiration that nurtures these movements. I had rarely been exposed through my learning and growing processes to such a resonant, affirmative, and passionate discourse. You urged me to feel privileged, to feel unique, to feel capable, and to feel creative regardless of the fears I might be trying to hide.

Building on my dream of being a successful teacher and mother, you have opened doors that I might have previously thought were closed. I'm learning how to be a nonconformist, a nontraditionalist, and a believer of the possible, both as a teacher and a mother. Would I ever give my students knowledge as a static, fixed, and neutral recipe that is spoon-fed in their silent mouths? Of course not. I'm learning how to internalize my consciousness of the unequal world in which I was born, not to dwell on its agony, but rather to externalize my understandings and be able to make a change in my life, or at least show my daughter that she should always struggle to be a person of action. In *Cultural Action for Freedom*, you describe this process as "conscientization," which can't exist in people "without a radical denunciation of dehumanizing structures, accompanied by the proclamation of a new reality to be created by men" (Freire, 1970, p. 46).

Paulo, though you are no longer in our world, my journey with your thoughts will never stop. There will be other Paulos who will continue your mission and your dream. As a believer in hope, I keep remembering your words: "Is the dream possible or not? If it is less possible, the question for us is how to make it more possible" (Freire and Macedo, 1987, p. 187).

Sawsan Abbadi

❦ Dawn Fontaine ❧

Fostering Change and Consciousness among Students and Colleagues

I cannot make myself alone, nor can I do things alone. I make myself with others, and with others, I can do things.
—Paulo Freire, *Pedagogy of the Heart*, 2004a, p. 73.

Fall 2002
Dear Paulo,

Thank you. It is with the deepest gratitude that I write to you. I could write on and on about the content of your inquiry and lifetime profession, but I'd rather humbly share with you how your words and passion have shaped my existence as an educator.

I recall my graduate school advisor introducing me to critical literacy, among many other ideas. Instantly, I was hooked. I began my work as an educator with strong political understandings about public education and its purpose and impact in this nation. Where you would call them the oppressed and the oppressor, I would call them the haves and the have-nots. It has always inspired me that real, substantive change for the betterment of all happens when ordinary people become empowered to make change. To foster this kind of change, I have chosen *conscientização*, or consciousness, as the guiding light of my philosophy.

You write that, as educators, we are what we do, and this is true for me. For many personal reasons, consciousness is important to me. If we are not conscious about what impacts us or how we impact others, we cannot facilitate change of circumstance.

It has been the process of fostering consciousness in young people that has touched me the most. It continues to be a road mixed with wonder, fear, responsibility, and reward. I've come to see this reciprocal process as planting seeds. To anticipate consciousness to unfold in my presence with all the young people who grace my day is both absurd and arrogant. I hope only to open the window and let the students find their own way when they are ready and prepared with the tools to be successful.

Paulo, your words have both inspired and soothed me. Whenever I feel overwhelmed, I am comforted by your wisdom and passion.

Dawn Fontaine

Summer 2007
Dear Paulo,

Several years after writing my first letter to you, I have again been afforded an opportunity to reflect on how your work has helped my teaching evolve over many years.

I still hold a commitment to building consciousness in the young people I serve. Along with educating young people, I now also work with my peers as a coach and a professor. I have learned that building their capacity to be conscious learners is sometimes more difficult than with young people. As adults, we have already written the scripts for justification or rationalization. We have come to accept injustice as a fact rather than a battle cry. When I am confronted with this challenge, I remember your words, "A pedagogy is that much more critical and radical the more investigative and less certain of 'certainties' it is. The more unquiet a pedagogy, the more critical it will become" (Freire and Macedo, 1987, p. 54). These words remind me to ask questions rather than give answers. When I do this, a wonderful thing happens, one which I am sure you have experienced many times: a partnership is formed. My peers and I become partners in uncovering the barriers to justice that are impeding the success of a young person. So again, I continue to be grateful for the work that you have done. It has been the foundation of my pedagogy and evolves with me as I enter different realms as an educator.

With respect and gratitude,
Dawn Fontaine

⬿⬿

⬿ Anaida Colón-Muñiz ⬿

Tertulias and Problem-Posing Education

> *Educators need to know what happens in the world of the children with whom they work. They need to know the universe of their dreams, the language with which they skillfully defend themselves from the aggressiveness of their world, what they know independently of the school, and how they know it.*
> —Paulo Freire, *Teachers as Cultural Workers: Letters to Those Who Dare Teach* (1998c), pp. 72–73.

March 21, 2007
Dear Paulo,

You probably don't remember me, but you have changed my life. I cannot imagine being who I am as an educator without you. You are a part of me. You set me on a path that helped me to view the world differently than when I started as a teacher.

I was a Teacher Corps intern at Bank Street College of Education in 1974. A group of us were completing our master of science degree while interning in a local school and engaging in community service. My internship was at P.S. 174 on 102nd and Amsterdam Avenue. While completing the required graduate courses at the college, I worked at P.S. 174 three days a week. I also taught a high school equivalency course in Spanish (GED) to adults at night on that same site. Bank Street College was a wonderful place, with its focus on constructivism and project learning and its foundation based on the theories of Piaget and Dewey. I had excellent teachers who also contributed to my professional development.

In spite of the wonderful experience we were having at Bank Street, a small group of us who were interested in bilingual education wanted more. We wanted to relate to the realities of the communities on the upper West Side in Manhattan, and Bank Street came from a position of privilege. Therefore, in addition to our other work, we read your book *Pedagogy of the Oppressed,* and we began to apply your ideas to our work. Our meetings were in the form of *tertulias,* informal gatherings of an intellectual nature, common in Spain and Latin America, where people engage in discussions on topics that interest them, and we would read a part of the book, then meet to dialogue about it. Then we began creating curricula that we thought would focus on building critical literacy in our students. For example, one member of the group, an artist, developed silk-screened posters depicting workers that—unlike the ones we had in the books in school, which showed women as nurses, and male doctors, and so on—instead were about the kind of work parents in our community did, and they included laborers and others who engaged in hard and menial work. They were large, and beautifully artistic, but also real.

Another curriculum effort we engaged in was using generative words with our students, where words such as *trabajo* (work), *el cheque* (the check), and *ropa* (clothing) began to surface. These words were important to our students' realities. For example, for many of my students who were on welfare, the monthly check meant a time for buying the food and clothing that they needed. These words led to developing curricula whereby a word as simple as *ropa* could help students gain consciousness about how clothing is made, who makes it, and its role in our economy and society. For example, we learned about how fabrics are made (for example, cotton and how it is grown and by whom, its historical significance, and so on). We learned about how workers are involved in every step of the process: the truck drivers who transport materials, the factory workers who sew the clothing, the salespeople at the store. We also discussed who owned the businesses and how profit was distributed—or not. It was an amazing experience that helped me grow as much as the students.

You changed my life as an educator and as a person. You helped me understand how to view the world, to question it, and to take my place in making it better, not just for me individually, but for the greater community. As a teacher educator, I share my experiences in the hope that they will serve to inspire other teachers as you inspired me. I take you with me wherever I go and whatever I do. As I began to understand the relationship of power and control, economy and privilege, my once innocent view of the world and the blind trust I had in those who govern us changed.

Thank you, Paulo, for helping me to understand that I am the protagonist of my life and that I can make a difference in this world by how I live it.

Yours in solidarity and fraternity,
Anaida Colón-Muñíz

Part 6: Politics

*This is a great discovery, education is politics! After that, when
a teacher discovers that he or she is a politician too, the teacher
has to ask, What kind of politics am I doing in the classroom?
That is, In favor of whom am I being a teacher?*
—Paulo Freire, *A Pedagogy for Liberation*, by
Ira Shor and Paulo Freire (1987), p. 46.

Without a doubt, Paulo Freire's most repeated and celebrated phrase is *education is political*, a sentiment he expressed in even his earliest written works and reiterated throughout the years. In one of his last writings, for instance, he mused: "My understanding of education as having a political nature came to mark me to such a degree, from a certain point in my experience as a man and as an educator, that I rarely fail to mention it" (2004b, p. 71). For Freire—and for many who have been influenced by his philosophy and pedagogy—the idea that education is political has great and lasting resonance. It means understanding that our work as educators is never neutral, first, because, as human beings, we are not neutral: we live our lives with our entire selves, and that is also how we walk into our classrooms—with our intellects, our feelings, our ideas, our desires and dreams, our biases and faults. Given this reality, the most honest action a teacher can take is to acknowledge our ideas and feelings, but without imposing them on our students and without letting them get in the way of our expectations and hopes for our students.

Paulo Freire was not unconcerned about the possibility that a teacher's ideas might unduly influence his or her students. Near the end of his life, he wrote: "Obviously, the freedom-loving critical educator's role is not to impose on the learner her taste for freedom, her radical refusal of the dehumanizing order; it is not to say that there is only one way to read the world—hers" (2004b, p. 20). In spite of the fear of unfairly influencing one's students, he felt that not doing so was *also* taking a political position. Thus, Freire believed that freely expressing one's position and ideas, and explaining the reasons for one's position and ideas to students, was, in the long run, both necessary and honest.

Second, teachers, Paulo thought, must take a stand in favor of their students, and doing so is also a political stance because education is political in another sense: because it is a human endeavor, education exists within an institutional context that is characterized by uneven power relationships. To view education as political, therefore, means understanding that all educational decisions (from the kind of texts one uses to the seating arrangements in a classroom; from the recruitment of teachers to the involvement of parents and families in the educational process; from curriculum standards to the use of high-stakes tests) are all political decisions.

The idea that education is political has had a profound impact on countless people around the world, especially educators who, once aware of this reality, begin to see their role differently. The letters in this section describe many ways in which education is political: they range from an author's reaction the first time she heard the idea that education is political, to reflections on the limit-situations of an unequal society, and the discovery that the CIA "owns literacy in cyberspace."

Elena Khatskevich

The Teacher-Politician

As passive individuals, learners are not invited to participate creatively in the process of their learning; instead they are "filled" by the educators' words.
—Paulo Freire, *The Politics of Education: Culture, Power, and Liberation* (1985b), p. 101.

Fall 2001
Dear Paulo,

I never knew that humility could be an important quality for teachers, and I could never imagine that humility requires courage, self-confidence, self-respect, and respect for others. Humility helps us understand that, as you have reminded us, no one knows it all, and no one is ignorant of everything. Many teachers don't succeed in their task of teaching because they act as if they know everything, that what they say is absolute truth without any possibility for amendment. Such attitudes make teaching rigid, and students will learn only one person's truth.

In *Teachers as Cultural Workers,* you also write that there are no themes or values of which one cannot speak, no areas in which one must be silent. This is very true regarding multicultural education. We, as teachers, should not shy away from many serious and important topics such as racism and sexism. If we keep silent about these things, we send a message to our students that this topic is wrong, that it is bad to discuss or reveal. But we cannot avoid racism if it exists in society. Our students are members of society, and our task is to empower them to eliminate racism.

Another striking idea in your book is that education is a political practice and that the educator is a politician because problems associated with education are not just pedagogical problems. You say that they may be political, ethical, and financial problems as well. My first reaction when I read those words was that teaching is such a great responsibility that I am not really sure if I am ready for this, if I am ready to be a teacher-politician. And if I were to become a teacher-politician, where is the guarantee that my political views are right, and if it is right to impose them on my students? Toward the end of the course in which I read your work, I realized that we don't *have* to impose certain political views on our students; we just have to be honest with them and let them choose what they want or prefer. We should trust that they will make the right choice.

Education is political because we, as teachers, are responsible for preparing citizens of the world and empowering our students to change the world for the better. Thank you for this wonderful book. .

Sincerely,
Elena Khatskevich

⸻ *Berta Rosa Berríz* ⸻

Building Community beyond Limit-Situations

> *More precisely, because we find ourselves subjected to countless limitations—difficult obstacles to overcome like the dominant influence of fatalist understandings of history or the power of neoliberal ideology, whose perverse ethic is founded on the laws of the market—there has never been a greater need to underscore educational practice with a sense of hope than there is today.*
> —Paulo Freire, *Pedagogy of Indignation* (2004b), p. 100.

December 2, 1999
Querido Paulo,

Many of us here know you by name and know how you read our world. We are finding our own language of struggle with our teachers and students in the literacy program. When I say *we*, I am referring to a group of five literacy resource specialists assigned the task of monitoring literacy services.* I am the administrative coordinator for literacy services within the Bilingual Department of Boston Public Schools. We are six teachers assigned a revolutionary task because building literacy is nothing less than a revolution within our context.

The starting point for the native language literacy program is organizing the delivery of native language literacy services within an oppressive system that imposes an antidialogical and noncommunicative banking method. We, on the other hand, focus on the students' view of the world as the generative place to begin. We want to go beyond this limit-situation.

The Native Language Literacy initiative was set up in response to legal action brought on behalf of students who arrive in our city from other parts of the world where their living conditions precluded schooling. Children aged nine to twenty-one come from difficult situations and enter another situation characterized by oppression. In the Boston Public Schools these students are gathered in small (limit fifteen) classrooms for a period of two years. Six specialists are assigned the role of monitors for the court-mandated requirements, and also resource specialists to develop the skills of teachers and administrators. Literacy teachers are challenged to use your approach—liberatory education—to literacy.

The human obstacles that we have to overcome have to do with an internalized sense of diminished self-worth. The children see that as old as they are, their mainstream peers already know how to read and write. In many cases, the teachers do not relate to their students as their own. The system has introduced a banking methodology to further attempt to keep teachers in their place. This includes the literacy team. The department, which is also reflective of the dominant system, does not promote community; instead, it promotes selected leaders. Our situation is but a microcosm of a global split in the new information age.

Here is how we see our revolutionary task: our goal is to build community that promotes literacy among us and with our network of schools. We start with our small group. In the literacy team, we are creating culture circles to develop our own thinking and build our working community. Our relationships with our schools are our primary resource. We come bearing gifts of support and validation. When we can, we work in teams to create study circles that promote literacy. Art and culture are always part of our generative themes. Our culture circles actively engage the human spirit while at the same time challenging reflection, reading, and writing.

I am the assigned administrator who insists on a *power-with* relationship (as defined by Kreisberg) with my colleagues. There is excitement about our new configuration. Within all of this, my particular interest is in the transformative use of culture. I want to nurture students' cultural identities as fertile ground for reading the world and the word. It saddens me to experience the opposition of those who come from our ranks and choose colonized ways of relating to me and to our program. I sometimes get lost in despair and hopelessness because of this. In my administrative role, I am far from my usual anchor, the children I teach. My place of hope is centered in my teaching community: Lydia, Lunine, Juan, and Olga. There is a certain magic in the fact that all of us, experienced and committed professionals with a common understanding of our work, have come to land here together. I find great hope in this.

In this spirit, together as the native language literacy team we dedicate this year of struggle to transform ourselves with our people. And you, Paulo, are here in our midst.

Con apreciación,
Berta Rosa

Note

*These literacy services were required in the consent decree that the Boston Public Schools negotiated with META (Multicultural Education, Training, and Advocacy), an advocacy organization that focuses on human and civil rights, including language rights in education.

☞ *Herb Kohl* ☜
Eating, Talking, and Acting: The Magic of Freire

> *I must confess that I am somewhat afraid of people who tell me that they do not like to eat. I become a little suspicious.*
> —Paulo Freire, *The Politics of Education* (1985b), p. 196.

Spring 2007
Dear Paulo,

This letter is to your spirit, since your inspiring presence is no longer with us.

I remember the first time we met at Jack London's house in Berkeley in the early 1970s. We had a *feijoada* in your and your wife Elsa's honor, a delicious stew full of meats, sausages, and black beans served with fresh tropical fruits and, as Elsa said, the aroma of Brazil. You were still in exile at the time, and the smells of your homeland moved you to eloquence. However, you didn't speak much English at the time, and my first experience hearing your spoken voice was in Portuguese, translated sensitively and thoughtfully by Elsa. I don't remember saying anything at the dinner, but I can visualize even now the pleasure with which you ate and spoke. Without understanding a word, I was struck by the fullness of your love for life—for ideas, food, people, justice. The image of your over-riding passion for life animated your books for me, since I found them overly dense and, though occasionally poetic, abstract beyond necessity.

The first time we actually talked was in 1977. I picked you up at O'Hare Airport in Chicago, and, since we were waiting for other people whose planes were late, we had a few hours to talk. After we introduced ourselves you asked me about my work. I mentioned my book, *Reading, How To*, which was influenced by your writings. Your response was perhaps the most flattering statement I have ever heard about my work: "I have that book in my small exile's library; it is one I think about."

At that moment exile was much on your mind, and you remarked about how exhausting and depressing it was to be unable to live in Brazil. I'm not sure where you had been before arriving in Chicago, but you were clearly discouraged. You said, not once, but a number of times, "I never want to hear the word *conscientização* again." It seems you had just been presented as the guru in residence at a "consciousness-raising" seminar, not by your doing, but by the North Americans that orchestrated the session.

In all the times we talked and I observed you with people, I had never heard you talk about individuals in negative ways, and the same was true this time. If I interpret it correctly, you were discouraged and angered by the equation of your revolutionary ideas with the ideas that drove the self-awareness and consciousness-raising movements. You said, "There's no *prache*, no praxis in their work." We talked about how many of the people you encountered in the United States mistook social transformation for personal transformation and applied categories that characterized the lives of the oppressed to their own lives. They individualized what you described as a collective educational process connected with political and social action. This is the dilemma of teaching your works and implementing your ideas in the United States. We are not at a historical juncture where revolutionary practice is possible, nor is there a Workers Party that, when you were engaged with it, had strong and explicit socialist ideals.

After speaking to many educators in the United States who said that they were inspired by your work and practiced your ideas, I became very uneasy. All of them were involved in struggling for social justice, were doing the best they could to open up their students to transforming the difficult circumstances of their lives, and improving the quality of community life surrounding their schools. They used some of your literacy tactics, built curricula around the lives and the vocabularies of their students. They did everything they could do as individuals and as comrades within small groups of their colleagues. But there was no engagement with a community that was awakening to the possibility that it could liberate itself from the external forms of economic and social repression. There was no radical political movement that connected them. Too often your ideas were turned into formulas for moderate change. I'm guilty of doing it on occasion. I use your pedagogy as much as I can but don't see the revolutionary potential of it in the United States. Praxis that emerges from your ideas does serve to help some students become open to their own potential and to engage in social action on a local scale. It also helps community groups clarify their own situation and potential. But very little of this praxis is revolutionary in your sense—it does not explicitly embrace fundamental change in the social and economic structures of U.S. capitalism.

In addition, and perhaps most important, adult nonliteracy is not the same issue in the United States as it was in Brazil when you wrote your books. Most people here are either literate or partially and selectively literate. The written word is not alien to them, as it was to many of the poor people you describe in *Education for Critical Consciousness*. That's why it's so important that toward the end of your life you talked about "reading the world" with more passion than you did about reading the printed word. The world is so hard to read and name—that is, to describe and encounter without deception. That challenge makes phonics or whole word learning and all the other attempts to provide print literacy seem minor.

Print literacy is one tool for reading the world, but there are multiple sources arising from culture, memory, history, value, and experience that contribute toward revolutionary consciousness. And, as you underline, without love, one cannot read or name the world or understand, through dialogue, the experiences of others. As you said in *Pedagogy:*

> Dialog cannot exist, however, in the absence of a profound love for the world and for women and men. The naming of the world, which is an act of creation and re-creation, is not possible if it is not infused with love. Love is at the same time the foundation of dialog and dialog itself. (Freire, 1970, p. 77)

A number of years ago I decided to teach a graduate teacher education course that had only one text, *Pedagogy of the Oppressed*. The idea was to do a close reading of your text and also read parts of the books you referred to in the footnotes. Each student also had to write a summary of what they read—not of what they thought about the text but what, from their understanding, it actually said. For most of the students this was a new experience. They were accustomed to being asked for their interpretations. I wanted them to look at what you intended.

Most of the students in the class had read excerpts from *Pedagogy* in other classes they had taken and considered themselves enthusiastic Freireians. After they finished reading your book and the texts from Fanon, Sartre, and others that you referred to, and discussing the ideas and structure of your work, the major conclusion was that you were too dangerous a thinker to follow. They agreed that many of your ideas were useful and worth trying out in the classroom, but making a revolution, actually working with oppressed people in ways that assisted them in mobilizing themselves and taking action, was too risky. I hope that the idea of risk was planted firmly in their minds and that some day they might, for moral reasons, be willing to become engaged in confronting systems of oppression in the context of collective struggle. But perhaps the current historical juncture in the United States is not right for revolutionary action. I know these students are decent, progressive people living in the belly of the beast during very difficult times. But the future is not predictable, and the time might soon be ripe for fundamental social and economic change. As my mentor, Myles Horton, once told me, things are always perking during what seem to be quiet times, since the passion for justice never dies and therefore there is no reason to abandon hope.

Paulo, one of the hardest things for U.S. educators who embrace your ideas is to publicly acknowledge an unambiguous rejection of capitalism and advocate some form of socialism. Currently we have no major socialist party in the United States, and the language of socialism is not used within the arena of education at all. The language of competition and what you call banking education rules supreme. Yet it is hard to imagine an authentic use of your ideas that is not explicit in its rejection of exploitation of any kind and a passionate identification with those to be educated. This means understanding "the yearning of the oppressed for freedom and justice, and by their struggle to recover their lost humanity" (ibid., p. 28). It also means understanding and respecting the knowledge and intelligence of the people you work with.

I remember an example of learning from poor, oppressed people that you described in *Pedagogy of Hope*. You said that you were at a peasant meeting and one of the members of the audience claimed ignorance and asked you, the expert, how they should go about solving their problems. Your response was to play a game of ten questions with one of the peasant leaders. Each was to ask ten questions of the other based in their own special knowledge. Your first question was "What is the Socratic method?" Not surprisingly the peasant didn't know the answer but responded with the question "What's soil liming?" You couldn't answer.

At the end of the questioning the score was ten for you and ten for the peasants. Your response to that was indicative of the profound way you draw people into their own learning:

> As I said good-bye, I made a suggestion. "Let's think about this evening. You had begun to have a fine discussion with me. Then you were silent, and said that only I could talk because I was the only one who knew anything. Then we played a knowledge game and we tied ten to ten. I knew ten things you didn't, and you knew ten things I didn't. Let's think about this." (Freire, 1994, pp. 46–47)

Your ideas about dialogue, the creation of culture, reading the world, and learning from the people have become guiding principles of my life and work. Your work is utopian and full of hope and provocation. Sustaining the battle for authentic democracy and the elimination of oppression is difficult and for many of us one whose fruits we will never experience. The question you raise in *Pedagogy of Hope* is: where shall hope be found when faith in the triumph of revolutionary struggles seems unfounded if not actually confounded by history? This is a constant worry for me, not strong enough to make me disengaged but one that tinges all my hopes for a just future with sadness. Your answer to this dilemma pointed to two sources of hope, one involving a reaffirmation and the other a dream. You reaffirmed the role people can play in making history and reminded us that history is process, that it has no end, and that its forms are neither set nor predictable but depend upon the moral actions and dreams of people. The second was to remind us to be utopian, and to pay attention to past efforts to build societies based on principles of justice and decency. As you said in the book:

> In our making and remaking of ourselves in the process of making history—as subjects and objects, persons, becoming beings of insertion in the world and not of pure adaptation to the world—we should end by having the dream, too, a mover of history.

There is no change without dream, as there is no dream without hope. Thus, I keep insisting, ever since *Pedagogy of the Oppressed*: there is no authentic utopia apart from the tension between the denunciation of a present becoming more and more intolerable, and the "annunciation," announcement, of a future to be created, built—politically, esthetically, and ethical—by us women and men. Utopia implies this denunciation and proclamation, but it does not permit the tension between the two to die away with the production of the future previously announced. Now the erstwhile future is a new present, and a new dream experience is forged. History does not become immobilized, does not *die*. On the contrary, it goes on. (ibid.)

I find your vision expressed beautifully in this quotation from Pablo Neruda's Nobel Prize acceptance speech, which he called The Splendid City:

I wish to say to the people of good will, to the workers, to the poets, that the whole future has been expressed by this line by Rimbaud: only with a *burning patience* can we conquer the Splendid City which will give light, justice, and dignity to all mankind. (Neruda, 1974, pp. 33–35)

Our work must be situated in this patience and in our own reading of the world and that of the people we teach. We must also be willing to take risks. Cultural action for freedom is a dangerous enterprise, and your spirit is an inspiration—it is as if you and Miles and other elders (by the way, I am seventy now) provide the energy and strength that keeps us going when we feel tired or discouraged or too angry to be effective.

Paulo, I'm honored that you are still with me and with us.

Best,
Herb Kohl

⌒

‿ *Eugenie Kang* ‿
Why History? An Open Letter to My Students

In this way, I insist that history is possibility and not determinism.
We are conditioned beings but not determined beings.
—Paulo Freire, *Pedagogy of the Heart* (2004a), p. 37.

December 2001
Dear Paulo,

Reading your letters has encouraged me to think about why I am a high school history teacher. Why do I teach? Why do I teach history? What value is there in learning history, and what do I hope my students will learn from it?

To continue with some of the questions that have been raised by reading your words, I've decided to try writing a letter to my U.S. history students about why history is important and what my hopes for them are. It's a work in progress, but I think it can be an interesting way to start the school year.

Dear U.S. History students,

What comes to mind when you hear the word "history"? Memorization? A barrage of names, events, and dates? Indifference? Boredom? But history does not have to be about the memorization of facts. When I think of history I think of making connections among people, actions, and ideas. History also evokes emotion in me. When I think of history, I feel joy and sadness, comfort and frustration, wonder and disbelief, strength and weakness, conflict and compromise, good and evil. Quite simply, history is powerful.

When we think of history we tend to limit our understanding to specific people and events. We need to see that history is not limited to, or manifested solely by, the most memorable individuals, treaties, battles, or speeches. History can be found in every human endeavor and reflects a wide range of emotion, reflection, and thought. There is history in art and architecture, in science and medicine, television and film, in literature and music, and in religion. Michelangelo's painting on the ceiling of the Sistine Chapel is history. The daring of Amelia Earhart is history. The televised Nixon-Kennedy presidential debate is history. The works of Langston Hughes and Toni Morrison are history. These and other actions and endeavors are connected to, and affect, a variety of other actions and endeavors.

History does not occur in a vacuum, nor can it be contained in one. The events we study do not just "happen." There are causes and effects. My elementary school teacher once showed our class how a drop of water in a pail causes a ripple, which causes another ripple, which causes another ripple. I believe that people, ideas, and events do the same. I believe that ideas, events, and people are affected by other ideas, events, and people and are connected in a variety of ways. Your personal and family histories are inextricably rooted in the past and will extend into the future. When we can see these connections with the past, we can have a better understanding of today's events and speculate about the events of tomorrow.

Take for example, the Civil Rights Movement. It did not just "happen." It did not begin with Ms. Rosa Parks's quiet yet powerful refusal to give up her seat on the bus, and it did not end with the assassination of the Reverend Dr. Martin Luther King, Jr. History teaches us that the roots of this struggle can be traced back to slavery and Reconstruction. Individual and group actions by African Americans to be educated, to provide for themselves and their families, to be treated with dignity and equality, and to have their voices heard did not just happen. They are connected to events, people, and ideas in the past. The study of history allows us to understand how the Civil Rights Movement continues to influence us today in areas such as education, employment, politics, and protest. Furthermore, not only has it affected Americans, it has also influenced individuals and movements outside the Unites States. Nelson

Mandela and the movement to free native South Africans from apartheid is but one example.

While it is important to draw connections between various endeavors and events, it is also important to make similar connections with those around us. History can help us do this. I invite you to think about your own history and share it with others. Consider that your history did not necessarily begin when you were born. Think about the connections between your life and the life of a family member. What were life and the world like when your parents and grandparents were growing up? Ask yourself how this influenced their lives. For example, did a relative participate in World War I, the Korean War, or the first Gulf War? Did they participate in protests during the Civil Rights Movement? Did a relative burn his draft card? Did your mother or grandmother burn her bra? Do your relatives remember when they heard that JFK was assassinated? How did the events of 9/11 impact your family? Ask them how they felt about these things. Listen to their stories because they are also your stories.

During the Korean War, while fleeing to the south to avoid the communism of the north, my mother was separated from her family after an air raid. She was only eight years old at the time. For a week she traveled alone, hungry and frightened. Her youngest sister, an infant at the time, was left behind in the north. To this day no one knows what became of her. Although I myself have not experienced a war, through my mother I can begin to understand how a war can affect individual lives. I see the Korean War as more than just another war that began on June 25, 1950, took place on the Korean peninsula, and ended with the territorial division of the country a number of years later.

Think about your own history, and ask family members about theirs. How do their stories differ from what you have been told by others? How are they similar? Why do you think they are different? I ask you these questions because it is important to understand that we all experience and interpret events differently. The fact that the experiences are different does not mean that one or the other is better or right. My mother's experience of the Korean War is in all likelihood different from the experience of a U.S. soldier. I believe these differences contribute to a more complete picture. Keep this in mind as you study history. In addition, you must ask yourself whether it is a complete interpretation. Whose interpretation is it, and why does it differ from others? Which people (men, women, the rich, the poor, different ethnic and racial groups, and so on) have been left out? You need to acknowledge that different interpretations are inevitable and invaluable to our learning and understanding of history and of one another.

I invite you to let history comfort, anger, inspire, empower, and teach you. I invite you to make connections with the past and with one another. History can evoke powerful thoughts, ideas, emotions, and connections in and between us if we let it. Let it.

Sincerely,
Ms. [Eugenie] Kang

∞

⇒ *Claire La Bonté* ⇐

A Teacher's Thoughts on the "War on Terrorism"

The power of the dominant ideology is always domesticating, and when
we are touched and deformed by it we become ambiguous and indecisive.
—Paulo Freire, *Teachers as Cultural Workers: Letters*
to Those Who Dare Teach (1998c), p. 6.

November 2004
Dear Paulo,

I am a coward, Paulo, I have to admit this much. I've grown up and been educated in a sheltered atmosphere, and I've pretty much had the privilege of working where I wanted to work. Don't get me wrong, I've had some restraints placed upon me (who hasn't?), but these have been pretty much of my own making.

Being a thinking and creative citizen involves more discipline than I've been able to muster over much of my career as a teacher, and it is only at this late date, as I approach fifty, that I'm really beginning to see what must be done, and that maybe I'm one of the ones who has to do it, to get involved. For years I've been preoccupied with raising my children while holding down a job as a teacher. Now I see that I must pay more attention to where I am teaching, and who I am teaching. I used to think that I had something my students needed and that they should be grateful to me for wanting to share my knowledge with them. How arrogant of me! I was talking *at* them and their families, and I was not listening to what they had to say to me.

I've been thinking about what you said about knowledge and growth, how we are the only animals who can think about how we know something, and that we should use the scientific method for examining how we know. This, you said, leads to growth. I agree. I can't help thinking about the events of the last three years, starting with the World Trade Center and Pentagon attacks. I remember thinking at the time, "Why do people hate us so much that they would do such horrendous things to us?" Was there something about Western civilization that so inflamed hatred toward us? Was it purely religious in nature, or was there more to it? Somehow, saying that we were attacked because we love freedom and democracy and we wanted the same for the rest of the world seemed a bit too naive, a bit too simple. There had to be more. I'm not sure what it is, but I know it involves a gross lack of understanding of the cultures and the mindsets of people on both sides. What has me most worried about this, though, is that people are not taking that step back, as you say we must, to try to look at the situation objectively and create some clarity, to see the situation for what it is—and it is confusing at best. It is only in this distancing that we can really come to know, understand, and appreciate the motives of our enemies, and thereby begin to work at eliminating those things that divide us in the first place. Why aren't we doing this?

Which brings me to the current situation in the West (that is, the United States and Great Britain in particular): we are so divided over the meaning of this war on terrorism. Some see it as a battle against those forces that would destroy all that we hold dear, our values and our way of life. Some see it as a divine call to spread our way of life to the rest of the world. But have we really examined our values and way of life, or are we just taking them for granted? Have we examined what we are doing and why we are doing it, first as individuals, and then collectively as a community and a nation, or have we become complacent in letting others define what it is we value and are willing to fight and die for? The situation is so confusing that I can easily understand how people would throw up their hands and let others do the thinking and worrying for them so that they can get on with their everyday lives. The trouble is, those who are doing the thinking and worrying for us aren't necessarily doing the dying, and that goes for both sides.

The last paragraph in your book of letters to teachers really slammed me when I first read it. What a warning!

> Knowing has everything to do with growing. But the knowing of the dominant minorities absolutely must not prohibit, must not asphyxiate, must not castrate the growing of the immense dominated majorities. (Freire, 1998c, p. 95)

Is this what has happened in the world? Is this what this war on terrorism is all about? Have the dominated majorities finally had enough and are they now fighting back in the only way the dominant minorities will listen to? Is there no hope for peace and reconciliation? I wonder, Paulo, if you had lived to see what happened on that terrible Tuesday morning, and how we Americans as a nation have allowed ourselves to be led to war, what you would have to say about it. All I seem able to do is shake my head, but there must be more a simple teacher can do. I dare to teach, yet I am such a coward. I can barely hear your voice, Paulo. What am I to do?

Claire LaBonté

⌒⌒

Shakira Alvarez-Ferrer

What I Learned in School: A Poem about Puerto Rico

> *My homeland is, above all, a space in time that involves geography, history, culture. My homeland is also pain, hunger, misery. It is also the hope of millions who remain hungry for social justice.*
> —Paulo Freire, *Pedagogy of the Heart* (2004a), pp. 39–40.

December 1999
Dear Paulo,

Pedagogy of the Oppressed made quite an impression on me. Sonia told us that sometimes, we have to read it five times to really understand it. Reading it, I am finding that the language I had for things seems less adequate than it once did. Or perhaps only that I am seeing the world as though it were new, and wanting to name it differently.

I wrote a poem about Puerto Rico, the country where I received much of my education, while reading your book, a poem unlike any I've written before. Nothing pretty in the language. Just saying what I needed to say.

> *Any situation in which some individuals prevent others from*
> *engaging in the process of inquiry is one of violence.*
> —Paulo Freire, *Pedagogy of the oppressed* (1970), p. 28.

Two plus two is four.
Atoms are smaller than molecules.
It is correct to say "I brought,"
    not "I brung,"
And on occasion *"Yo traje,"*
    but only during *la clase de español.*

George Washington is the father of our country.
    (*Pero misi,* of Puerto Rico?)
    No. Of the United States.
    (*Misi, misi,* was George Washington a *gringo?*)
    The correct word is American.

There were slaves in the South.
    (Of what, *misi?*)
    Of the United States!
    (I heard there were slaves here, *misi.*)
    Well, yes.
    (Then why can't we talk about that?)

In 1898, there was the Spanish-American War.
    Puerto Rico came under American rule.
    (How did that happen, *misi?*)
    They came to make life better for the people.
    (How?)

Then the Americans came to live on the island.
    (Like you, *misi?*)

They brought a governor with them.
  (But what about elections, *misi?*)
Those came later.
  (But when?)
Fifty years later.
  (Half a century?)

They made Puerto Rico into a democracy.
  (Without elections? But I thought you said ...)

They had public schools for everyone, so everyone
  could learn to read and write.
  (But how did the Americans know Spanish reading?)
In English.
  (But *misi,* didn't the people speak Spanish?)

Puerto Rico became a Commonwealth.
  (Like Massachusetts?)
  No.

The first governor of the Commonwealth was Luis
  Muñoz Marín. He was a great man.
  (He was a *popular,* right?)
Yes.
  (*Misi,* what are you?)

He was governor for a long time. Since then, Puerto
  Rico has remained a Commonwealth.
  (Hey *misi,* is it true we're a colony?)
  No! Com-mon-wealth. *Estado Libre Asociado.*
  (But my neighbor says ...)

Time for recess.

Sincerely,
Shakira Alvarez-Ferrer

∽

⸙ *Linda Brodkey* ⸙
Radical Politics, Writing, and the CIA

If our schools, from the earliest grades, were to devote themselves to
the work of nurturing in students a taste for reading and writing
and were to maintain that nurturing throughout their school
lives, there would possibly be fewer graduate students who spoke
of their inability to write or their insecurity about writing.
—Paulo Freire, *Teachers as Cultural Workers: Letters*
to Those Who Dare Teach (1998c), p. 24.

Spring 2007
Dear Paulo,
   One of the first things I did after learning about this collection of letters to
you was "Google" the key words "literacy in U.S." The first entry is "The World
Factbook," a site registered under, owned by, hosted by the CIA (www.cia.gov/). I
queried because I was curious about worldwide literacy rates by country. Now I'm
even more curious about how the CIA came to be the first entry. And I can't help
wishing you were still here. More than anyone else I've ever known, I believe you
would appreciate my curiosity.
   I suppose it is common knowledge that the first site listed by a search engine is the
one with the most "hits." That would mean that the CIA registered/owned/hosted
literacy site on Google gets more hits than either UNESCO or the Department of
Education, two that one might reasonably expect to see at or near the top. And yet
the CIA site is not nearly so visible on other well-known search engines (for example,
ASK or Yahoo). I mention these facts and my musings because they seem to me at
once peculiar and ominous. The facts are peculiar because I'm not accustomed to
associating the CIA with education, and ominous for the same reason.
   I understand that for many people the name Paulo Freire is wholly synonymous
with the word *radical*. That's true as far as it goes. You *were* radical, even profoundly
radical. Yet you were an intellectual as well as political radical. You taught us to short
shrift neither our desire for institutional reform nor our belief that teaching is a
worthy use of intellect. When I first became interested in teaching writing I needed
someone I respected to respect my choice. Most of my professors were disappointed
that I preferred "writing" to reading. Later still, when my work on adult literacy
undermined my belief in the democratic intentions of public education, I once
again turned to you. I was not looking for a mentor. I was looking for someone who
understood that well-intentioned people may not fully understand the hypocrisy of
advocating reading as the one and only measure of universal literacy.

In saying that reading is not the sole measure, I do not mean to underestimate its importance to individuals or society. Reading is critical. But surely reading is not enough. It is the first step. Full citizenship requires readers who also write. Without writing we play no active role in the directions we are encouraged to follow, take no critical part in making the laws we are bound to follow. While it may be what most politicians mean by literacy, literacy reduced only to reading suppresses the incipient power of literacy. It most assuredly ignores what you meant by literacy.

Readers must be writers if literacy is to mean anything beyond reading and following directions. Literacy campaigns that teach reading at the expense of writing are less about empowering people than staffing institutions. Perhaps that is why this volume is such a fitting testament to you. I can think of no one else who could have appreciated more a volume of letters written by students and teachers. I suppose one could argue there is no better way to honor writers than reading their work. But I believe there is no better way than writing to honor you, Paulo, you who understood full literacy to be the foundation of participatory democracy.

That said, I still worry that if the CIA "owns" literacy in cyberspace, it may also own literacy in geographical space. It strikes me that perhaps the best way to remember and honor you is to make certain that universal literacy education takes some part in the defense against such hegemony.

Yours,
Linda Brodkey

Part 7: Love

I do not believe in loving among women and men, among human beings, if we do not become capable of loving the world.
—Paulo Freire, *Pedagogy of Indignation* (2004b), p. 47.

The word *love* is not heard very much in the current discourse on education today, and this is true both in the United States and around the world. Sadly, the most commonly heard words in education today are such terms as *rubrics, templates, adequate yearly progress, accountability, underperforming,* and other terms associated with market- and measure-driven views of education. Nonetheless, in my many years of experience with classroom teachers, I have found that the most effective teachers are those who ground their work in love. This is not a soppy, sentimental love, and it is not just a matter of patting a student on the back. The love they speak about is a *critical* love, a love that demands, and expects, nothing but the best from students, a love that believes that students can engage with the world, and that they have a right and a responsibility to change it.

Teachers with whom I have been fortunate to work over the years believe that their work, in order to be transformative, must be imbued with love (Nieto, 2003). They agree with Che Guevara (1965), that "[at] the risk of seeming ridiculous, let me say that the true revolutionary is guided by a great feeling of love." In this sense, the teachers with whom I have worked have been true revolutionaries: they love their students, and they work tirelessly on their behalf. Moreover, they are clear about this: neither rubrics, templates, nor adequate yearly progress brought them to teaching, nor do these things keep them there. It is love that is at the heart of what they do.

The letters in this section describe in numerous ways what it means to love one's students. From trying to find a way—and the time—to love them, to defining daring as love, they explore the many ways that teachers struggle with the notion of love, as one of them says, "in spite of it all."

∞

⌒ *Kristen French* ⌒

A Love Letter to Paulo

We must dare, in the full sense of the word, to speak of love without the fear of being called ridiculous, mawkish, or unscientific, if not antiscientific.
—Paulo Freire, *Teachers as Cultural Workers: Letters to Those Who Dare Teach* (1998c), p. 3.

October 24, 2000

Dear Paulo,

I am writing this letter of love to you as both teacher and learner transformed by your work. In fact, I would like to begin by thanking you for several tremendously powerful words that have resonated within me: *hope, dreams, justice, dedication, radicalism, freedom, discipline, courage, politics,* and *love.* I was struck by the impact they had on me as I actively read *Teachers as Cultural Workers* (1998c), but also the importance of teaching and living by them. I am sure that as I continue to read your work and grow as a teacher and intellectual, I will add to this list.

As I read your letters in your book, I imagined the teachers you write about who value freedom for students but maintain authority without becoming authoritarian. The teachers you describe walk and speak with honesty and integrity. They are neither weak nor arrogant, and they consistently evaluate their thoughts and actions. These are the teachers I want to emulate. After reading your letters, I felt compelled to honor the two teachers I have known who embodied these traits. Their dedication to creating democratic relationships between the teacher and student, one of mutual respect, demonstrate that profound transformation *is* possible. For instance, when I read your story about Carla, an uneducated, dirty-faced girl, I was deeply moved. You wrote: "[S]he wandered around as a lost soul, and what was worse, she was lost from herself, a kind of nobody's little girl" (ibid., p. 57).

Metaphorically, I was Carla. Without the mentorship of kind, courageous, thoughtful, and ethical teachers who were able to see the beauty beyond my "dirt," I may not have been able to transform myself into an intellectual and a teacher. Like Carla, I had discovered—or rediscovered—myself, and I began to believe in my own potenial and self-worth. I now have the courage to create a hopeful future for my family, children, and students. You write that

> the task of the teacher, who is also a learner, is both joyful and rigorous. It demands seriousness and scientific, physical, emotional and effective preparation. It is a task that those who commit themselves to teaching develop a certain love not only of others but also of the very process implied in teaching. It is impossible to teach without the courage to love,

without the courage to try a thousand times before giving up. In short, it is impossible to teach without a forged, invented, and well-thought-out capacity to love. (Ibid., p. 3)

In writing this, you honor the profession of teaching and the teachers I have known who love their students unconditionally without fear or disappointment. You remind us that our job is to have compassion, love, and the drive to improve our society by inviting our students to participate in becoming change agents themselves. This love moves beyond simply "caring" for our students; it also means maintaining the courage to fight for their success despite the difficulties we may face in doing so.

You also remind me of the profound effect that teachers have on students of all ages, whether they are young children, young adults, or adult students. Having had incredible role models as an adult, role models who "walk the walk," has made an indelible impression on me as a teacher, and you, Paulo, remind me to be true to the visions of these remarkable educators. Knowing the love of teachers and also loving my own students—some like Carla—inspires me to continue teaching.

You also write:

We must dare so that we can continue to teach for a long time under conditions that we know well: low salaries, lack of respect, and the ever-present risk of becoming prey to cynicism. We must dare to learn how to dare in order to say no to the bureaucratization of the mind to which we are exposed every day. We must dare so that we can continue to do so even when it is so much more materially advantageous to stop daring. (Ibid., p. 3)

Our ability to develop democracy within our classrooms and society is obstructed by those who lead us to believe that our work is not valuable. We are an underprivileged educated community by mere choice of profession, although we belong to an elite group of great social thinkers such as Socrates, Plato, and you. Thank you for reminding us that our power is phenomenal. Sometimes we need the words of great educators to push our thinking and reignite our passion to move our dreams of justice, love, and freedom forward.

I have been most fortunate to see the teaching that you described in your letters. I am therefore called to be a radical teacher myself. By that I mean that I must believe in what I teach, teach to the best of my ability, show compassion for my students, and provide strong academic support while creating loving learning environments in which students may be empowered to struggle for their own freedom and for a truly democratic society. I keep your words close to my heart: "[As] educators we are politicians; we engage in politics when we educate. And if we dream about democracy, let us fight, day and night, for a school in which we talk to and with the learners so that, hearing them, we can be heard by them as well" (Freire, 1985b, p. 68).

As I conclude this love letter to you, dear Paulo, I wonder why as an adult having struggled within our public schools for several years, I had not been introduced to your teachings? Why wasn't I taught about your philosophies in my teacher education program? I believe that you represent change and action, which the current educational and political system is not ready for. It is time to change this ideology, and I want to be a part of it. In fact, I began by sending a copy of your book three thousand miles from where I now sit to my teaching colleagues so that they too could be transformed by your words of love and justice. By continuing the cycle of love, anything is possible!

Thank you, Paulo!

Kristen

☞ *Alexis Nasdor-Jones* ☜
Learning to Love My Students

> *I love children. I may be wrong, but I think children also love me a lot.*
> —Paulo Freire, *The Politics of Education: Culture,*
> *Power, and Liberation* (1985b), p. 197.

Dear Paulo,

When I first read your book, I hated it. On each page I understood just one phrase, maybe? I did not understand why each sentence had so many parts. By the time I reached the end of the sentence, I had forgotten the beginning. Just as you wrote, it is true that a student can be taught something new, and it means nothing to them because they are not ready to receive the information. This was true for me, but when I read your book a second time I was ready to read it. In between readings, I had read other works and had important experiences that allowed me to engage with and re-create your text through the lens of a first-year teacher.

As a first-year teacher I struggled to make critical pedagogy an organic and authentic part of my classroom curriculum and environment. Each week I left school feeling guilty and bored because I knew that a lot of the problems in my classroom were linked to this lack of a multicultural perspective in my teaching. I felt guilty because I knew better; I had great ideas but got sidetracked by the stresses of first-year teaching. I was bored because I was not tapping into my own talents and interests.

In this frustrated state, I began reading *Teachers a Cultural Workers*. As I read each chapter, I found many of your statements reassuring. Though in your other works there are important messages, from this text I focused on two important messages for me, right now as a learner and a teacher.

It takes time to develop. Though obvious, it was reassuring to read that. Since I was so frustrated with myself, reading it just made me take a step back to revisit how to incorporate critical pedagogy into my classroom. It made me repeat to myself that, of course, my critical literacy attempts are not going to be wholly successful the first time. Each following step will be an improvement upon the first.

Love your students. I first read this and thought, I do not love my students. I have a migraine, and if I have to repeat, "Please show me how we sit at circle," one more time I'm going to have to change careers. As I continued to think about this statement, "Love your students," I started to smile at the child who does somersaults to his workspace, but then dives right into his math work. He is so enthusiastic about figuring things out. He wants to be a part of our classroom community, and he jumps out of his seat excitedly anytime Spanish or Puerto Rico is mentioned. I want to hear his opinions as we inevitably discuss Puerto Rico and its relationship with the United States. I want to hear his questions and answers as we discuss the fundamental needs of all people and how those needs are—or are not—met. I am intrigued by his thought process as he considers why a white man would dump food on a black woman's head, when all the woman was doing was sitting at a lunch counter trying to order a snack. When I first read "Love your students," I was not ready to hear that, but as I thought about it, I decided that though frustrated, I *do* love my students and I am excited to learn with them. Now as I think about it, diving into a critical pedagogy curriculum might be the way to pull my classroom community and curriculum together.

My frustrations with my first year of teaching stemmed from my own idealism and expectations for my classroom and curricula. Reading and reconstructing your text allowed me to reflect on the reality of my classroom and my expectations. As I consider your work, I appreciate that you do not offer specific practices for the elementary classroom, but rather a philosophy to influence those practices. This enables me to understand and think about how your philosophy applies to my specific students, their needs, and their sociopolitical context.

Yours,
Alexis Nasdor-Jones

⁓ *Ruth Harman* ⁓

Teaching with Tenderness and Compassion

> *It is impossible to talk of respect for students, for the dignity that is*
> *in the process of coming to be, for the identities that are in the process*
> *of construction, without taking into consideration the conditions in*
> *which they are living and the importance of the knowledge derived*
> *from life experience, which they bring with them to school. I can in no*
> *way underestimate such knowledge. Or what is worse, ridicule it.*
> —Paulo Freire, *Pedagogy of Freedom* (1998a), p. 62.

November 2002

Dear Paulo,

When I was twenty-two years of age, I read *Pedagogy of the Oppressed* for the first time. Even then, despite my lack of training as a teacher, I was filled with energy when reading your words. This semester, I have read two of your books: besides rereading *Pedagogy*, I have also read *Teachers as Cultural Workers: Letters to Those Who Dare Teach*. It is now as a seasoned teacher and administrator in the United States, far from my fishing village near Dublin, Ireland, that I feel the wisdom and depth of your words.

In *Teachers as Cultural Workers* you show such understanding of the plight of teachers in our repressive society and also such vision about how we, cultural workers and educators, can transcend our conditioning and teach with compassion and tenderness. You also point out several strong traits to succeed as cultural workers: we need to be hard working, directed, courageous, disciplined, motivated, and relentless. We cannot fall down and weep when the tide turns against us. We need to remain standing even if guns are pointed at us.

Your message to teachers is an inspiring and galvanizing one. It is so important to stress the fact that students are the teachers of teachers. For all our university education and academic discourse, we teachers are not the knowledgeable ones. When teaching inner-city teenagers and adults in New Orleans, I found myself being guided by my students. If they could come to class through bullet-holed doors and past crack houses, leaving behind perhaps five or six children with a relative after working a long day somewhere far off from their homes, I could come to my classes prepared and with my heart open for whatever dialogue we would have.

At the beginning I was intimidated. I was out of the safe sanctuary of my university world of books and schooled students. I felt I was speaking a different language from my inner-city students, and I despaired of finding a key to get them talking to me, to get them writing in a loose way, to let them forget the scars they carried from their experiences in the inner-city public schools. And it took time. I would come with long lesson plans and discard them once we got some hot topic going. For two years I was with them two evenings a week, and I watched some grow as writers, some fall off, some stay in the same spot. But those two years gave me so much energy and appreciation for this lively and courageous group of students. They were the teachers: they were coming to get their G.E.D. despite troubles at home, unemployment, ill children. They would come and give more than I gave.

Yes, Paulo, we need the courage to keep on going, the direction to know where we are going, the compassion and tenderness for all our students. and the patience to remain with those who fail time and time again and those who challenge us. But also, Paulo, as you say, the students are our guides.

Every time I read you I cannot help thinking of Thich Nhat Hanh and his teachings. You remind me of him in that you are direct and probing in your message. You talk about compassion but you also talk about the need to be strong and directive in class when need be. You probe the nature of the self and the need to strip off layers of cultural conditioning if we want to make a difference. You write about the political nature of teaching: we cannot ignore the inequities in our schooling system, in housing, in employment, in academic access, and in quality of life issues. I used to talk to my students a lot about N.I.M.B.Y. ("not in my backyard," that attitude of dumping undesirable waste, undesirable industry, and undesirable pollutants in the gardens and neighborhoods of those who cannot fight back). But we need to reflect carefully on how N.I.M.B.Y.-type attitudes have molded all of us. We need to carefully strip ourselves of our own capitalist and egocentric tendencies so that we can meet our students halfway.

Thank you, Paulo, for making us think and talk about education in transformative ways. If we could only bring all teachers and students into our cultural circle and begin a dialogue that would break down the iron armor of greed, individualism, and cravings in ourselves and others. "Peace is every step," as Thich Nhat Hanh would say. Each pebble will cause a ripple on the water; each teacher and student engaged in true dialogic learning will cause a ripple in all those they encounter. We need to begin small and humble in order to sow seeds of true compassion and understanding.

Your student forever,
Ruth Margaret Harman

☙

❧ Kelley Crisp ☙

Colonialism, the English Language, and a Teacher's Love

> *It is imperative that we maintain hope even when the harshness*
> *of reality may suggest the opposite. On this level, the struggle for*
> *hope means the denunciation, in no uncertain terms, of all abuses,*
> *schemes, and omissions. As we denounce them, we awaken in*
> *others and ourselves the need, and also the taste, for hope.*
> —Paulo Freire, *Pedagogy of the Heart* (2004a), p. 106.

November 2005
Dear Paulo,

I wish that you were here so that I could talk to you about the Marshall Islands. I look back on my experience in the Marshall Islands with some sadness—the way English is being spread like something sacred. I know that it isn't that simple. I know about Bikini and Kwaj and the GDP, all of that dependence on American green that came out of exploitation. I know that exploitation still exists; that the

United States is still using the Kwajalein lagoon for missile firing practice; we call it the Star Wars missile defense system. I know that the Marshallese people who lived on the tiny islets that make up the Kwajalein atoll have been pushed onto a tiny islet called Ebeye, an islet with a population density that is greater than that of Calcutta. I know some of the people who are benefiting from U.S. money. The *Iroij* (traditional leader based on land inheritance) of the Kwajalein atoll is living on Majuro and spending money on bodyguards and travel and drinking at the Tide Table (a local bar in Maj). I know that the United States is trying to extricate itself from this predicament that it created by gradually limiting its outlay of money to rental of land (Star Wars again). And I know that there are great disparities in wealth and access that are culturally related and also influenced by Western contact. The Iroij traditionally divided up the natural wealth of the islands: the fish, the coconuts, the pandanus, and the breadfruit. But now there is all of this money. And when I learned about critical literacy, I wanted to take that critical literacy and wrap it up in a package to take with me to the Marshalls. Some present! Just another imposed American point of view.

But it is not that simple, either. There is also migration between the United States and the Marshalls and English taught as sheltered immersion so that the oral language of the people, the Marshallese language, doesn't make it in the schools past the fifth grade. And there is rice and diabetes and just plain the people don't fish as much anymore. I saw a pig slaughtered and I went to my first *kemmem* (this is a celebration if a baby makes it to the second year) and I sat in a circle and ate shark with my fingers. I wasn't much good at weaving mats. And on that tiny coral atoll with 180 people on a two-mile-long boomerang-shaped islet, I am not sure how English fits in.

What next, Paulo, what do I do next? Colonialism, now that is a strange thing to say about me and three fifth-grade boys sitting on coral rock and looking at my guide book to Micronesian reef fish. We were so close together that I thought of puppies, so close that we were stuck together by salt and sun and sea emulsion. Love is not missing here, but what is?

I know you would acknowledge my heartbreak, but I know that you would also feel my hope. I have been changed by my experience, and I hope that I have not been a part of changing a fragile balance between old and new ways of being. Inevitably things change, but I think it matters *how* they change. My biggest hope is that Marshallese people will make the decisions about how future change takes place.

I have very little influence on how change can take place in the Marshall Islands, but I can make suggestions to World Teach for different readings to include for their *Selected Readings,* a compilation given to volunteers. I know this seems small, but reading and what and how we read are important. You write: "Acquiring literacy does not involve memorizing sentences, words, or syllables—lifeless objects unconnected to an existential universe—but rather an attitude of creation and re-creation, a self transformation producing a stance of intervention in one's context" (Freire, *Education for Critical Consciousness*, 1974, p. 48).

It would be educationally relevant to include articles about the importance of teaching indigenous languages in the classroom and the importance of using the Marshallese language in English language classes. It would be important to include articles on the job possibilities for Marshallese people and articles on classroom practices and content that might be more relevant and meaningful to Marshallese learners. These are useful directions to explore. It would be even more useful to talk about those articles with the volunteers. I hope that this is a realistic goal, even though I realize how tricky it might be to pull off. There are many assumptions being made by World Teach and the MOE (Ministry of Education) about the spread of English and how good and empowering it will be for the Marshallese people. In my experience, this just wasn't always true. In any event, what I am proposing is small, but I hope it might prove useful.

Thanks for listening,
Kelley Crisp

⟶ *Jennifer Burk* ⟵
Love as Daring

Educators must ask themselves for whom and on whose behalf they are working. The more conscious and committed they are, the more they understand that their role as educators requires them to take risks, including a willingness to risk their own jobs.
—Paulo Freire, *The Politics of Education: Culture, Power, and Liberation* (1985), p. 180.

December 15, 2005
Dear Paulo,

After reading your book *Teachers as Cultural Workers: Letters to Those Who Dare Teach,* no longer can I look at teaching as merely a means to bring students to educational success; it is so much more than that. With a compassionate, guiding hand, your letters showed me how teachers are, above all else, learners in their own mistakes, doubts, and fears, and that true teaching is not only helping students to achieve academically but also supporting, encouraging, affirming, and loving them as special individuals who all have a powerful voice to share and enrich within the classroom.

"Dare" is truly the right word to use, for it is certainly not easy to stand against the tide of traditional, limiting pedagogical practices that constantly threaten to overwhelm even the most well intentioned and dedicated of teachers. And it is also a huge gamble to take the chance to make a lasting difference in even one student's life, or to let oneself be washed away by the tide of monocentric education practices and pedagogies.

So thank you, Paulo. Thank you for showing me what it truly means to dare, and just how empowering such daring can be.

Warm regards,
Jennifer Burk

∽

∼ *Stephanie Doyle* ∼
Love, in Spite of It All

I am a teacher full of the spirit of hope, in spite of all signs to the contrary.
—Paulo Freire, *Pedagogy of Freedom* (1998a), p. 94.

December 6, 2005
Dear Paulo,

I am not a hero. I am not famous or acclaimed in any way. But I am a teacher.

Why am I a teacher? I teach to see my students smile when they see me in the hallway or in class. I teach for those *"aha!"* moments when my students understand a concept. I teach to reach my students in ways that nobody else will ever reach them. I teach because life is a wonderful gift that I want to share with students. I teach to make a difference in the world, by reaching one little person at a time, who I know will become big people who I believe will change the world themselves, and as you put it in *Teachers as Cultural Workers* (1998c), become "strong *presences* in the world" (p. 33). Simply, I teach because there is no other choice for me.

I would be lying if I said that I have never had doubts about teaching. I have doubts more often than not. But I have not, as you say, "let the fear of what is difficult paralyze [me]" (ibid., p. 27). I have worked with tough colleagues, students, and parents. I have taught in a city that carries so many negative connotations that people continually question my motive for working in such a place. I have faced the difficulties that come when one loves and cares for their students almost too much. I have worked incredibly hard (and continue to do so) to get through state requirements that are changing daily. But who hasn't? I am just beginning my teaching career and have a long way to go before I can look back and feel satisfied at what I have done. Doubts and fears creep in occasionally, but I have not, and will not, let that stop me from doing what I know is right and what I love.

You write: "Without the democratic intervention of the educator, there is no progressive education" (ibid., p. 57). You speak of the "constant commitment to justice, liberty, and individual rights, of our dedication to defending the weakest when they are subjected to the exploitation of the strongest," and that "there is beauty in the ethical struggle" (ibid., p. 56). This is something that I have seen and have been a part of, but could not have put into words before becoming a teacher. Before this, I never knew I could have so much love for twenty-nine children, all from different backgrounds and life experiences, all with different personalities and intentions. I have come to realize that being a teacher is not just about what goes on in the classroom, but also about what goes on outside the classroom, in the lives of our students and their families, and that as teachers, we must be a part of this nonschool life in order to be fully committed to educating these children. We must fight for our students' rights in and out of the classroom and ensure as best we can that they are able to live to their fullest potential.

I have so much to learn, not just about teaching but also about life in general. I have always been and will continue to be a lifelong learner, and it is my hope that this shows in my teaching. Reading your letters has brought me to a better understanding about how to become a more effective, aware, and loving teacher.

Respectfully,
Stephanie Doyle

— *Mike Hayes* —

Teaching as Relationship

In truth, I feel it is necessary to overcome the false separation between serious teaching and the expression of feeling.
—Paulo Freire, *Pedagogy of Freedom* (1998a), p. 125.

December 6, 2005
Dear Paulo:

When I decided I wanted to become a teacher, I was worried that my parents would not think it was a rigorous enough career (I found out that this was not something I needed to worry about—they are very proud of what I do). I figured I wouldn't last more than five years. I thought that teaching would become dull once I had "figured it out." I had somehow been trained by society not to value the intellectual nature of the job I was choosing for myself.

What I have found is not what I had expected. Teaching is amazingly intellectual. Knowing your content is the easiest part of the job. What makes teaching intellectual are the children: I must find a way to take what I know and understand and help the students have their own understanding of it. Doing this for one child is a challenging task. Doing it for a whole class, with its myriad of identities and ways of learning, the task becomes quite daunting.

To address this task, in *Teachers as Cultural Workers*, you wrote about the indispensable qualities of progressive teachers. There are three that I want to stick on my chest and carry into the classroom every day—*humility, lovingness,* and *permanently seeking justice*. Without humility, we will not grow as teachers. I quickly learned humility when I entered the classroom and found out just how intellectual it is. I never want to lose the feeling that there is more I can learn as a teacher.

The word I think of when you say lovingness is *relationship*. The power of the human relationship to overcome the obstacles to learning should never be ignored. If a teacher cannot love the children for who they are and show them this love, he or she should not be teaching. This quality of seeking justice will come out of the love. If we truly love our students, we will have the courage to fight for them.

Your writings talk to what teaching really is—one of the most challenging and intellectual pursuits one can undertake. Your message to teachers is empowering in a time when we truly need it. The message we are given by our society is that we are valued only in our ability to have our students perform well on a test. I do give some value to these tests, and I do think we need to prepare all students to do well on them. However, I do not think that they are the only measure of who we are as teachers and who our students are academically. When the focus is only on the performance by your students on a test, teaching becomes a rote, passionless job.

Thank you for your courage.

Mike

⌘

⌘ *Tracy Walker* ⌘

Time to Love

I have a right to be angry, to show it and to use it as a motivational foundation for my struggle, just as I have a right to love and to express my love to the world and to use it as a motivational foundation for my struggle because I live in history at a time of possibility and not of determinism.
—Paulo Freire, *Pedagogy of Freedom* (1998a), p. 71.

November 24, 2004
Dear Paulo,

I am a middle school teacher. I love the middle school level. I love being a part of the great change that my students experience during this tumultuous time of their lives. What is hard, however, is time. I seem to do no more than swim in time like I'm caught in a current in the ocean, getting a glimpse of where I am only when I float up with the crest of a wave. Back down in the trough, it is just water all around me.

I would like to share with you a medley of school life as seen through my eyes. Every image is true and none are exaggerated. This medley is a snapshot of my sixth-grade humanities classroom. It made me feel better to write it, and I hope in reading it you can stand there in my room with me on some days. My classroom is a gray room lit with fluorescent light, covered with a thin film of yellow chalk dust and filled with furniture. Up above us all is a big, ticking clock, and it bears down on us all, fitting us into the frames of its day. I imagine the sound of the first bell of the day, and I can see them all now as they were.

Damien stood in front of me with the book and peered out over the rims of his bent glasses. In the back of the room, four kids tripped through the door giggling and K. C. dropped his set of glow pens on the floor and scrambled to collect them. Damien had one side of his bent glasses hooked over his left ear and the other side stuck out against his head. He reached up with his middle finger and pushed them into his forehead. "How much longer do we have?" he asked. He squinted when I pointed at the clock.

"The bell rings at eight twenty. When the big hand is on the four." K. C. yelps and has the last glow pen in his hand. Then there is Bobby complaining and Marcus in tow with the guinea pig clutched to his chest. Marcus has guinea pig hair all over his black T-shirt and Bobby wants to hold it. The secretary calls a list of names to the office during break so as not to interrupt class time. Aimee is outside on the wet grass of our school, an escapee from class. She is blowing through Mrs. Noel's giant conch shell and shouting at Greg, who is clapping yellow chalk from the erasers against the school brick. I look at Damien, then at the book Damien is holding, one for drawing pencil sketches of plants. "I can't see the clock," he tells me. He goes out in the hall to get a drink behind his glasses.

Hanna sits at her desk before class every morning and works on her story. She tells me she looks like her mom, and she does. She writes so lightly with her pencil that her words are wispy. I sit on a stool to talk to her when Greg comes back through the door running, and I get up to yell. Suddenly there is green poster board blocking my view. Millie and Mandy tell me they have discovered that the prime meridian runs through Greenwich, England, because of the observatory operating there since the 1600s. This is true. I bend over to ask Lucia if she has finished her world map, and scowl at her when she makes excuses. The bell rings. We all open to page forty-nine.

Andrew cannot read, and he is a very fat little boy. We are learning all about Eastern and Western dragons, and he has brought in his T-shirt, a beautiful Celtic design with a dragon. Ramos is sharpening his pencil again. We admire the shirt until Andrew waddles off with Bobby to what he calls the "special room." On page forty-nine Dwayne yells that he read this yesterday, and Crissy reminds me that she has been sick. I say we are on page forty-nine, and is it a question for the group or a personal question? The hands go up and down. The office calls for Melanie to go to the dentist. Ramos grinds his pencil. We admire her new braces with the yellow plates, and Chad says braces make your tongue numb for about two weeks but after that you can't feel it. Melanie slams the door. It's quiet. Ramos grinds his pencil and looks at me and pulls the pencil out of the sharpener and looks at me and sticks it back in and grinds. We do start reading the story. We are reading *Tuck Everlasting*, a story about a family who drink from a spring and get eternal life. We all agree it would be no good to be twelve forever. We all like the story, and when the protagonist, Winnie, almost runs away from home but doesn't, we share stories about when we did the same thing. I hope that everyone has an okay story about home to share. We read. For a while there is the quiet posture and stillness in the room of people reading to themselves in another world, and Johnny played with the lead in his pencil, not knowing the sounds.

The bell rings again. I guess K.C. does not bring lunch money or lunch to school. He tells me every morning how hungry he is. The vice principal comes into my room while I am sitting again with Hanna looking at her wispy writing and drawings of cats, and he tells me that K.C. has been getting free peanut butter sandwiches for four days now and that has got to stop and admires the cats. The break is over, and I am yelling at the front of the room that it's time to start. I am thinking about peanut butter, and we look at the world and Kristopher says that Greenland is part of Europe. We work hard; you've got to know how elevation is related to climate and where the Gulf of Mexico is, or what's the longest river in the United States. Mandy has twelve trophies she has won at a bowling tournament, and she would like to show them to the class. We figure out the latitude of Boston, and I send seven students to learn about the doldrums, the Sargasso Sea, and scurvy. I confiscate a large bag of mini-marshmallows that K.C. is secretly trying to eat from out of his desk. Veteran's Day is coming up, and so is our social studies test. We know about all the continents and oceans, longitude and what it's like to get your locker stuck. We take out our planners and write that there is a test tomorrow and that we have to get permission from our parents to use the Internet.

When we are done with the lesson, Robbie raises his hand from the back of the room and asks if I want to see the three-legged frog that he caught when we were down doing restoration at our adopted wetlands last week. Alicia says she does not want to go to band today. Her family didn't buy her an instrument, she says is why. The school rents only baritone trumpet. Who wants to play baritone trumpet? Not O'Delia. The kids are saying that Tabby is a Bambi hunter because she missed school on Friday to go hunting with her family and brought in a deer leg to science class. The vice principal comes on the intercom about the magazine drive and says that tomorrow is treasure card day and that all sales are double prizes. I am asked a lot of questions about this, and Mandy is pulling all her bowling trophies out of her bag. Damien shows me his perfect picture of English Holly. The bell rings and the second class of my day is waiting at the door.

I think sometimes that what's hardest about this kind of day and what I do is the pace of it all. The necessity to jam-pack these snippets of love and woven treasure and discovery into neat, forty-two-minute packages callously sliced by the ringing of the school bell leaves me little margin. I have my attendance lists with the one hundred and some names on it, and I stand in the doorway, shepherding in and out, chasing them down for their homework and lending out pencils. There is so much work to do, and at 2:25 when the last school bus pulls away it is utterly silent.

Help me to have the strength and the patience and the calm to bring love to that cramped and poorly swept little room every day, Paulo. Help me to keep my inner peace, not to linger in cynicism, and most of all, to love what I do and to have the drive and the courage to do it well. Daniel is counting on me to tell him what time it is, and I keep my eye on the clock.

Sincerely yours,
Tracy Walker

Part 8: Study/Dialogue

The act of study, in sum, is an attitude toward the world.
—Paulo Freire, The Politics of Education: Culture,
Power, and Liberation (1985a), p. 3.

For Paulo Freire, the act of study was an indispensable aspect of being human. It was a disciplined and difficult task that required time, attention, and perseverance.

During the 1980s, for a number of years Paulo visited us for a month at a time at the University of Massachusetts. During his stays, he was always gracious about meeting with students, faculty, or community people (and we filled up his calendar with seminars, major talks, visits to community centers, and so on). But he also made it quite clear that he needed time to read and to study. He brought books and articles with him, and he spent time in his apartment reading, learning, and writing.

Paulo never saw himself as "finished" in terms of learning, and it is this same spirit of education as an active and even physical activity that differentiates his view of learning from more passive expressions of learning. In contrast to active or liberatory education, he decried "domesticating" or "banking" education, the kind of education that lends itself easily to empty nutritional metaphors where leaders "digest" knowledge and "regurgitate" it. As seen in Freirean terms, to study is a physical and even aggressive activity. "In fact," he wrote, "a book reflects its author's confrontation with the world" (ibid.).

In this section, the letter writers have taken Paulo seriously, and they do indeed interact with him: they critique his writing as too dense for most teachers to follow, among other criticisms, but they also thank him for broadening their vision of learning. In the process, they reread, retheorize, and re-create him, and themselves.

⌒

⸎ *Tina Clark* ⸎
The Need to Study

Teachers who do not take their own education seriously, who do not study, who make little effort to keep abreast of events have no moral authority to coordinate the activities of the classroom.
—Paulo Freire, *Pedagogy of Freedom* (1998a), p. 85.

November 17, 2004

Dear Paulo,

Oh, Paulo! How your work has frustrated me! Your work requires one to be a scholar, a philosopher. One would need the intelligence of ten individuals to sort out your words and their meanings. I struggle. I read and then I read again, the same paragraph over and over, trying to decipher your meaning, your message. I am left in despair, feeling ill-equipped and of little intelligence. What does this mean? How does that translate? Why does Paulo torture me so?

But … I am intrigued. I continue to read, to decipher, and, finally, to grasp the meaning of your words. I read everything not once but twice. I want to know. I want to understand. I like the frustration and torture; they challenge me. Is that your trick? Are you tricking me into something?

I think you want me to read your work not once but twice. I think that you want me to fumble and ponder your message. You like that. All that talk about educators being political and modeling the values of democracy. I think that you feel that educators need to study, that educators need to stand up and say, "I am competent, and I am a political advocate!"

Wait! Reflecting back, I did understand your work. I got it! I had to use your words to read your work. I had to study, reread, and understand instead of memorize. How ingenious of you! Not only did I learn new ways to bring freedom, democracy, and political activism into my classroom, but I also learned how to bring freedom, democracy, politician activism, and a new respect for my profession, teaching, into my life.

Thank you, Paulo Freire.

With love and much admiration,
Tina Clark

P.S. I bought two more of your books to go along with *Teachers as Cultural Workers.* They are *Pedagogy of the Oppressed* and *The Politics of Education.* Any clues on how to read them only once?

⇜ Martha Barquero-Checkwicz ⇝

Weekly Conversations

An individual's preparation for learning, studying, is before anything else a critical, creative, re-creating activity.
—Paulo Freire, *Teachers as Cultural Workers: Letters to Those Who Dare Teach* (1998c), p. 18.

November 27, 2004
Dear Mr. Freire:

Today I sat down to write you this letter of complaint. As a graduate student, I first approached your book *Teachers as Cultural Workers: Letters for Those Who Dare Teach* with the same mindset that I had approached most of the textbooks throughout my graduate studies. The class that I was reading the book for was officially the last class that I was required to take for my master's degree, so my experience with "required texts" was extensive and at this point teetered on uninspired—not because the idea of teaching or learning about teaching had lost its luster, but because the bureaucratic process of becoming a "highly qualified" educator (the term used in the punitive No Child Left Behind legislation in the United States) had at times become overly controlling. As in many other classes that I had taken, I looked through the syllabus of the class and plotted my course of action to "get through" this last class and get on with the business of teaching.

Well, Paulo, I wasn't quite counting on having you along for the ride. You see, my professor thought that your work was instrumental to my perspective of the profession, so she assigned your book for the class. On a weekly basis she assigned one, two, or sometimes even three of the letters that you so diligently crafted for people just like me. So besides reading the typical scholarly work that is often assigned at this level of learning, I was also required to read your letters.

At first I wasn't sure what to make of your book. I looked at the old man on the cover, comfortable and somehow comforting as well. Quickly I read the foreword by Donaldo Macedo and Ana Maria Araújo Freire, and suddenly I began to get the bigger picture. I knew that this was not going to be just another textbook for me, and yet I approached it with one hand on my heart and the other full of pessimistic regret and disbelief. At times I wondered if your experience and wisdom were misplaced for my time and in this country. After all, what similarities did Sao Paulo, Brazil, and Chicopee, Massachusetts, really have? As it turns out, more than I expected!

I was inspired by your directness and encouraged by your faith in those of us who have chosen to become educators in spite of the political, cultural, and even physical hurdles that we are faced with daily. I came to regard our weekly "conversations" as my own private mentoring discourse with you, because although at times I did not fully understand what you were trying to say, I knew that eventually I would. I appreciate your willingness to combine equal measures of advice, warning, and experience in your writing. It was almost as if you knew exactly what I was encountering in my classroom with some of the children, with some of my colleagues, and with some administrators. But most of all, it was as if you were aware of some of the things that were going on inside of me, knowing about my fear, my frustration and ultimately about the joy of being an educator and giving me advice on how to keep the right perspective in the face of it all. Now, as I close this book and experience the end of my coursework, it occurs to me that the business of teaching (which I have been so eager to get on with) is the same as the business of learning and, at once, the business of living.

And so it seems that I have come to the end of my letter without explicitly stating my complaint—a task that I set out to do with the utmost passion. So here it is: Paulo … why didn't I know about you sooner? I think of how much better I would have understood other materials, having understood that it wasn't about consuming every last word of the texts that I was reading, but about engaging in a dialogue with the authors. I also think of what a different mindset I would have had approaching the tasks that now amount to a letter on a college transcript.

Thank you, Paulo, for having the courage to anticipate the value of your advice to all of us who sometimes lose hope or heart in molding the present and the future—both those of our students and our own.

Respectfully,
Martha Barquero-Checkwicz

◌

◈ Phil Lawrence ◈

Critically Analyzing Paulo

Deep down, this must be every author's true dream—to be read, discussed, critiqued, improved, and reinvented by his or her readers.
—Paulo Freire, *Teachers as Cultural Workers: Letters to Those Who Dare Teach* (1998c), pp. 30–31.

December 9, 2005
Dear Paulo,

My initial impulse was to write a letter expressing frustration with your writing style, but after reading the first draft I became embarrassed for myself. I can do better than this, I thought. So I went back and reread my journal entries from earlier this year and reread the introduction, the first words, and the first letter of your book *Teachers as Cultural Leaders: Letters to Those Who Dare Teach*. That is enough for now, I have decided, because reading further I came upon my own resistance to the material. This resistance is a marker for me with your work and others. As you say, "If I am really studying, seriously reading, I cannot go past a page if I cannot grasp its significance relatively clearly" (p. 18). I would say that it is better for me to approach your work slowly if I am going to do it at all. I am engaged, as you say, in the "struggle to meet the timing of knowledge" (p. 23). I realize I am not quite ready for all you have to say. I suspect that once I gain a better understanding of your thinking we will not agree on everything and the fun will begin. I have had glimpses of this already, but I am not ready to "take you on." It is you who put this into perspective for me, or I should say, it is my reading of you that has brought me to this particular conclusion, which I hope is not a conclusion at all but merely a beginning.

Here is an example of what might be in store. On pages 24 and 25 of the first letter, "Reading the World/Reading the Word," there are no fewer than eight themes: the impossibility of study without reading and writing; the insecurity of students surrounding writing; the need to nurture reading and writing at an early age; the importance of learning to learn; study as burden; study as pleasure and happiness; the refusal to accept mechanistic and idealistic interpretations of history. This is immeasurably dense writing. I can imagine spending quite a bit of time on those two pages alone.

On page 24, I read: "In the literate cultures, without reading and writing it is impossible to study, to seek to know, to learn the subjectivity of objects, to critically recognize an object's reason for being." Maybe that is true, but I think it is also debatable. Other writers and writings come to mind on the subject of literacy: Walter Ong and *Orality and Literacy, The Dark Side of Literacy* by Shilpa Manish Jain, and even your friend Ivan Illich and *Deschooling Society*. I doubt that any one of these authors would necessarily disagree with you, but the statement as written has such finality it takes on the weight of a generally agreed-upon assumption. Is it really impossible to critically recognize an object's reason for being without reading or writing? What do you mean by "recognize an object's reason for being?"

Do you see what I am trying to get at here? When I read something that I intuitively do not understand or agree with, I start to take the sentence apart. That stops me, or at least slows me down. Your sentence is a huge statement that underpins much of your thinking. It is ironic that I argue with you using the very tools that you regard as essential to any genuine discourse. What I think is left out of your assumption is other ways of knowing and critically analyzing the world. What comes to mind is the use of visual art, film, dance, performance, and music to understand life and living. All of those forms have elements of literacy in them, so they may not represent the best argument. Nonetheless, I believe your assumption is worth exploring. My desire to unpack this assumption comes from two things: one is my objection to the word *impossible* as it relates to study, and the other is a sense (an intuition or yearning perhaps) that there are other forms of understanding and knowing that are not logo-centric and yet contribute to a more just and equitable world. Perhaps I am just playing with definitions of literacy; only time and research will tell.

Thank you for inspiration,
Phil Lawrence

Maria José Botelho

Rereading the Text

Indeed, studying is a difficult task that requires a systematic critical attitude and intellectual discipline acquired only through practice. This critical attitude is precisely what "banking education" does not engender.
—Paulo Freire, *The Politics of Education* (1985a), p. 2.

December 10, 1995
Querido Paulo,

The last time I heard you speak was in the spring of 1991 at Harvard University. At the time you were talking about your experience in taking over the São Paulo public schools. I came to you for encouragement to continue my work with teachers, who were primarily from working-class, European-American backgrounds. I sat in the front row and listened intently.

Many years have passed and once again our paths have crossed, this time through your text. This is my sixth reading of your seminal work *Pedagogy of the Oppressed,* and once again I've taken something new away from it. I still remember the first time I heard your name: I was an undergraduate at the University of Massachusetts, Amherst, listening to a lecture by Professor Bob Suzuki, who taught courses in multicultural education. He mentioned your work; I could not believe my ears: a scholar with a Portuguese surname! My affinity to you was our common heritage, which occurred at some point in history when my country colonized your country. You were close enough to being Portuguese.

I ran out and purchased your book the next day. I wanted to know what a Portuguese-speaking person had to say. Reading *Pedagogy of the Oppressed* was a liberating event. It described my educational experience in the United States and helped me understand that, indeed, I was an intellectual being and that only limited amounts of my knowledge were permitted within my school experiences. My cultural and linguistic knowledge stayed at home; I was never invited to speak, read, and write/think in Portuguese. I could take part in literacy events only after I learned English. School literacy practices led me to look for knowledge outside myself and mistrust my understandings about the world. In reading your book, I began to speculate on learning and teaching possibilities for me and the teachers I worked with; I experienced a new level of understanding and *conscientização*.

Your book has traveled with me to many places: it was useful when I was a children's librarian; it was useful when I studied anthropology and conducted fieldwork; it was useful when I worked with early childhood and elementary school teachers; it provided guidance when I taught preservice teachers and graduate students; and, of course, it was critical in my work with adult learners and families. Its application is widespread.

Paulo, your book has been part of my personal and professional growth; it's a resource to return to again and again. But this time around, I finally was able to name some of the discomforts I have felt with it. Your book poses three problems for me:

1. the register you chose to write it in is not accessible by the common person;
2. your portrayal of the oppressed at the onset of the problem-posing process is a passive one; and
3. your omission of the teachers' responsibility to explicitly teach and live the democratic process within their classrooms.

At times your book reads like a religious text, with many spiritual overtones. It is a complex text and not one that would be easily accessed by the oppressed. I am not suggesting that it should be a self-help book, but a book that a diverse group of people can sit down with and begin the process together.

Secondly, you seem to suggest that the peasant or the oppressed are passive agents in the reality that they find themselves in. But my lived experience as a Portuguese American woman of peasant, working- and middle-class background and my dissertation research, as well as the critical ethnographic research that I have read, have helped me to take notice of how the oppressed exercise power every day. Creativity, resistance, and action are central to these social processes.

Lastly, your text seems to suggest that liberation will happen organically. I don't think so. I think a final step to rehumanizing pedagogy is making democratic practices explicit, with the teacher modeling and talking about and inviting learners to take part in socially reconstructive activity within the classroom. This process demystifies the culture of power and creates spaces for the exercise of power that benefit the classroom community and beyond.

Thank you for your scholarship. My dialogue with you does not end here, but will continue throughout my life as I live, learn, teach, and research toward social change and justice.

Paz,
Maria José Botelho

Postscript: August 31, 2007

Many years have elapsed since I wrote this letter, Paulo. During this time, I have immersed myself in your other writings and the work of other scholars (for example, theorists of critical multicultural education, feminist poststructuralism, critical ethnography, cultural studies, and critical literary theory), and I have engaged in critical teaching and in personal and collaborative research. My new understandings about power and language further expand on my critiques of your work as I outlined above. Paulo, you conceptualize *conscientização* as a linear process, flanked by the oppressed and oppressor, a one-directional framing of power. While *conscientização* is a coming to know one's place in the world, as we question and take action against sociopolitical practices that maintain and contribute to social oppression, it is a complex and recursive process. My understanding of power has moved from power that is *owned* and one-directional (top-down, as Marxism describes) to power that is *exercised* and circulated by all of us on a daily basis. This complex view of power illuminates the collusive and resistant practices that linear, top-down, and fixed understandings of power overlooked. Our teaching and research practices are expressions of how we exercise power.

I have come to know that people have similar and differing experiences with oppression (that is, different racisms and classisms). Each of us possesses multiple identities and lives within a power structure that vests us with different amounts of power and privilege, depending on those identities. For example, while I have lived many forms of classism, I am vested with white privilege because of my European American heritage. However, the white privilege that I have benefited from is a departure from the white privilege described by Peggy McIntosh (1988), for example, because in many ways, her research tends to conflate white privilege with class privilege.

How we use language plays a key role in how we exercise power and use our privilege. Our language use can maintain, circulate, perpetuate, and/or challenge dominant ideologies that reflect the present power relations of class, race, and gender. For example, I could explain the current high dropout rate of Portuguese high school students in Toronto (where I am a faculty member at the University of Toronto) as a reflection of this community's lack of a "culture of literacy," as was described in a recent newspaper article. Explaining this dropout rate as a lack of this community of students isolates this cultural group from the sociopolitical factors that have constructed the situation in which they find themselves in the first place. Certainly, school literacy practices are implicated, as are socioeconomic factors.

When we read power in our language, teaching, and living practices, that is, locating the possibilities for exercising power, we become aware of how we perpetuate social inequities (for example, class, race, and gender) through social interactions and practices. (Keep in mind that language is a social practice.) In doing so, we become conscious of how we may oppress and collude with racist and classist ideologies, for instance, and how resistance and agency can translate into local democracies. (I am building here on Gibson-Graham's [1996] construct of "local socialisms.") Local democracies are social transformations at the community and interpersonal levels.

These transformations can happen within families, schools, and at the neighborhood level. While these small democracies will not reconstruct our society overnight, such transformations will reconstruct how we practice society locally, developing equitable habits of living among us, and affording us with moments of collaborative power. Reading power has helped me understand that I cannot blame everything on capitalism and has also helped me to envision other ways of being in the world.

∞

$\backsim$ Romina Pacheco $\backsim$

Beyond "Getting the Reading Done"

It's not possible to read critically if one treats reading as if it were a similar operation to buying in bulk. What's the point of boasting of having read twenty books—twenty books! Really reading involves a kind of relationship with the text, which offers itself to me and to which I give myself and through the fundamental comprehension of which I undergo the process of becoming a subject. While reading, I'm not just a captive of the mind of the text as if it were simply a product of its author.
—Paulo Freire, *Pedagogy of Freedom* (1998a), p. 3.

November 26, 2004
Querido Paulo:

I am really happy to be writing you this letter; I only wish I could write it in Spanish, my mother tongue, because writing in English frustrates me at times. Nevertheless, I should "not let the fear of what is difficult paralyze [me]" (Freire, 1998c, p. 27) as you stated in one of your letters.

I shall begin by thanking you for your wonderful words, for I find them very encouraging. As a young educator, I am constantly being bombarded with negative messages. Your words, on the other hand, have given me hope and encouragement to continue working toward the liberation of our society. In your own words, "we must dare so that we continue to teach for a long time under conditions that we know well" (p. 3). I'm here to tell you that I dare to teach, and by this I do not mean just standing in front of a classroom having students repeating words like parrots. No, I want to encourage those around me to reflect, create, experiment, critically think, question, challenge, and transform the world into a safer space for everyone.

Additionally, I want to express my gratitude for encouraging me to write. The discipline you suggest one should have when reading and writing is beginning to help me. I am starting to dare to teach through written words. Unfortunately, previous experiences have done such a good job of discouraging me from writing that it is going to take me a while before I can explore my potential to the fullest. But again, your advice to "not let what is difficult paralyze you" helps me to fight thoughts of oppression inside me.

I also want to share a dilemma that has been running through my head ever since I came in touch with your argument about the importance of having a dialectical relationship with the texts we read. You write that the reader should take time to process a reading piece and question its source. Although I find your argument compelling, I can't help but wonder how it is possible to have such a dialogue when one must meet a class deadline? Most professors do not seem to think about these things when assigning weekly readings. As a consequence, week after week I find myself trying hard just to get the reading "done" before class; most of the time I do not have time to "converse" with the author or to reread the book as a way to understand it fully. However, that is not going to stop me; I will continue my path through this world, there is no turning back.

Your *last words* really stood out for me. For example, the way you talk about the relationship between "growth" and "knowledge" is fascinating. You are absolutely right: how can there be growth without knowledge, or how can there be knowledge without growth? But at the same time I appreciate how you argue that growth should not be an excuse to oppress others, not even if it is coming from minorities. How can we make those in power understand your thoughts? Perhaps we should have our politicians read a copy of your book!

Finally, I want to say that I will not forget the value that practice and theory have in our work toward freedom, and that as an educator and a political agent I have both the right and the responsibility to fight for it. For these words of wisdom and many more:

Obrigada,
Romina Pacheco

Jeff Duncan-Andrade

To Study Is a Revolutionary Duty

If we reflect on the fact that our human condition is one of essential unfinishedness, that, as a consequence, we are incomplete in our being and in our knowing, then it becomes obvious that we are "programmed" to learn, destined by our very incompleteness to seek completeness, to have a "tomorrow" that adds to our "today." In other words, wherever

there are men and women, there is always and inevitably something
to be done, to be completed, to be taught, and to be learned.
—Paulo Freire, *Pedagogy of Freedom* (1998a), p. 79.

June 1, 2007
Dear Paulo,

It seems appropriate that I am writing my first letter to you while on my first trip to the country of your birth. I came to Brazil to give two presentations on how your work has influenced mine. Letter writing is a much more intimate act than presenting, and therefore infinitely more difficult.

This letter presents a particularly difficult challenge because it is asking that I articulate your mentorship of my work. There is simply not enough room in this initial letter to you to capture the depth at which you have impacted my life and my teaching. In fact, I am sure I cannot even fully comprehend it because every time I revisit your work I find something new that challenges me to rethink what I have been doing. So, my hope with this letter is to give you some sense of how I came upon your work, how it has influenced my pedagogy as a high school teacher, how it has influenced my pedagogy as a teacher of teachers, and, finally, how it has led me to formulate my own pedagogical theory, which attempts to connect those two endeavors.

Let me start with some back-story that led me to your work. In 1995, I had been teaching English literature for three years at Westlake Junior High in Oakland, California, and I had never even heard of you. Each of those years I received a March 15 letter of nonrenewal, and in each of those years I also received a "Best Teacher" award from students at the school. When the start of the new school year would near in late August and the school had not found someone to fill my position, they would hire me back with another "emergency" contract. The reasons for my multiple "nonrenewals" (read firings) were largely the same as the reasons I received accolades from my students. I did things differently from most of my colleagues, I challenged time-honored rules and traditions, and I used a pedagogy and curriculum that encouraged students to do the same.

At the time, I struggled to understand why I was being punished by the leadership of a miserably failing school when my methods were clearly having a positive effect on student engagement and achievement. My students, predominantly of African, Latin American, and Southeast Asian descent, did well in my classes, particularly the students that most of my colleagues complained about as unruly and unmotivated. Parents liked the work I was doing with their children. I believed, wrongly I guess, that the people involved with Westlake Junior High expected me to push and challenge all students.

That belief persisted despite my better wisdom from having attended schools with similarly low expectations of the majority of its students. I recall schooling experiences when students were explicitly discouraged from dreaming beyond their circumstances. In most cases, these forms of discrimination are explained away as minor deterrents that most people encounter in their lives, microaggressions against hope. But the frequency with which they happened over time and the lack of challenges to their normality in school culture crushed the spirits of the overwhelming majority of my classmates. As one example, I vividly remember telling my high school math teacher and soccer coach that I wanted to go to the University of California at Berkeley. He laughed out loud in front of the class and told me that Berkeley would never take a student like me.

Years later, after I had graduated from U.C. Berkeley, my father revealed that my math teacher was not the only one who felt that way about me. When I was given a "special admit" to Berkeley, the director of financial aid requested to meet privately with my parents. He told them that they should not be surprised when I returned home before completing my first year at Berkeley. He said I had not attended schools that could properly prepare me for the rigors of such an esteemed institution. Experiences such as these led me to want to become the teacher-coach-counselor that I did not have, one who encouraged critical thinking, hope, and a sense of purpose in all students. The fact that I fall short of that goal every year does not discourage me; it reminds me that I must work harder and be humble enough to critically reflect on my practice as I seek the impossible: perfect pedagogy.

True to this pursuit, discouraging reviews from my administrators in hand, I accepted an appointment to teach an ethnic studies class to a group of thirty East Oakland 9th-grade students in the summer of 1998. I accepted this position because it allowed me to move on to the high school level with many of my Westlake students, but I was struggling to understand the double standard of my calling. On the one hand, the local educational leaders openly admitted that schools like Westlake were failing miserably. On the other, measures that I was taking to effectively confront that failure were punished. It was during that summer, amid my confusion about my calling, that I was introduced to your work. That moment was one of the most significant in my life. It set off a shift in consciousness that has indelibly changed my understanding of myself, my life's purpose, and the nefariousness of deliberate, systematic miseducation.

Another teacher in the summer program handed me a copy of *Literacy: Reading the Word and the World.* He told me he thought I would like what it had to say. It was perfect timing because my treatment inside schools had me believing that there was something wrong with *me.* The more I read, the more I found my critique of the institutions and my pedagogical instincts affirmed. The book gave me clarity about my purpose as an educator. It justified my resistance of the malaise that had embittered and disenchanted most of my teaching colleagues.

The passage that most influenced me comes from the Second Popular Culture Notebook that you used in your adult literacy campaign in São Tomé and Príncipe. You quote "The Act of Studying," stating:

> A text to be read is a text to be studied. A text to be studied is a text to be interpreted. We cannot interpret a text if we read it without paying attention, without curiosity; if we stop reading at the first difficulty. ... If a text is difficult, you insist on understanding it. ... To study demands discipline. To study is not easy, because to study is to create and re-create and not to repeat what others say. To study is a revolutionary duty! (P. 77)

No single passage has more profoundly impacted how I instruct my students about the importance of study. I have posted it in my classroom, and I often reference it when students wonder why I am so demanding. I am so heavily affected by this passage because it transformed the way that I thought about studying for myself. I had never thought of study as a revolutionary act. Before reading your book, study was a means to an end. Studying was a burden, something I had to suffer through to get a degree, or to access opportunities and places to which people from my family had never been invited.

To a large degree, this was the promise I gave to my students. My teachers had never told me that there was any other use for studying, and I had never read anything that suggested that possibility. Even though I connected to my students, and found ways to inspire and motivate them, before reading your work I was mostly reproducing the same logic systems that I had been taught in public schools. I convinced my students that the system was a game, and that like any game it had rules. Even if they did not come from families that had histories of winning at this game, they could learn the rules and beat the game, just as I had. For the most part, my pre-Freire promise to my students was that studying would allow them to plug into an economic system that had historically exploited their communities. It would allow them the option to go from exploited to exploiter. (As I read more of your work I acquired the language to name this pattern of social reproduction as the suboppressor component of the oppressor-oppressed paradigm.)

I suppose I still agree with this logic to some degree—better them than us. But, reading your work helped me to understand studying as something greater than an individual act; it is a "revolutionary duty." This passage from your work helped me to understand the difference between learning to earn and learning for freedom. Learning to earn is undoubtedly the law of the land in most U.S. classrooms, and it has very little to do with studying. The learn-to-earn paradigm is the pursuit of knowledge for personal gain—it is learning how to become a more effective cog in the economic engine of capitalism. But the studying you were talking about was revolutionary, it was learning for freedom. I came to understand the freedom that lies in study when that study is dedicated to an intellectual discipline that challenges the prevailing logic of injustice. As these skills developed, my study progressed toward the creation of a new worldview—freedom. I could actually envision a radically different world, which meant I no longer had to accept the current conditions as inevitable. As I became a student of freedom, I developed the understanding that a major part of my revolutionary duty was to share that path to freedom with others who find themselves trapped in the logic of learning to earn.

The opportunity to share that path presents itself every day that I teach. But, as you are aware, there are always moments in teaching when the opportunity to have an impact on an individual student is heightened. For me, this opportunity often presents itself when students ask me: why do we have to learn this? Prior to reading your work, I would have given them answers similar to those given to me by my teachers, all of which are both unsatisfactory and unmotivating. That is, I would have been dismissive, with something like "Because I said so," or I would have been compliant with the status quo by saying, "Because it's what rich kids learn, and when you go up against them in college I want you to be ready to compete." Those answers reflect my own training as a student, but they also reflect my ignorance about the depth and significance of that question. It is shameful that so many teachers are unable to give a profound answer to this question. Why should a student learn from me if I cannot answer that question in a compelling way?

Paulo, your work unlocked an answer to this question for me. Now, when students ask me this question, I have two responses for them. First, I turn the question back onto them, and I ask them why they think they should learn. Most claim they don't know or throw back stock responses similar to the ones I used to give. Once I have them thinking about answering their own question, I give them the passage about the importance of studying from your book. I read it to them and I tell them that I did not understand the importance of study until I read that passage. Next, I tell them that somewhere there is a five-year-old child they have never seen, and that child is counting on them to study. In ten years, when that five-year-old is fifteen, their paths will cross. In that moment, they will either change that child's life by sharing knowledge and purpose from what they have studied, or they will miss that opportunity because they have not prepared themselves for it. I tell them that is what you meant when you said that studying is a revolutionary duty, because to be truly revolutionary is to prepare oneself to serve the next generation so that each generation inherits a better world. Finally, I tell my students that every time they get tired or frustrated with what they are studying, I want them to picture that five-year-old because they are not just studying for themselves. They are studying for that child, and that child simply cannot afford for them to give up. We go back to your text and we are both reminded of your challenge—that we insist on understanding that which is difficult, and that this type of study, revolutionary study, is not easy; it demands discipline.

I think most young people understand this, and it helps explain the disconnection between young people and school. We underestimate young people and their desires when we paint them as shallow consumerists. They may be socialized to value consumerism, but the young people I work with end up there mostly as the result of the absence of a viable alternative. They continually ask us why they should learn from us because they have not given up hope that we can offer something more to life than the pursuit of fortune and fame. But, when we fail to offer them a compelling narrative about that alternative possibility, most young people come to see school as an extension of a morally bankrupt society. If studying is a revolutionary duty, then using our studies to inject the promise and the hope of a more just society is a revolutionary imperative. Your words have taught me this lesson, and I pledge to express my gratitude for this freedom by responding with equal vigor and sincerity each time my students ask me to explain why they have to study.

Eleven years have passed since my first encounter with your work. I remain a high school teacher in my community, but I am now also a teacher of teachers. The responsibility that comes with supporting and mentoring aspiring critical pedagogues has helped me to understand your reasons for describing study as a process of creating and re-creating. I have worked in the last couple of years to study my own practice and the practice of other effective urban educators so that I can help more teachers get access to pedagogical strategies that are effective and give them some explanation about why those approaches work. This process of studying effective pedagogy has led me to be increasingly self-critical as I turn these examinations onto my own teaching. This self-reflexivity is also particularly useful when I work with new teachers because they get to hear about my own struggles as a teacher, and through these struggles I can impart the relationship between effective pedagogy and a lifelong commitment to study and critical self-reflection.

To advance your efforts to stimulate dialogue about critical pedagogy, I have used my study and work with teachers to develop a next iteration of your *Pedagogy of Indignation*. As your wife states in the book, that title was chosen as a counterbalance to your other writings where you articulate so much of your commitment to pursuing and promoting pedagogy that is imbued with hope, love, *conscientização*, and freedom. But in each of those previous books your indignation about the conditions facing the masses has always been obvious to me. You have said many times over that we cannot be pedagogues with any of those aforementioned traits if we are not indignant about the existence of conditions that oppress. Likewise, you have cautioned us to balance our anger with an awareness that the future is not predetermined; anger should be partnered with critical hope that we have the capacity (and responsibility) to act and change oppressive conditions.

Your sagacious advice has been essential because my indignation at miseducation in poor communities is fueled by the fact that it is deliberate. We know how to educate poor children. We have the knowledge and capacity. We lack the courage. We are cowards. Nothing angers me more than cowardice, because cowardice is the confluence of someone knowing what is morally right, having the capacity to act on that moral imperative, and still deciding against that action. Because the educational system in this country has the knowledge and capacity to provide a quality education to all children, and chooses to act as though it is tirelessly trying to figure out how to do that, we have systematic cowardice. Systematic cowardice, particularly in regard to services for young people, is the reflection of a morally bankrupt society.

As a response to this cowardice, I have begun to write, speak, study, and share an adaptation of the pedagogy of indignation that I call THUG LIFE Pedagogy. I borrow the term from Tupac Shakur, someone I am sure you knew both in name and in spirit, but perhaps not for his full body of work. Tupac, despite his death in 1996, remains wildly popular among young oppressed peoples around the globe. To be sure, the medium of music and poetry that Tupac used to deliver his message is key to his popularity. But I am convinced that the longevity and extent of his popularity are the result of the portions of his work that speak to the righteous indignation that festers in almost every person who detests injustice. Only twenty-five at his death, Tupac had just begun the development of a theory of humanization for oppressed peoples that drew from their indignation. He argued that oppressed people would need to search within themselves and their communities for freedom, and that this would require adults to pay special attention to children who are born into a society that hates them. For Tupac, hate that is passed to children through the cycle of social inequity destroys communities. He gave his theory an acronym THUG LIFE (The Hate U Gave Little Infants Fucks Everyone), a deliberate turn of phrase against the racist stereotype of urban men of color as street thugs. In an interview, Tupac explained:

> By "thug" I mean, not criminal or someone that beats you over the head. I mean the underdog. The person that had nothing and succeeds, he's a thug because he overcame all obstacles. It doesn't have anything to do with the dictionary's version of "thug." To me "thug" is my pride, not being someone that goes against the law, not being someone that takes, but being someone that has nothing, and even though I have nothing and there's no home for me to go to, my head is up high. My chest is out. I walk tall. I talk loud. I'm being strong. … We gonna start slowly but surely taking our communities back. Regulate our community. Organize. We need to start taking care of our own. We gotta start somewhere, and I don't know about anything else, but this, to me, is a start. (Lazin, 2003)

Like Tupac, I believe that the hatred/rage/hostility/indignation that results from any group of people systematically denied their right to food, clothing, shelter, education, and justice will ultimately cause a society to implode. Likewise, properly channeled, those legitimate feelings can be developed into the courage to act and fundamentally change the direction of a society, even in the face of the broader society's cowardice. In fact, the necessary courage to dramatically and justly alter the direction of an empire might only be found among those who suffer under its oppressive weight. This is the type of young person that a THUG LIFE Pedagogy aims to nurture.

Tupac referred to these young people as roses that grow from concrete. They are the ones that prove society's rule wrong. They keep the dream of a better society alive, growing in spite of the cold, uncaring, un-nurturing environment of the concrete. In his poem "The Rose that Grew from Concrete" he wrote: "[L]ong live the rose that grew from concrete when no one else even cared." He expanded this metaphor in his song "Mama's Just a Little Girl," writing: "[Y]ou wouldn't ask why the rose that grew from concrete had damaged petals. On the contrary, we would all celebrate its tenacity. We would all love its will to reach the sun. We are the roses. This is the concrete. And these are my damaged petals. Don't ask me why … ask me how."

My hope for THUG LIFE Pedagogy is to influence educators (current and future) in urban and poor communities to grow more roses from the concrete. With respect to supporting and developing our current group of teachers, we are challenged by the fact that the majority of the teachers are outsiders (racially and socially) to our communities. I find that a growing number of teachers have been exposed to your work in their teacher training programs, and a growing number of them find it valuable. Sadly, most people who use your work to train teachers do little to help new teachers interpret its relevance for U.S. urban K–12 classrooms. Many teacher educators do not even mention the fact that your analysis emerged primarily from your experience working with adults. It seems so critically important to me that we understand your pedagogical recommendations, particularly your critique of the banking model of education, as an analysis of work you did with adults. You were working with students who chose to come to your classroom. We are working with students who are mandated, by threat of legal repercussions, to come. You were working with students who had the wisdom that comes from surviving and subsisting into adulthood, in spite of the hatred given to them as infants. We are working with children who, like any children, have not had the lived experience of adults to guide their decision-making and therefore need a more deliberately structured and disciplined environment.

Sadly, the result of these decontextualized teachings of your work often lead to two more forms of oppressive pedagogy that we must battle against. The first of these is a pedagogy guided by fear. Many teachers are so afraid of being labeled as oppressive (read racists) that they shy away from their responsibility as the adult and educational leader in the classroom. They shirk their duty to exercise authority for fear of being authoritarian, which results in classrooms that lack structure and discipline under the auspices of being nonoppressive and democratic. As teachers, they are exactly like the parents you describe in the first letter of *Pedagogy of Indignation,* complacent authorities who think of themselves as champions of freedom but find themselves vexed by the "tyranny of freedom." Far too many of these teachers who may consider themselves to be well meaning use democratic sensibilities and social justice leanings to defer to students on decisions that are the teacher's responsibility. In so doing, they fail to establish themselves as a legitimate adult authority with a clear plan for the direction of their students. Inevitably, when the class has spiraled out of control and the teacher decides to hold the young people to some random rule of discipline, the requisite respect of the students is lacking. The two most common results of this situation are equally bad. Either students refuse to recognize the authority of the teacher to the point that the teacher gives up on the class, or the teacher shifts to the role of uncompromising dictator, regains some semblance of control, and then interprets the authoritarian approach to be the most effective one with our children.

Of course, it is usually our students and families who get blamed for this, and the archetype of the unruly ghetto child unable or unwilling to stake a claim to her/his education is reified. Insert culture of poverty "experts" to the rescue who pimp the failing of these teachers with their snake oil solutions that situate the problems with students and the families. Their solution: a "pedagogy of poverty" (a term coined by Martin Haberman): "back to basics" drill and kill scripted literacy, social studies, and mathematics lessons; zero-tolerance discipline policies; high-stakes testing; one-size-fits-all standards-based instruction; and phenomenally expensive all-inclusive in-service programs for teachers. The latter of these are particularly disturbing because they are designed by people from outside our communities to help teachers from outside our communities to understand the "culture of poverty" that vexes our communities. The widest-selling of such programs, Ruby Payne's *aha! Process,* claims that teachers should teach their students to examine individuals who have attained prosperity to learn the hidden rules of wealth creation. She argues that teachers should be trained to help individuals who are intent on improving their economic lot. Year after year, these regressive pedagogical methods produce identically low test scores and achievement patterns, and questions from teachers wondering how critical pedagogy might help break the pattern. Does critical pedagogy mean that we are not supposed to prepare students to do well on tests anymore? Does it mean that we should throw out state and national standards? Does it mean that college is unimportant? Does it mean that we should not be preparing young people to enter the economy? What does this look like in a classroom? Won't I lose my job if I teach these things?

These questions reflect the second outcome of misinterpretations of your work—pedagogical decisions guided by a false binary. Teachers trained as critical pedagogues sometimes believe they must choose between academically rigorous teaching and teaching for social justice. This false binary is largely the result of the aforementioned pedagogy of poverty whereby teachers are trained to believe that an academically rigorous pedagogy does not have time for critically investigating the material conditions of the society. An academically rigorous pedagogy focuses on skill development to prepare students to score well on state and national achievement tests, most of which are norm-referenced and tend to be more useful (and accurate) as indicative of parental income than of intellect. I find that many teachers believe in the value of a critical and socially just pedagogy, at least on a theoretical level. But, under the pressure facing their students to perform on a battery of tests by which their ability as teachers will be judged, they find much more job security in teaching to the test (learn to earn) than teaching students to think critically (learn for freedom). The bitter irony of this decision is that even when they teach to the test, their students don't usually end up doing any better.

To caution teachers against buying into the existence of this binary, I return them to your first letter in *Pedagogy of Indignation* where you write:

> The progressive educator does not allow herself any doubt with respect to the right boys and girls from the masses, *the people,* have to know the same mathematics, physics, or biology that boys and girls from the "happier parts" of town learn. At the same time, she never accepts that the teaching of any discipline whatsoever could take place divorced from a critical analysis of how society works. (P. 20)

The disciplined classroom environment, producing the academic rigor and critical social awareness of which you speak, is the foundation on which THUG LIFE Pedagogy is built. Ultimately, THUG LIFE Pedagogy is an effort to ground your theory of critical pedagogy in the U.S. K–12 urban context so that teachers understand that all of the standards that students will be tested on are taught when you employ a critical pedagogy. There is no binary; you cannot have critical pedagogy without academic rigor and you cannot be academically rigorous without drawing from critical pedagogy.

Despite the small number of teachers who struggle to apply critical pedagogy in U.S. urban contexts, I remain hopeful about its potential to improve classroom pedagogy because most teachers I encounter want to be great at what they do. Contrary to prevailing public and governmental opinions, the majority of teachers I come across are more in need of guidance and critical support on how to be effective than they are of mandates and threats. THUG LIFE Pedagogy allows me to encourage, support, develop, and incite educators to grow roses in the concrete. It provides a framework from which to study, and it highlights the work of the best teachers I meet so that people no longer ask why the roses' pedals are damaged. Instead, they ask *How can we grow more?*

Working with teachers who are already in the classroom will not be enough to radically alter the quality of education given to most children. I recognize that we must also become more diligent about growing future educators in our communities. This coincides with your insistence that study include the act of creating and Tupac's insistence that we pay attention to nurturing more roses in the concrete. And, so, I end this letter to you with a promise: I will create and re-create THUG LIFE Pedagogy based on my understanding as a practitioner of it. I will be an educator growing roses in the concrete, nurturing and mentoring those roses so that they can return to the community to grow rose gardens. My promise is to study and practice THUG LIFE Pedagogy so that it too might grow like a rose from the concrete—it is my revolutionary duty.

In solidarity,
Jeff Duncan-Andrade

Michael Greene
More than Turning Pages

The act of study should not be measured by the number of pages read in one night or the quantity of books read in a semester. To study is not to consume ideas, but to create and re-create them.
—Paulo Freire, *The Politics of Education: Culture, Power, and Liberation* (1985a), p. 4.

December 6, 2005
Dear Paulo,

Though we've never met, I've felt you were someone I'd like to learn more about since first hearing about you from my son's father-in-law, who grew up in Brazil. From Sonia's description of you I'm impressed by your sense of unpretentiousness in lectures, and your desire to express warmth and connection through touch with those near you. So much of what you write in *Teachers as Cultural Workers: Letters to Those Who Dare Teach* applies more broadly, of course, than to teachers within the context of public school education. We all interact with numerous institutions and in many contexts of human relationships, and your insights apply across this spectrum.

Thanks, first of all, for encouraging me as a student who also teaches in several contexts. You speak of the importance of really interacting with texts, and the time this takes if one considers learning as more than consuming so many pages of text. (This was especially challenging for me when pursuing my first graduate degree while also working full-time—a thousand pages of outside reading required in addition to the papers assigned for a course, for example.) Your words serve as a good reinforcing reminder of what the goal of all my study is, after all—not just to pack in more knowledge, but more reflective insight, so my theory and praxis are well informed and integrated well with each other.

You also have given me a better appreciation for "reading" my students and the contexts of their lives. I'm appreciating more and more what my students possess in prior knowledge and experience as I help them with learning English (one of the contexts in which I teach). And as a teacher, being both competent with regards to the content and cooperative in the learning process with my students are essential. Because you speak from such a concrete context, the situation in Brazil, your practical insights for teachers are so helpful—dealing with one's fears, the essential character qualities of progressive teachers, and the constant need to reflect, together with my students, on what and how I'm teaching/facilitating the learning process.

In some ways, the contexts of your students and mine could be viewed as opposite ends of the spectrum. Most of your life's work has been among the poorer classes; my present work is among the "elites" of the university world. Yet people are people, and for those with access and opportunity, there is the responsibility to use such resources wisely and in ways that serve the needs of others. One of the compelling strategies in working in higher education is that influencing some of the "influencers" of society is one of the best ways to make positive impacts for good throughout society.

Having said that, I find myself reflecting and praying for insight as to how I might use what teaching resources I have to better reach underserved members of the educational community at large. Your model of matching your words with principled action, even at great personal cost, is inspiring.

Sincerely,
Michael Greene

Part 9: Freedom

Freedom is a must, a constant challenge.
—Paulo Freire, *Pedagogy of Freedom* (1998a), p. 86.

Freedom, as we commonly think of it in the industrialized, developed West, is made up of individual rights: the right to speak, to think, to congregate, to worship, and even, in the United States, to carry guns. While many of these freedoms are also valued in other societies, those in poor nations generally refer to freedom in terms of much more basic needs: freedom from hunger, from abuse, from homelessness, from disease, from ignorance.

On yet another level, freedom is made up of social and community rights: the right to explore truth together, the right to be heard and to hear others, the right to learn from one another, the right to challenge one's condition and fight for a better life. The "constant" challenge of freedom, then, exists on several planes, but for Freire, it was the communal level that most inspired and moved him to action. In one of his last books, *Pedagogy of Freedom*, a book that Stanley Aronowitz described on the cover as his "last will and testament," Freire described freedom in this more expansive and collective way: "The socio-political solidarity that we need today to build a less ugly and less intolerant human community where we can be really what we are cannot neglect the importance of democratic practice" (ibid., p. 46).

Democratic practice, for Freire, could not be alien to schools. The democratic impulse is strong, and for him, it needed to be evident in all spheres of life, including schools. At the individual level, he often railed against the arrogance of teachers and academics who believe they own the truth, those who silence their students as if they have nothing to say. But democratic practice goes beyond individual interactions and relationships. Even more important, democracy needs to be apparent in schooling as an *institution*. Given the market-driven neoliberal agenda of the past two decades in the United States and elsewhere, the significance of democratic practice in schools—not to mention in other institutions—has been nearly obliterated (Apple, 2006). The result is that the "public" has been largely taken out of our lives, with fewer and fewer institutions focused on the "public good." This has certainly been the case with schools, which have become the site of ideological confrontations between those who see them as important laboratories for democratic life, and others who view them as little more than preparation for limited job skills. Donaldo Macedo and Ana Maria Araújo summed up this dilemma well in their foreword to one of Freire's last books:

> What is rarely discussed in the North American school debate is the fact that public schools are part and parcel of the fabric of any democratic society. In fact, conservative educators fail to recognize that a democratic society that shirks its public responsibility is a democracy in crisis. A society that equates for-profit privatization with democracy is a society with confused priorities (Macedo and Araújo Freire, 1998, p. x).

We end the book with letters that Paulo would have loved. Centering on democracy, freedom, and utopian dreams, these letters lead us to an imagined and hoped-for future, to, in Maxine Greene's words, "new beginnings and a vision of possibility."

⌒ Bekisizwe S. Ndimande ⌒
Pedagogy of the Township: A Letter to Paulo Freire

It is up to us to make history and to be made and remade by it.
—Paulo Freire, *Daring to Dream: Toward a Pedagogy of the Unfinished* (2007), p. 7.

August 26, 2004
Dear Paulo Freire:

I first engaged vigorously with your scholarship and your ideas on education when I was midway through graduate schoolwork at the University of Massachusetts, Amherst, back in 1997. In seminars in which we read your work, particularly in Professor Sonia Nieto's multicultural education seminars, your scholarship evoked a mixture of excitement and disenchantment at the same time. On the one hand, I was fascinated to learn about your ideas in relation to the role of education within the sociopolitical and economic structures in societies; on the other, I was disenchanted because it was the first time I fully realized the dehumanizing elements of Bantu education in apartheid South Africa, an educational system in which I was educated. But I am getting ahead of myself.

I come from the poverty-stricken black township of Daveyton, approximately twenty miles southeast of Johannesburg, South Africa. The poverty of Daveyton is similar to that

---

I would like to thank Sonia Nieto, Marcus Weaver-Hightower, and Alvaro Hypolito for their thoughtful comments on this letter.

of the urban working-class areas you knew in Brazil, such as the poor areas of Recife, one of the poorest sections in the northeast of that country. Of course, the conditions may not be exactly the same, but there are probably some aspects that cut across both situations, For instance, the struggles of black South Africans toward becoming *subjects* rather than *objects* in their education, and the struggles against apartheid may well be similar to the struggles of the descendants of enslaved peoples in your own country, Brazil, which struggled toward emancipation from slavery and against an alienating education system. Besides growing up poor in the segregated black township, I am also a product of the banking education that you so eloquently describe in *Pedagogy of the Oppressed.*

As you would know, South Africa gained political independence in 1994, and we were heralded worldwide as one of the exemplary democracies in the late twentieth and early twenty-first centuries. Independence, though, has been paradoxical in that South Africa is increasingly experiencing homelessness, a series of health care crises, unemployment and underemployment, racism in public schools, privatization of public services, and the increasing gap between the rich and poor, among other challenges. Hence a high percentage of black people continue to live under the poverty line, and that leads to their social marginalization.

Our educational system has changed from Bantu education to an outcomes-based education curriculum, a change that at times brings ambivalence. While I am excited that Bantu education is gone, I am also apprehensive about the direction in which the education reform is headed. Of course, you would be the first to know what "outcomes-driven" education does to a society riven by social inequalities, precisely because "outcomes-driven" education does not invite the epistemologies of students from marginalized communities. You taught us through your work that education should be an encounter between women and men, mediated by the world in order to name the world, not just to produce "outcomes" without much deliberation about the type of world we are trying to name or create. Wouldn't this type of education turn marginalized peoples into objects and (re)produce a culture of silence that leads to continuing domination by people with power?

Besides "outcomes-driven" education, most public schools in South Africa are still unequal in terms of educational resources. Formerly white-only public schools generally have greater resources, while formerly black-only public schools remain under-resourced. This has resulted in public schooling remaining stratified. The difference may seem to be related more to money than race, but since money often correlates with and is distributed according to race, racial distinctions have re-emerged. As you probably would know, too, the postapartheid government passed a law that requires public schools to desegregate. This means that schools previously reserved for whites only are now required by law to have open enrollment and to accept black students from under-resourced township public schools. Yet there is a growing problem of unequal treatment and racial discrimination within wealthy public schools that have begun to enroll black students.

Let me hasten to tell you that I am the first to support desegregated schooling; I believe that any form of segregation is oppressive and racist and should not be allowed to exist in a democratic society. In fact, I perceive the desegregation of schooling in

South Africa as a partial victory for the oppressed groups who have been fighting for many years for social justice, including equal educational opportunities. However, I am concerned not only about racial discrimination but also about the acculturation of black students into white culture, the lack of curriculum content that represents children of the "Other," and the Anglicizing curriculum, all of which are widespread, troublesome phenomena that exist in most of these desegregated public schools.

A year ago, I talked to a group of black parents who transferred their children to desegregated schools in suburban areas that, under apartheid, had been reserved for whites.* Most of the parents expressed delight that their children now had the right to enroll in formerly white public schools because of the cultural economy associated with those schools. However, like me, these parents also expressed apprehension about the acculturation of their children at these institutions. They told me they were concerned about their children losing cultural values, especially the loss of language. Thandeka and Noluthando were part of this group, and they spoke about their thoughts and concerns regarding the cultural loss in these schools. Let me first present Thandeka, a working-class mother who lives in the township and sends her daughter to a desegregated school in a suburban area for the sake of the greater resources available at that school:

> I don't want my child to change. Our family structures are different from white family structures. How do you handle a situation where your child is unable to talk to her grandparents because she doesn't know SeSotho and speaks English only? There won't be any communication in the family. We don't want them to lose "Ubuntu." "Ubuntu" is their identity. Do you want to tell me that if the white people [of South Africa] can learn to speak SeSotho, then they would change their culture to that of BaSotho? It won't happen. We don't want to be whites, either.

The second comment is by Noluthando, who is a relatively middle class woman. She has a steady job in the city; her family has recently moved to a suburban area, yet she is also concerned about the cultural loss of her children in formerly white-only schools. This is what Noluthando had to say:

> Did you know that white teachers in these white schools teach "third languages"? Instead of hiring at least a black teacher to teach indigenous languages, they ask a white teacher to do it. A white teacher teaches indigenous languages in such a way that the language sounds English. This means a child learns IsiZulu in English ... what a joke!

It seems to me that these are strong and compelling testimonies from parents who believe that education for their children will bring a better future. Yet at the same time they are mindful of the trade-off—that is, the dangers of cultural loss in their children. In *Pedagogy of the Oppressed* you talk about *cultural invasion* as an antidialogical action, a phenomenon that doesn't create a space for equal dialogue, but instead functions as a divisive tactic that serves the privileged group whose culture occupies the center stage in social institutions. In your astute analysis of this phenomenon, you point out that the cultural invaders "impose their own view of the world upon those they invade and inhibit the creativity of the invaded by curbing their expression" (p. 150). Thus, those whose language is deemed "appropriate"

---

*These are fictitious names.

become authors and actors of the culture—the subjects—while turning the "Other," whose language is deemed not "appropriate," to an object status.

As expressed by Thandeka and Noluthando above, the dominance of the white discourse in public schools, schools that are supposedly multicultural, can cause black children to look down upon their own indigenous languages as if they were inferior and uncivilized, with a consequential effect of losing their cultural identities. For me, the culprit here is not the child neglecting her or his own language, but the school discourse that validates some languages and invalidates others. We have witnessed this unfortunate cultural degradation happen in other nations, too, when, through education, the indigenous communities, and especially the children, are made to believe that their own cultures are not as worthy as the white culture. Ngugi wa Thiong'o (1986) and Frantz Fanon (1967), for instance, have brought this widespread phenomenon to our attention in the contexts of Kenya and Martinique, respectively.**

A few years ago I discovered that my own fourteen-year-old nephew did not know how to read or write in our mother tongue, IsiZulu, because his desegregated school does not consider IsiZulu a language worth teaching in the early grades. In his school they were given options to learn the language only after grade six. Think of what will happen to "minority" languages in these communities ten years from now! In fact, it is incorrect to say that IsiZulu is a "minority" language in a nation where 79 percent of the population is black and does not speak English as a mother tongue. This is indeed a disturbing practice in school curriculum. With this alone, I find myself thinking more and more of your teaching about education being a humanizing practice that should assist and encourage all people to become fully human in their own right, not lead toward assimilation to other people's cultures. If desegregated schools promote cultural invasion, where the cultures of the "Other" become endangered species, education would no longer become a liberatory practice. And if students' cultures are not represented in the curriculum content, they begin to see themselves as less legitimate and undeserving of leadership roles in the classroom. This perpetuates their low self-esteem and even promotes ignorance of their cultural heritage. On the contrary, liberatory education engages students to challenge the curriculum content and create critical possibilities to change the world. Liberatory education does not assimilate people, but helps them to support broader struggles for cultural, political, economic, and social recognition.

In *Pedagogy of the Oppressed,* you stated that the pedagogy of the oppressed is the pedagogy of people engaged in the fight for their own liberation. Allow me to quote you here because for me this is one of the crucial tenets of your arguments:

> No pedagogy which is truly liberating can remain distant from the oppressed by treating them as unfortunates and by presenting for their emulation models from among the oppressors. The oppressed must be their own example in the struggle for their redemption. (P. 39)

The educational situation in public schools that has excluded other cultures is complicated, and I believe that the reforms in postapartheid South African social

---

** I am mindful that Ngugi and Fanon's work transcended the nations of Kenya and Martinique. Fanon, for instance, lamented the colonial behavior of black folks he came across in France.

policy tend to further incapacitate those who are marginalized and poor. I do not mean to insinuate that marginalized and poor people have no agency to liberate themselves, nor that the postapartheid government has back-pedaled so that its policies are no different from the previous apartheid regime. Rather, I situate this state of affairs within a larger context in education reform initiatives. You reminded us many years ago that education doesn't happen in a political vacuum; rather, it is a political act that is mediated by competing ideologies.

In the last two decades or more, there has been a shift in political ideology internationally, and South Africa is not immune to that shift. Throughout the world we witness rightist movements that are not only opposed to progressive social policies but also committed to the agenda of marketizing the world. We are often told that if we can have faith in markets and their order, things will turn out well for everybody. In education we are now supposed to promote and implement a market-driven, outcomes-based education, rather than focus on a liberatory education based on students' sociocultural realities. This is deeply troubling, and I wonder what advice you could give us about this educational challenge.

I do not want, however, to give an entirely glum picture of education, as if there are no progressive possibilities in some classrooms. In the midst of all these education reform challenges, some educators (I include myself on that list) are able to engage their students in what I call a Freiran teaching praxis. As a teaching assistant for Professor Marianne Mimi Bloch at the University of Wisconsin-Madison, I teach preservice teachers in a course that is intended to help prospective teachers understand the importance of the connections among home, school, and various communities, as well as to embrace the richness of the diverse contexts in which children's learning takes place. In my own teaching, I have been trying my best to introduce liberatory education to my students, a practice strongly encouraged by Professor Bloch herself. This I do individually or collaboratively with my fellow teaching assistants. Each time I read critical reflections in my students' journal entries, I feel a glimmer of hope of the impact problem-posing education can have on future teachers. Yet we constantly need to engage rigorously in our classrooms, so that student teachers become more critical in their thoughts and actions.

I am entering my final year as a Ph.D. student working with Professor Michael W. Apple at the University of Wisconsin-Madison. It is a widely known tradition that graduate students who work with Michael meet every Friday afternoon to critically discuss issues in local and international politics, education reforms, economy, social justice, social activism, and so forth. We also have committed scholars and activists other than Michael's students who participate in the Friday seminar once in a while. I have observed, with a great deal of attention, how Michael bestows accolades to activists or scholars who are engaged in crucial community work, especially those working with oppressed peoples. For instance, this is what he would say about their critical work on social justice issues (and I am paraphrasing): "I have spent time with Paulo Freire in Brazil. He was very committed to the issues you mentioned here this afternoon. I am certain that Paulo would be very proud of your work." That comment alone gives testimony to your pioneering work in critical education for social justice.

On days when I get dejected about the situation of marginalized students in public schools, or when I witness conservative educational policies implemented, I go back to my old copy of *Pedagogy of the Oppressed* and reread your ideas. I am writing this letter to thank you for awakening my critical consciousness on these complicated and at times contradictory issues in education. This has enabled me to understand the crucial role of education—namely, that a good education is one that contributes to social justice and helps improve people's lives. If you were still around you probably would help with more nuanced strategies to reinforce my understanding of your ideas so that I could share them with teachers and communities in my native country and in other places where I teach college students. I'm optimistic, though, that the current educational reforms in South Africa and in other nations will eventually seek to address the concerns of those who have been marginalized and denied quality education for many decades. Hence, I would like to end with a note of hope about the education of our children, a hope that largely originates from your inspirational work in critical educational studies.

Best wishes,
Bekisizwe S. Ndimande

PS: Two years have passed since I first wrote this letter. I successfully completed my doctoral studies in 2005 and subsequently accepted a faculty position at the University of Illinois at Urbana-Champaign. I left shortly afterward for a visiting position in South Africa. As I revise this letter, I am sitting in my little office at the University of Pretoria, where I will serve as a visiting fellow for the next two years before returning to the University of Illinois. I'm currently teaching an online course that critically examines the stereotypical images and the skewed portrayal of African histories and cultures in school textbooks and in other forms of regimes of knowledge. My course aims to dispel the myth of a monolithic Africa. I constantly encourage my students to engage with the readings and pedagogy in a Freiran praxis—which I believe can develop critical ways of learning that will contribute to the liberation of the oppressed.

Theresa Jenoure

Feathers

Dreams are visions for which one fights. Their realization cannot take place easily, without obstacles. It implies, on the contrary, advances, reversals, and at times, lengthy marches. It implies struggle.
—Paulo Freire, *Pedagogy of Indignation* (2004b), p. 32.

January 15, 2007

Dear Paulo,

Yours were big ideas. And each one of them seemed like a personal invitation to try them on for size—to offer my own interpretations, and accounts, complete with familiar names, faces, places—the details of neighborhoods, schools, teachers I had known. And as we, your students, looked into these big ideas, we shared our enormous hunger for social change, each of our needs smelling, tasting, and feeling different, though somewhere beneath it all lay a faith that we were gathered together for a purpose so much larger than any of us alone. Yes, yours were big ideas: Faith, Imagination, Joy, Dialogue, Emancipation. Ideas that quite frankly, took me by surprise. I mean, they didn't sound like "school" words.

It was 1978, and I had graduated from college only a few years earlier. I had majored in philosophy, and from the first course my freshman year had fallen completely in love with this field, this discipline. Me and philosophy: a perfect fit. I remember how my head would swim sometimes. Immersed in a warm, blue water of notions and possibilities, a landscape of language about the known and the unknown that took me far out, away from any shore where my feet might touch bottom. I loved it! You see, I was a young girl from the housing projects in the Bronx, and already I had known remarkable things. I had seen people who lived in my building head for work, to bars, to church, to steal, to play the numbers, to work second and third jobs, to care for grandchildren and great-grandchildren. We walked fourteen flights of stairs sometimes when the elevator was broken. We fought our way to and from school, dodged drunken men, and knives or bullets in the hedges. And in spite of the teachings that came through these remarkable things, they threatened to tie me down.

I was a young girl with big ideas, too. Big dreams and a huge confidence. A girl with ways of thinking about things that not only by-passed the mundane but hid desperately from the convention of details—from the nuts and bolts. I had little patience for what seemed to be a waste of time: understanding how things work, like an engineer; or calculating certainty, like a mathematician; or putting things in logical order, like a lawyer. No, I had hoped and prayed my way out of the Bronx and into college, had sipped from that mysterious, sweet cup of philosophy, and here I was, looking for a graduate program to study further.

As fate would have it, I applied to a master's program in philosophy and was rejected. Accepted at the School of Education, I took what I viewed at that time as my consolation prize. Not my first choice. Not even a remote desire, actually. I equated "education" with structures and methods, with instructions and prescriptions, with ailments and death. The death of my passion for philosophy, and an end to my fascination for those questions that answer questions, and go round and round, admitting that perhaps there are no answers. It seemed to me that education was a morgue full of dead things, like rules, policies, guidelines, plans. You see, I was an improvising musician, self-directed, always looking for the truth of the moment. And even in music I outran the rules of permanence and desperately ran from convention, from the written score, from the arrangement of sounds composed in black and white. I was committed to exploration and most of all, to uncertainty.

Paulo, I met you at the beginning of the master's program, and at first it seemed too good to be true. There I was, reading your words, and even though they were new to my ears, they were ancient to my heart. Words and phrases like "dangerous," "transforming the world," "liberation," "subjectivity"—words that painted large, luminous images and offered opportunities for me to explore not only what you might mean but also who I might be, and want to become.

It has now been almost thirty years since I first met you on my personal, metaphoric Road to Damascus, that wonderful road where Saul met the resurrected Christ and changed his name to Paul, a change that marked a new way of walking that road. Paulo, this story is mine, too, because when I met you I imagined that you knew the same people from my neighborhood. So many people with very little hope, with tremendous anger and confusion, but with so much fight. We were the people who had tired of the world's "right answers" about who we were, and who, in many ways, felt isolated from that oppressive, defining world. You looked deep into our psyche, mine and theirs, and now I know, your own, too. You used those words: fear; humility; courage; impatience; insecurity. And so, on this road, I met your big idea—this notion that teaching might be a political act. That was when I changed my name—when I knew I was where I was intended to be. Your ideas were my own, just not yet fully shaped, and I imagined that your words were what mine might sound like if I had been full grown.

As I scan the horizon, your teachings are skyscrapers punctuating a blue, open, dome. Only now I know that you erected your big ideas with our help. We were the small but determined force that cleared the road so that someone else could gather the dirt, and others would mix it with water, and others still would form the bricks for your great building. We read, debated, cried, and shouted. And today, maybe because I was never any good at remembering the details, the formulas, the instructions, the score, the choreography—anything really, that might tie me to an old moment that could contain me, I am left with something much richer: a sense of the things you meant, the flavor, the energy, the essence, the spirit. I learned that there were others who cared less about the punctuations that preoccupy us when we "read the word" and who are desperately hungry to "read the world," or to understand life context and human connection. For me, your teachings have always resonated with my own passion for the improvised work because they've encouraged me to discern and intuit.

This story is an example: I had been at a conference in Arizona a few years ago and found myself in a conversation with a like-minded man, a university professor and visiting scholar from Tanzania.

"I want to lose the script," I said, referring to my mounting frustration with the limitations of a written, predetermined syllabus.

"That's a good thing," he assured me, almost without hesitation.

"You think so? I mean, I want to know what would happen if I didn't have it. There's something so contrived and hardening about it."

Then he said the perfect words: "Jesus didn't have a script, a syllabus all written out, prepared to hand out to his students, his disciples. He took his finger and wrote out responses to questions in the sand as they arose. They came with needs, and he responded as those needs arose. He really taught!"

I said, "I want to teach like Jesus," marking a precious moment for me. Paulo, he brought me something like what you brought me when I first read your encouragement for us to "read the world." The world: something big, that revolves and is constantly touched by light, even when we are asleep.

I want to share something else with you. It is something small maybe, but of great importance to me. It's an entry from my journal that I wrote about a month ago. I want to share this because I think it may explain more about my journey. I wrote it after having taught a group of in-service teachers in South Carolina who are part of an advanced degree program, all of whom already have masters' degrees in education. The group had been together for a year, and I was their instructor for an intensive two-weekend course. This journal entry has everything to do with you because the things I've desired most in my teaching are spiritual growth and freedom. Of course, in a historical moment when these words are suspiciously didactic, I say them to you knowing that if anyone will understand their meaning, you will. I have always understood your words to be spiritual because they have encouraged transcendent possibilities. And I say this not because I know anything about your beliefs concerning the body and the essence, or earth and heaven. I say this because as I have worn your teachings and lived their deep wisdom over the years, I find that they have been key to my own flight—my evolution. They tie us together in love. They beg us to feed something other than the body, or even the mind. And maybe you never said such a thing, or would never use such a word as *spiritual,* but I wear your teaching like a work of art that takes on new meaning the moment it is made for a public, no longer the sole domain of its creator. That said, Paulo, here is my entry:

Today was a day unlike any other. It started this morning at six o'clock when my husband called to wake me. I could only half-remember the dream. I told it to him like I usually did, letting it unfold to me as the words came forward. I told him: "IN THE DREAM, I had to order for someone very important who was catching a flight overseas. It was my job to see that this person got their food in time. So, I called a Chinese restaurant—it's an exclusive, high-end place. The wait staff is very stoic and simply dressed. I place my order, and as soon as I do, I'm immediately frozen. I'm nervous. I'm worried. The person who took my order is supposed to give it to their delivery service. But, will they remember? Will they get it there on time? Did they understand what I said? Did I speak slowly and clearly enough? Did the order make any sense? Will they even care? Will it all happen the way I want it to? I'm feeling lost, angry, anxious, out of control."

As the story and its details unroll for my husband at just a few moments after I've awoken from the dream, another piece of it comes to me. It sits so firmly, solidly in the front of my mind. I don't even know how I might have missed such a key detail. I wonder if I would have found this piece had I not been relaying the dream so carefully, like I'm looking for clues—for that missing piece—a lost part of me. But, here I am telling Michael again about my dreams—those parts, those precious treasures redeemed at the oddest, unexpected moments. It comes to me like a shell by my toes as the sea tosses it and the tide dances backward, as if to say: 'Here, it's your turn now.

Let's see what you can do with this.' Thankfully, I look down and pick it up from its buried spot angled in the sand. And I finish the story—or, what I now know about it. "The restaurant's delivery service is called Feathers," I tell my husband, trying to grasp it before it escapes—flies away. "Feathers?" He's interested, but more in the helpful way he likes to facilitate, mostly because he knows I love and need this solid exchange, the questions, basic and uncomplicated. I'm thinking. More than thinking, I'm welcoming this place in myself. I make lots of room for the full story—all the details, the emotions, the smells, even the sound of my heartbeat as I anxiously wait for the food. Of course, this is all about my faith—the way it mocks me. The way I pray and then doubt that I've been heard, been understood. Is there simply too much commotion in the cosmos for my urgent order? And, I haven't come to just any ordinary fast food take out place, or a neighborhood diner. No, I've ordered from the most reputable gourmet establishment. I can see the white linen, the black suits, the shiny shoes, simplicity of line. And in spite of all the signs, the blessed assurance, I make my request with utter trepidation. But as I say its name, its meaning makes itself known. It settles somewhere deep and safe inside me, though not yet fully accessible. *Feathers*: light; swift, sure flight; great speed. *Feathers*: delicate, belonging to a creature so unlike me.

Left to marvel at the beauty of what's unfolding, I stand in front of my class a few hours later, still covered and protected by the dream. I slowly write the word *Feathers* on the chalkboard behind me, and I tell my story to this group of public school teachers enrolled in my graduate level research course. I don't know where it will lead us. I tell them that, too. My usual way is to begin class by asking my students to make connections in their learning—to bridge any significant insights or observations about work we have done in a previous session to the start of our new day. My usual way is to listen to them and occasionally comment. But today, Feathers has grabbed my arm and written its name on the boards in large capital letters. This is not a usual day. I tell my dream. I tell it exactly as I told my husband, only now, with a little more authority: "This dream is not only for me. It's for all of us," I say. I feel fragile. I'm a single object placed in front of our classroom. The tables are set in a square. My students sit behind them, and I'm at the front of the square configuration. This morning I am small and alone. I have nothing to back up this unusual story. No jokes, no theories, no research. Only my dream in its three-hours-old condition. Already it is myth, losing energy. It has begun to settle among the many stories I tell to make myself more real. Stories of the miraculous. I tend to love the odd, unlikely pivoting from mundane to supernatural. And my students are poised and ready for this offering on this morning.

"I had a dream, too." Michele is an ambitious, young, dark brown woman with a tight, thin frame and mischievous eyes that penetrate. The group immediately shifts their attention to Michele, whose story now rides on mine. She looks at me and says, "In my dream I was wearing your glasses." The group loves this. My glasses are French vintage brown tortoise shells, circa 1950. Unusual and bold, they create a scholarly, but fashionable, almost costumelike appearance. "When I had on your glasses I felt like you," she starts. We all laugh really hard. There's a feeling like we're going somewhere today. "I felt like you and I even talked like you." I'm in Georgia for this course, so compounding my New York City roots, West Indian and Latino cultural references, graduate degrees that spit out occasional terminologies, cadences accrued over twenty years of living in New England, and gritty 1960s black pride shouts from time to time (by the way, no one in this group knew who Angela Davis is. When I showed my immediate surprise, disappointment, and horror at this, a middle-aged white woman explains in a self-satisfied, matter-of-fact voice that this isn't unusual, since she says 'the 1960s were before my time.' 'Have you heard of the Civil War?' My response shoots out from a tight trigger. We're used to bringing our real selves to each other).

Michele keeps going: "When I had your glasses on I knew all this stuff. I was really sure of myself. But when I took them off, I was just me again." The group loves it. We're all laughing and talking. This dream. Our dreams: Michele's and mine. We're webbed in a wonderful place high above the reach of yesterday's anxieties about research and its dense, impenetrable ways. Ways made even more elusive by a previous research instructor who hammered the rules to this group like old, rusty nails. Today, our dreams are opening us from inside. And, I ask with confidence, already knowing the answer as I look into wide eyes that are so ready to come with me: "Can we agree on something that I know will take us to a very high place today?" They're ready. Some nod. I hear affirming sounds. I say, "Let's let go of everything today. Let's not let anything hold us down. Let's expect great things. Let's make our needs and desires fully known—to ourselves and to each other. Then, let's let Feathers deliver."

Paulo, can you see the connection between your big ideas and what they have borne in me? We had brought our dreams to each other, me and my students. Not only the figurative ones, but literal ones, which under ordinary circumstances might never have found their way into the classroom. Yes, something insignificant that happened while we were asleep, while we set aside the pressures and conscious efforts toward "learning." We used our dreams, with all their messages of fear, distrust, insecurity, expectation, incongruity, humor, ambition. We bore witness to those great teachers that emerged from unexpected places. We wondered and waited together. We cleared a sacred space among ourselves where great learning could happen. Then, we wrote the answers in the sand. And so I thank you for helping us Read the World.

Terry Jenoure

⌘

❧ Margaret Allard ❧

Layers of Understanding

I cannot be a teacher without exposing who I am.
—Paulo Freire, *Pedagogy of Freedom* (1998a), p. 87.

Fall 2005
Dear Paulo Freire:

My friends have said that you encourage students to address you by your first name, but I do not want to risk disrespect. I have recently read *Teachers as Cultural*

Workers: Letters to Those Who Dare Teach. This book is equally inspirational and intimidating because I am both moved to do more to motivate learners and, at the same time, fearful of my own ineptitude. The story you wrote about the teacher who was intimidated by his class is a frightening tale. There is a fine line between a persona of strength, confidence, and openness and a persona of fear. You might say that that line is not so fine. Perhaps that is true, but within one individual teacher, that humanness (and I remember that you guided us to acknowledge our fallibility) does not dispose on us equal amounts of each attribute, each and every day. When you vowed never to allow that to happen to you, I vowed never to let fear transform my pedagogy to that of authoritarianism. Not only would authoritarianism negatively impact my learners but it can also deny my very core and my reason for being, not just for being a teacher.

I do have knowledge of myself, and I continue to explore this self through my poetry writing, meditation, chanting, and reading the scholars. Other than education as a political act, the all-encompassing theme of your book seems to be summed up in your statement "I too am made by history." This is a statement that a teacher can make on the first day of a semester to influence the communication between teacher and learner and the critical curriculum. This statement can also be used to generate a discussion of critical historical perspectives. It can also foster humility as well as self-worth and cultural identity. For the teacher, this statement could generate information about each of our histories.

You have said that freedom has a lot to do with what we inherited and what we acquired. You refute the idea that cultural inheritance is static, and you state that impediments to freedom in education are primarily connected to historical, cultural, social, economical, and ideological structures. I agree that we are consciously aware of our conditioning and are not predetermined by it. In your examination of the goal of the dominant class with respect to the dominated class, you address the point of teachers being from a dominated class although they teach learners from both the dominant and marginalized groups. You say that the dominant class gives no pretense that those who are different are equal and that it wants to maintain the differences and keep its distance and recognize and emphasize the inferiority of those who are dominated. Again you point out that educators are politicians and have a responsibility to know scientifically the concrete world of students.

Finally, you use the definition of knowing as a social process, whose individual dimension cannot be forgotten or devalued. Therefore, you show us, the novice teachers, that knowing is not, and can never be, a purely cerebral act.

I am grateful for your inspiration, and as I grow and learn more, I intend to reread your book again so that my new self may reach another layer of understanding.

In gratitude,
Margaret Allard

⌒ ⌒

⌒ *Andrew Habana Hafner* ⌒

We Dare: To Teach, to Learn, to Love

It is imperative that we maintain hope even when the harshness
of reality may suggest the opposite. On this level, the struggle for
hope means the denunciation, in no uncertain terms, of all abuses,
schemes, and omissions. As we denounce them, we awaken in
others and ourselves the need, and also the taste, for hope.
            —Paulo Freire, *Pedagogy of the Heart* (2004a), p. 106.

December 4, 2001
Dear Paulo,

I will not claim to know you very well yet, although I hear your name being mentioned frequently and your thoughts and ideas held in high regard by educators I admire. As a student of education, that is certainly enough for me to take special notice, especially since you have been immortalized in time like the great prophets who came to speak to people about struggling for a greater vision and to dream and strive for something better. It is often hard to know as a teacher which voices you should follow: the government, the community, the intellectuals, the individual, the self. That is why your simple lessons for me are so fundamental in our political education project of working against oppressions, which forces us to walk a fine line between service and disservice to those we teach.

Like the wise man on the street sharing great visions, you wrote plainly in your *Letters to Those Who Dare Teach* that educators should teach from a self founded in love, trust, and humility. Such simple words stick with me years later as I encounter new challenges that raise questions about how I contribute to a more just world if I dare to continue to teach. I hear your call to the service of education transformed by teachers learning from students and students having the space to become teachers. The liberatory experience of education is in being wise enough to allow ourselves to be taught, rather than thinking that through our teaching we work toward liberating others from oppression.

I think perhaps more than any other specific thought or insight that you have articulated, I take lessons from your commitment to the struggle itself, a struggle of the heart, a labor of love. I respect the fact that you love your people and country so much that you risked losing them and were sent into exile. You took the risk and it paid off for you as time carried you back home to your country and your people, whom you inspire.

In different ways, I have struggled for that connection and commitment to people and places in the Philippines, a liberating struggle for love in finding myself, in finding my community, in schools, in family, in friends, in language, in words, in service. I believe that personal relationships are somewhere at the heart of transformative learning, which is why I appreciate your discussion of education from inside and outside school walls and what is at stake in terms of real-life issues. I recall making a long trip to a barrio school in the hills of a Philippine province to work with a solitary underpaid teacher who ran a one-room schoolhouse for young children. Sometimes students walked over two hours on foot each way to get to school to get their education, to become literate, to know numbers, to learn of the world. I was completely humbled by the commitment to come together around teaching and learning, a vision that school was worth the daily journey. And on the other side of the same world, but over different adversities and difficult paths, I have seen teachers in American schools with the same commitment to go to the boundaries of the system to reach children and their imaginations, showing their vision in a glimpse of community-centered education. I am also inspired by my courageous high school students who have made epic journeys across deserts, cities, and oceans to arrive in a new terrain of struggle in classrooms, cafeterias, and textbooks.

So, while I know your labyrinth of words can sometimes lose us readers, you also return with the deafening simplicity of thought that encompasses profundity. Indeed, I find the most profound thoughts take few words to encapsulate, as it is often the attempt to overexplain that confuses the point. We often do not want to accept simple answers. The same perhaps is true of your lesson about teaching and learning. The task before us is simple in its essence. It is a struggle that seems clear, and if we existed in a vacuum, it would be straightforward and unconstrained. Your life experiences and teachings, however, testify that education is not simplified by context, but rather complicated by politics. And I would agree, while at the same time, I lament the fact that we human beings are such a bittersweet creation. As you have described, the beauty of education lies in its liberatory dynamic, and yet, people allow political agendas and power structures to possess education so that it, too, becomes oppressive. It should not be so, but so it is. And there lies the nobility of your commitment to struggle. I hope that I, too, can follow your example of sacrificing for community to affirm humanity. My intellect finds it a coincidence, while my spirit feels it fate, that your words have come to me with such truth as did those of another Brazilian named Paulo whose message I have cherished in his fable *The Alchemist* (Coelho, 1993). It is a literary daydream about following your heart in walking your own path through life, looking for signs appearing in people, places, and things that guide us if we open our hearts and minds to feel them. It is a fable of a long journey of a simple person with big visions who ends up finding that he had to journey unexpectedly far and long to discover precious things so near. It is a lesson of realization and consciousness. In our journey of education, the simple things that students or colleagues might say to us can have profound meaning if we are paying deeper attention with a heart of love, trust, and humility. We talk so much talk about knowing what is best for our children, yet they often have already told us and we just haven't heard. As teachers, we have powers of great collaboration, and we have seeds of tremendous divisiveness that inhibit our liberatory goals of building community in and through schools.

Just as I have read *The Alchemist* many times like scripture, I hope to continue to discover that your words and passion too will inspire and guide me to live a true and honest life, to dedicate myself humbly to an educational mission that is greater than myself. I sense from you that for those who have the privilege to decide to struggle, it is committing to the struggle itself that is most liberating. Our liberation is in struggling not just for those but with those who have no other choice but to struggle because it is their existence.

Yours,
Drew Habana Hafner

Brahim Oulbeid

Teaching and the Struggle for Democracy

> *It is truly difficult to make a democracy. Democracy, like any dream, is not made with spiritual words but with reflection and practice.*
> —Paulo Freire, *Teachers as Cultural Workers: Letters to Those Who Dare Teach* (1998c), p. 67.

November 20, 2004
Dear Paulo,

My first meeting with your writing was "The Act of Study," in which you discussed the meaning of studying. I agree with you when you said that "studying is above all thinking about experience," and "an attitude towards the world" (p. 3). As I started reading your letters, I became aware of the fact that the task of teachers is not an easy one. After all, teaching is not about the transfer of knowledge from teacher to learner as many people and even some teachers still believe. It is more than that. Education should not be separated from politics. Educators should be involved in a political struggle for democracy and freedom.

I have learned from your writings that teachers need to be committed to help their learners interact with the surrounding environment to better understand the world, to question their living conditions, and therefore to take action to make change. I have learned from you that responsible citizens cannot be produced unless we listen to students at school, talk to them and with them, accept and respect their identities and cultural values.

When you talk about Brazil in regard to the educational system and how it operates, I feel as if you are talking about Morocco, my country of origin, or any other country in Africa, Asia, or South America. Teachers in all these countries lead a miserable life because of the factors you talked about (low salaries, lack of respect, and so forth). I found your argument about teachers not to feel insecure or disrespected true and relevant to most new teachers. I would add that they should believe that their task is a noble one, and that, as you mentioned, they need to fight to regain the respect and consideration that they deserve.

I am sure that your ideas about empowering students are the clue to the reform of education in the world. But these ideas seem hard to achieve in a world where teachers still feel insecure about their abilities to bring about change, are afraid of their superiors, and still stick to the prepackaged educational materials. It is only with the collaboration of politicians and educational staff that reform in education will see the light of day and we will be able to build a democratic society.

Sincerely,
Brahim Oulbeid

∞

⟶ *Maxine Greene* ⟵

New Beginnings and a Vision of Possibility

The world is not finished. It is always in the process of becoming.
—Paulo Freire, *Pedagogy of Freedom* (1998a), p. 72.

August 7, 2007
Dear Paulo,

I am happy to have another chance to come in touch with you, to recall moments of encounter with you, to rediscover the lasting meanings of your work, certainly in my life. I am grateful to Sonia Nieto for gathering a chorus of diverse voices to bring alive memories that make you present once again. I am sure all of us agree that we never needed a model of reflective action as much as we do today in this time of spreading apathy and thoughtlessness. A model, yes, but one that awakens those who attend, that urges them on to new beginnings. I must say, however, that—dream as I might of creating a new and significant "pedagogy of the oppressed" for New York's young people and students—it has been impossible for me to duplicate your unique sensitivity and insights, particularly with regard to "the lives of others" very different from my own. (And then I remember, when we were celebrating your marriage to Nita at my house, your walking around telling people, "I am not a peasant." What you had in mind, I am sure, was the conviction that, whatever the class or ethnicity, we share the human condition, that our differences need not keep us apart.) And, of course, I have never worked among suffering and deprived people in Brazil, Chile,

Haiti, Tanzania, and the other places where you have left your mark. Nor have I had the opportunity to find out whether I had the capacity to act with that combination of tough-mindedness, scholarship, ingenuity, and tenderness that have won you such regard and unconditional love wherever you have been.

I first heard you speak at the Highlander Folk School, then in Knoxville, Tennessee. I remember people crowding in with sleeping bags, either because they had traveled distances or were prepared to spend the night, if necessary, listening to you speak. The school at that time was established in a white frame house with scars of bullet holes on the porch—bullet holes, Myles Horton said, left over from the days when the Klan tried to disrupt their activities and make the integration that distinguished Highlander impossible.

Horton, who had been fighting for civil rights and integration for years, would never bow to racism or any form of segregation. It is not surprising that you and Myles, for all the cultural differences between Brazil and the North American South, shared so many interests and commitments, especially when it came to overcoming the internalized oppression that thrust so many into silence and feelings of powerlessness.

Like many of my friends and colleagues, I became increasingly familiar with your ideas through my reading of your works and through attendance at meetings and conferences at Harvard, Amherst, Teachers College, Michigan, Chicago, and the Graduate Center of the City University here in New York. You must have been moved and sometimes perplexed by the enthusiastic responses you received. Students everywhere resonated to your talking about "banking education," even those who recognized the connection with John Dewey's transactional and experiential views. There were always those as well who heard the echoes of Marxism, existentialism, and theories of liberation in what you were saying, even as there were a few who recognized the influence of hermeneutics and the anticipations of critical theory.

This is where I would relish another face-to-face talk with you. How would you have us cope with the gap between the stock of knowledge brought to discussions by those of us privileged enough to go to graduate schools and those less fortunate? Those of us fortunate enough to develop cosmopolitan views? I remember an occasion when you were waiting to speak at the New School, and you and I were talking about adult education and Myles's approach to the process in the Appalachian Mountains, among miners, fighters for voting rights, and even people struggling for school lunch programs. You went to the podium and began speaking about language: vernacular language, the "language of power," critical literacy, the use of dictionaries. Unexpectedly a man ran down the aisle, obviously angry. He said that he was a "late learner" and could not be expected to keep up with what you had just said. As I recall, you addressed yourself to the man's integrity, his potentiality, his right to "name the world" from his point of view, and—somehow or other—help the rest of us to see.

How can we ground our pedagogies in lived experiences without trivializing or demeaning what lacks conceptual form? How can we infuse the arts and humanities with insights from your pedagogies? How can we relate imagination to our concerns for social change?

How can we awaken even the angry ones to the thought of new beginnings and a vision of possibility?

Sincerely and gratefully,
Maxine Greene

References and General Bibliography

Introduction

Freire, P. (2004a). *Pedagogy of the heart.* New York: Continuum.

Freire, P. (1985). *The politics of education: Culture, power, and liberation.* South Hadley, MA: Bergin and Garvey.

Freire, P. (1970). *Pedagogy of the oppressed.* New York: Seabury Press.

Freire, P. (1998c). *Teachers as cultural workers: Letters to those who dare teach.* Boulder, CO: Westview Press.

Freire, P (1978). *Pedagogy in process: The letters to Guinea-Bissau.* Translated by Carman St. John Hunter. New York: Continuum.

Freire, P. (1996). *Letters to Cristina: Reflections on my life and work.* New York: Routledge.

Shor, I. (Ed.) (1987). *Freire for the classroom: A sourcebook for liberatory teaching.* Portsmouth, NJ: Boynton/Cook Publishers, Heinemann.

Freire, P., and Macedo, D. (1987). *Literacy: Reading the word and the world.* South Hadley, MA: Bergin and Garvey Publishers.

Shor, I., and Freire, P. (1987). *A pedagogy for liberation: Dialogues on transforming education.* Grancy, MA: Bergin and Garvey Publishers.

Freire, P., and Macedo, D. (1995). A dialogue: Culture, language, and race. *Harvard Educational Review* 65, no. 3: 377–402.

Freire, P., and Macedo, D. (1997). Scientism as a form of racism: Freire and Macedo. World Wide Web: http://www.Hb.wmc.edu/pub/researcher/issueXI-2/ freire-macedo.html. Date unknown (April 5, 1997).

Giroux, H. A. (1988). *Teachers as intellectuals: Toward a critical pedagogy of learning.* Granby, MA: Bergin and Garvey.

Apple, M. W. (2006). *Educating the "right" way: Markets, standards, God, and inequality,* 2d ed. New York: Routledge.

National Commission on Excellence in Education (1983). *A nation at risk: The imperative for education reform.* Washington, DC: U.S. Government Printing Office.

Meier, D., and Wood, G. (Eds.) (2004). *How the No Child Left Behind Act is damaging our children and our schools.* Boston: Beacon Press.

Nichols, S., and Berliner, D. C. (2005). *The inevitable corruption of indicators and educators through high-stakes testing.* Tempe, AZ: Educational Policy Studies Laboratory, Educational Policy Research Unit, Arizona State University. Available at http://edpolicylab.org.

Johnson, H. L., and Salz, A. (2008). *What is authentic educational reform? Pushing against the compassionate conservative agenda.* New York: Lawrence Erlbaum Associates, Taylor and Francis Group.

Kalantzis, M., Cope, B. l., Noble, G., and Poynting, S. (1990). *Cultures of schooling.* London: Falmer Press.

Castles, S. (2004). Migration, citizenship, and education. In J. A. Banks (Ed.), *Diversity and citizenship education: Global perspectives* (pp. 17–48). San Francisco: Jossey-Bass.

Apple, M. W. (2006). *Educating the "right" way: Markets, standards, God, and inequality,* 2d ed. New York: Routledge.

Gillborn, D., and Youdell, D. (2000). *Rationing education: Policy, practice, reform, and equity.* Philadelphia: Open University Press.

Gonçalves e Silva, P. (2004). Citizenship and education in Brazil: The contributions of Indian peoples and blacks in the struggle for citizenship and education. In J. A. Banks (Ed.), *Diversity and citizenship education: Global perspectives* (pp. 185–214). San Francisco: Jossey-Bass.

Carnoy, M. (2004). Foreword. In P. Freire, *Pedagogy of the heart* (pp. 7–19). New York: Continuum.

Shor, I. (Ed.) (1987). *Freire for the classroom: A sourcebook for liberatory teaching.* Portsmouth, NJ: Boynton/Cook Publishers, Heinemann.

Shor, I., and Freire, P. (1987). *A pedagogy for liberation: Dialogues on transforming education.* Granby, MA: Bergin and Garvey Publishers.

Freire, P. (1970). *Pedagogy of the oppressed.* New York: Seabury Press.

Freire, P. (1998c). *Teachers as cultural workers: Letters to those who dare teach.* Boulder, CO: Westview Press.

Part 1: Beginnings

Freire, P. (1998c). *Teachers as cultural workers: Letters to those who dare teach.* Boulder, CO: Westview Press, p. 3.

Freire, P. (1970). *Pedagogy of the oppressed.* New York: Seabury Press.

Freire, P. (1998c). *Teachers as cultural workers: Letters to those who dare teach.* Boulder, CO: Westview Press.

Reading the Class: Mary Cowhey

Freire, P. (1998a). *Pedagogy of freedom: Ethics, democracy, and civic courage.* Lanham, MD: Rowman and Littlefield, p. 126.

Freire, P. (1998c). *Teachers as cultural workers: Letters to those who dare teach.* Boulder, CO: Westview Press, p. 47.

Yolen, Jane (1992). *Encounter.* San Diego: Harcourt Brace Jovanovich.

Macedo, D., and Freire, A. M. A. (1998c). Foreword. In P. Freire, *Teachers as cultural workers: Letters to those who dare teach* (p. xi). Boulder, CO: Westview Press.

Belpré, P. (1969). *Santiago.* New York: F. Warne.

Williams. S. (1990). *I went walking.* San Diego: Harcourt Brace Jovanovich.

Gannett, R. S. (1948). *My father's dragon.* New York: Random House.

Freire, P. (1998c). *Teachers as cultural workers: Letters to those who dare teach.* Boulder, CO: Westview Press, p. 48.

Freire, P. (1998c). *Teachers as cultural workers: Letters to those who dare teach.* Boulder, CO: Westview Press, p. 48.

Angelou, M. (1996). *Life doesn't frighten me.* New York: Stewart, Tabori, and Chang.

Freire, P. (1998c). *Teachers as cultural workers: Letters to those who dare teach.* Boulder, CO: Westview Press, p. 48.

Freire, P. (1998c). *Teachers as cultural workers: Letters to those who dare teach.* Boulder, CO: Westview Press, p. 49.

Lionni, L. (1982). *Let's make rabbits*. New York: Pantheon Books.
Freire, P. (1998c). *Teachers as cultural workers: Letters to those who dare teach*. Boulder, CO: Westview Press, p. 50.
Ibid, p. 50.
Ibid, p. 51.
Ibid, p. 65.
Ibid, p. 66.
Ibid, p. 68.

Thirty-Nine First Days: Mary Ginley

Freire, P. (1998c). *Teachers as cultural workers: Letters to those who dare teach*. Boulder, CO: Westview Press, p. 51.
Dickinson, E. (1960). I dwell in possibility. In T. H. Johnson, *The complete poems of Emily Dickinson*. New York: Little, Brown and Co.

Part 2: Fear/Courage

Freire, P. (1998c). *Teachers as cultural workers: Letters to those who dare teach*. Boulder, CO: Westview Press, p. 27.
Shor, I., and Freire, P. (1987). *A pedagogy for liberation: Dialogues on transforming education*. Granby, MA: Bergin and Garvey Publishers, p. 54.

Teaching for the First Time: Sarah Hamlett

Shor, I., and Freire, P. (1987). *A pedagogy for liberation: Dialogues on transforming education*. Grancy, MA: Bergin and Garvey Publishers, p. 60.

Fear of Disappointing: Angélica Ribeiro

Freire, P. (2004b). *Pedagogy of indignation*. Boulder, CO: Paradigm Publishers, p. 122.

More Questions than Answers: Lynn Sisco

Shor, I., and Freire, P. (1987). *A pedagogy for liberation: Dialogues on transforming education*. Granby, MA: Bergin and Garvey Publishers, p. 55.

Lessons from Paulo: Nancy Costa

Freire, P. (1998c). *Teachers as cultural workers: Letters to those who dare teach*. Boulder, CO: Westview Press, p. 28.

Fighting for Democracy: Dalia Mostafa

Freire, P. (1994). *Pedagogy of hope: Reliving Pedagogy of the oppressed*. New York: Continuum, p. 124.

Modeling Democratic Principles: Laila Di Silvio

Freire, P. (1994). *Pedagogy of hope: Reliving Pedagogy of the oppressed.* New York: Continuum, p. 119.

Easy to Say, Not to Do: Tzu-Pei Kuo

Freire, P. (2004b). *Pedagogy of indignation.* Boulder, CO: Paradigm Publishers, p. 21.

Defying the Paralysis of Fear: Elizabeth Robinson

Freire, P. (1998c). *Teachers as cultural workers: Letters to those who dare teach.* Boulder, CO: Westview Press, p. 48.

Teaching for Liberation: Kathy McDonough

Freire, P. (1998c). *Teachers as cultural workers: Letters to those who dare teach.* Boulder, CO: Westview Press, p. 58.

Freire, P. (1998c). *Teachers as cultural workers: Letters to those who dare teach.* Boulder, CO: Westview Press.

Part 3: Pedagogy

Freire, P. (1998a). *Pedagogy of freedom: Ethics, democracy, and civic courage.* Lanham, MD: Rowman and Littlefield, p. 108.

Shor, I., and Freire, P. (1987). *A pedagogy for liberation: Dialogues on transforming education.* Granby, MA: Bergin and Garvey Publishers, p. 27.

Shor, I., and Freire, P. (1987). *A pedagogy for liberation: Dialogues on transforming education.* Granby, MA: Bergin and Garvey Publishers, p. 13.

On Being a Teacher: Daniela Alvarez-Bradley

Freire, P. (1998c). *Teachers as cultural workers: Letters to those who dare teach.* Boulder, CO: Westview Press, p. 34.

Saying Yes to Teaching: Lisa Varandani

Freire, P. (1998c). *Teachers as cultural workers: Letters to those who dare teach.* Boulder, CO: Westview Press, p. 44.

Teaching Vows: Hera Zinno

Freire, P. (1985). *The politics of education: Culture, power, and liberation.* South Hadley, MA: Bergin and Garvey, p. 21.

The Courage to Teach: Carolina Rothkegel

Freire, P. (1985). *The politics of education: Culture, power, and liberation.* South Hadley, MA: Bergin and Garvey, p. 177.

The Responsible Learner: Elaine Stinson

Freire, P. (1970). *Cultural action for freedom.* Cambridge, MA: Center for the Study of Development and Social Change, p. 1.

A "Stealth Coup" Threatens Us: Ira Shor

Freire, P (1978). *Pedagogy in process: The letters to Guinea-Bissau.* Translated by Carman St. John Hunter. New York: Continuum, p. 9.

Shor, I., and Freire, P. (1987). *A pedagogy for liberation: Dialogues on transforming education.* Grancy, MA: Bergin and Garvey Publishers, pp. 61–62.

Shor, I., and Freire, P. (1987). *A pedagogy for liberation: Dialogues on transforming education.* Grancy, MA: Bergin and Garvey Publishers, pp. 31–32.

Can Popular Education Work in U.S. Educational Settings?: Andrée Rose Catalfamo Fee

Freire, P. (2007). *Daring to dream: Toward a pedagogy of the unfinished.* Boulder, CO: Paradigm Publishers, p. 64.

Freire, P. (1996). *Letters to Cristina: Reflections on my life and work.* New York: Routledge.

Heaney, T. (1995). Issues in Freirian pedagogy. Available at: http://nlu.nl.edu/ace/Resources/Documents/FreireIssues.html. June 20, 1995 (April 5, 1997).

Collins, M. (1995). Critical commentaries on the role of the adult educator: From self-directed learning to postmodernist sensibilities. In Welton, M. R. (1995), *In defense of the lifeworld: Critical perspectives on adult learning.* New York: State University of New York Press.

Pedagogy of Love: Carlos REC McBride

Shor, I. and Freire, P. (1987). *A pedagogy for liberation: Dialogues on transforming education.* Granby, MA: Bergin and Garvey, p. 36.

Testimony to Teaching: Elizabeth Rendón

Freire, P. (1998a). *Pedagogy of freedom: Ethics, democracy, and civic courage.* Lanham, MD: Rowman and Littlefield, p. 64.

Freire, P. (1998c). *Teachers as cultural workers: Letters to those who dare teach.* Boulder, CO: Westview Press.

Part 4: Praxis

Freire, P. (1998a). *Pedagogy of freedom: Ethics, democracy, and civic courage.* Lanham, MD: Rowman and Littlefield, p. 30.

A Good Vision, Not an Easy One: Jacqueline Pinn

Freire, P. (1998a). *Pedagogy of freedom: Ethics, democracy, and civic courage.* Lanham, MD: Rowman and Littlefield, p. 38.

Teaching as Advocacy: Toni Hochstadt

Freire, P. (1985). *The politics of education: Culture, power, and liberation.* South Hadley, MA: Bergin and Garvey, p. 43.

Questioning, Teaching, Growing: Kerri Warfield

Freire, P. (1998a). *Pedagogy of freedom: Ethics, democracy, and civic courage.* Lanham, MD: Rowman and Littlefield, pp. 89–90.

Seeds of Solidarity: Deb Habib

Freire, P. (1994). *Pedagogy of hope: Reliving Pedagogy of the oppressed.* New York: Continuum, p. 8.

Context Matters: Wendy Seger

Freire, P. (2004b). *Pedagogy of indignation.* Boulder, CO: Paradigm Publishers, p. 63.
Ibid., p. xiii.
Ibid., p. xvii.
Ibid., p. 74.
Ibid., p. 15.
Ibid., p. 14.
Ibid., p. 62.
Ibid., p. 83.

Daily Acts of Praxis: Adriana Morehouse

Freire, P. (1998a). *Pedagogy of freedom: Ethics, democracy, and civic courage.* Lanham, MD: Rowman and Littlefield, p. 86.

Learning Moments: Tom Wilson

Freire, P. (2007). *Daring to dream: Toward a pedagogy of the unfinished.* Boulder, CO: Paradigm Publishers, p. 85.
Horton, M., and Freire, P. (1990). *We make the road by walking: Conversations on education and social change.* Philadelphia: Temple University Press.
Freire, P. (1985b). *The politics of education: Culture, power, and liberation.* South Hadley, MA: Bergin and Garvey
Freire, P. (1970). *Pedagogy of the oppressed.* New York: Seabury Press.
Colón-Muñiz, A., Park, P., and Wilson, T. (forthcoming). *Memories of Paulo.* Rotterdam. Sense Publishers.
Fromm, E. (1989). *The art of loving.* New York. Harper and Row, pp. 116–17.
Fromm, E. (1989). *The art of loving.* New York. Harper and Row, pp. 118–19.
Freire, P. (1998c). *Teachers as cultural workers: Letters to those who dare teach.* Boulder, CO: Westview Press, p. 41.
Freire, P. (2004b). *Pedagogy of indignation.* Boulder, CO: Paradigm Publishers, p. 12.

The Challenges of Aligning Cultural Integrity with Social Justice: Sara L. Young

Freire, P. (2004b). *Pedagogy of indignation.* Boulder, CO: Paradigm Publishers, p. 6.
Freire, P. (1998c). *Teachers as cultural workers: Letters to those who dare teach.* Boulder, CO: Westview Press, p. 49.
Freire, P. (1998c). *Teachers as cultural workers: Letters to those who dare teach.* Boulder, CO: Westview Press, p. 58.

Changing the World a Little Bit: Amadee Meyer

Freire, P. (2004a). *Pedagogy of the heart.* New York: Continuum, p. 36.

Radicalizing the Reading of the World through Art: Patty Bode

Freire, P. (1985). *The politics of education: Culture, power, and liberation.* South Hadley, MA: Bergin and Garvey, p. 21.
Ibid., p. 40.
Ibid., pp. 28–29.
Ibid., p. 34.
Ibid., p. 33.
Ibid., p. 53.
Ibid., p. 19.

Chatting across Texts, Geography, and Time: Michelle Fine

Freire, P. (1998c). *Teachers as cultural workers: Letters to those who dare teach.* Boulder, CO: Westview Press, p. 6.

Questions and Quandaries from the Academic Borderlands: Jason G. Irizarry

Freire, P. (1985). *The politics of education: Culture, power, and liberation.* South Hadley, MA: Bergin and Garvey, p. 178.
Delpit, L. (1995). *Other people's children: Cultural conflict in the classroom.* New York: New Press.
Lorde, Audre. 1984. *Sister outsider: Essays and speeches by Audre Lorde.* Freedom, CA: Crossing Press.
Flores-Gonzalez, N. (2002). *School kids/street kids: Identity development in Latino students.* New York: Teachers College Press.
Freire, P. (1970). *Pedagogy of the oppressed.* New York: Seabury Press.

Part 5: Conscientização

Freire, P. (n.d.). *The Ladoc "keyhole" series.* Washington, DC: Division for Latin America, United States Council of Churches, p. 10.
Freire, P. (n.d.). *The Ladoc "keyhole" series.* Washington, DC: Division for Latin America, United States Council of Churches, pp. 3–4.
Freire, P. (n.d.). *The Ladoc "keyhole" series.* Washington, DC: Division for Latin America, United States Council of Churches, p. 5.
hooks, b. (1994). *Teaching to transgress: Education as the practice of freedom.* New York: Routledge, p. 22.

Pieces of the Puzzle: Stacie Tate

Freire, P. (2004a). *Pedagogy of the heart.* New York: Continuum, p. 94.

The Fire of Conscientization Still Burns: Ramón Vega de Jesús

Freire, P. (n.d.). *The Ladoc "keyhole" series.* Washington, DC: Division for Latin America, United States Council of Churches, p. 6.

Althusser, Louis. *Lenin and philosophy and other essays. Monthly Review Press* (1971): 101.

Freire, P. (2002). *Education for critical consciousness.* New York: Continuum International Publishing Group, pp. 36–38.

Brown, K., Figueroa, E., and Sayers, D. (1997). Yet another path he blazed: Paulo Freire, the pedagogy of distancing, and technology. *Taboo: The Journal of Culture and Education* 2, pp. 154–56.

Brown, K., Cummins, J., Figueroa, E., and Sayers, D. (1998). Global learning networks: Gaining perspective on our lives with distance. In E. Lee, D. Menkart, and M. Okazawa-Rey (Eds.), *Beyond heroes and holidays: A practical guide to K–12 anti-racist, multicultural education and staff development.* Washington, DC: Network of Educators on the Americas.

Vega de Jesús, R. (August 2004). Voices: A cross-cultural binational study of Puerto Rican circular migrant students (CMS). Unpublished dissertation, University of Connecticut, Storrs, CT. Dissertation Abstract International, 65, 4477.

Lessons in Humility: John Raible

Freire, P. (1998a). *Pedagogy of freedom: Ethics, democracy, and civic courage.* Lanham, MD: Rowman and Littlefield, p. 54.

Freire, P. (1970). *Pedagogy of the oppressed.* New York: Seabury Press.

Berliner, D. (2006). Our impoverished view of educational reform. *Teachers College Record, 108* (6), 949–95.

Spring, J. (2007). *Deculturalization and the struggle for equality: A brief history of the education of dominated cultures in the United States* (5th edition). Boston: McGraw-Hill.

Nieto, S. (2004). *Affirming diversity: The sociopolitical context of multicultural education.* New York: Longman (2d edition, 1996; 3d edition, 2000; 4th edition, 2004, by Allyn and Bacon).

Barab, S., and Roth, W-M. (2006). Curriculum-based ecosystems: Supporting knowing from an ecological perspective. *Educational Researcher,* vol. 35, n. 5, pp. 3–13.

Nieto, S. (1995). From brown heroes and holidays to assimilationist agendas: Reconsidering the critiques of multicultural education. In C. E. Sleeter and P. L. McLaren (Eds.), *Multicultural education, critical pedagogy, and the politics of difference* (pp. 191–220). New York: State University of New York Press.

Illich, I. (1970). *Deschooling society.* New York: Marion Boyers Press.

Kahn, R., and Kellner, D. (2006). Resisting globalization. In G. Ritzer (Ed.), *The Blackwell companion to globalization.* Malden, MA: Blackwell Publishers.

Teaching Became a Revolution: Ernest Morrell

Freire, P. (2004b). *Pedagogy of indignation.* Boulder, CO: Paradigm Publishers, p. 7.

Freire, P. (1970). *Pedagogy of the oppressed.* New York: Seabury Press.

A New Way to Read the World: Diana Caballero

Shor, I., and Freire, P. (1987). *A pedagogy for liberation: Dialogues on transforming education.* Grancy, MA: Bergin and Garvey Publishers, p. 36.

Freire, P. (1996). *Letters to Cristina: Reflections on my life and work.* New York: Routledge, p. 123.
Freire, P. (1994). *Pedagogy of hope: Reliving Pedagogy of the oppressed.* New York: Continuum, p. 8.

Of Rage and Hope: Sawsan Abbadi

Freire, P. (1998c). *Teachers as cultural workers: Letters to those who dare teach.* Boulder, CO: Westview Press, p. 51.
Freire, P. (1998c). *Teachers as cultural workers: Letters to those who dare teach.* Boulder, CO: Westview Press, p. 15.
Freire, P. (1998b). *Pedagogy of the oppressed.* New York: Continuum Publishing Co., p. 14.
Freire, P. (1998c). *Teachers as cultural workers: Letters to those who dare teach.* Boulder, CO: Westview Press, p. 89.
Freire, P. (1970). *Cultural action for freedom.* Cambridge, MA: Center for the Study of Development and Social Change, p. 46.
Freire, P., and Macedo, D. (1987). *Literacy: Reading the word and the world.* South Hadley, MA: Bergin and Garvey Publishers, p. 187.

Fostering Change and Consciousness among Students and Colleagues: Dawn Fontaine

Freire, P. (2004a). *Pedagogy of the heart.* New York: Continuum, p. 73.
Freire, P., and Macedo, D. (1987). *Literacy: Reading the word and the world.* South Hadley, MA: Bergin and Garvey Publishers.

Tertulias and Problem-Posing Education: Anaida Colón-Muñíz

Freire, P. (1998c). *Teachers as cultural workers: Letters to those who dare teach.* Boulder, CO: Westview Press, pp. 72–73.
Freire, P. (1970). *Pedagogy of the oppressed.* New York: Seabury Press.

Part 6: Politics

Shor, I., and Freire, P. (1987). *A pedagogy for liberation: Dialogues on transforming education.* Grancy, MA: Bergin and Garvey Publishers, p. 46.
Freire, P. (2004b). *Pedagogy of indignation.* Boulder, CO: Paradigm Publishers, p. 20.

The Teacher-Politician: Elena Khatsevich

Freire, P. (1985). *The politics of education: Culture, power, and liberation.* South Hadley, MA: Bergin and Garvey, p. 101.

Building Community beyond Limit-Situations: Berta Rosa Berríz

Freire, P. (2004b). *Pedagogy of indignation.* Boulder, CO: Paradigm Publishers, p. 100.
Kreisberg, S. (1992). *Transforming power: Domination, empowerment, and education.* Albany: State University of New York.

Eating, Talking, and Acting: Herb Kohl

Freire, P. (1985). *The politics of education: Culture, power, and liberation.* South Hadley, MA: Bergin and Garvey, p. 196.

Kohl, H. (1974). *Reading, how to.* New York: Dutton.

Freire, P. (2002). *Education for critical consciousness.* New York: Continuum International Publishing Group.

Freire, P. (1970). *Pedagogy of the oppressed.* New York: Seabury Press, p. 77.

Freire, P. (1970). *Pedagogy of the oppressed.* New York: Seabury Press, p. 28.

Freire, P. (1994). *Pedagogy of hope: Reliving Pedagogy of the oppressed.* New York: Continuum, pp. 46–47.

Neruda, P. (1974). *Toward the splendid city.* New York: Noonday, pp. 33–35.

Why History?: Eugenie Kang

Freire, P. (2004a). *Pedagogy of the heart.* New York: Continuum, p. 37.

A Teacher's Thoughts on the "War on Terrorism": Claire LaBonté

Freire, P. (1998c). *Teachers as cultural workers: Letters to those who dare teach.* Boulder, CO: Westview Press, p. 6.

Freire, P. (1998c). *Teachers as cultural workers: Letters to those who dare teach.* Boulder, CO: Westview Press, p. 95.

What I Learned in School: Shakira Alvarez-Ferrer

Freire, P. (2004a). *Pedagogy of the heart.* New York: Continuum, pp. 39–40.

Freire, P. (1970). *Pedagogy of the oppressed.* New York: Seabury Press, p. 28.

Radical Politics, Writing, and the CIA: Linda Brodkey

Freire, P. (1998c). *Teachers as cultural workers: Letters to those who dare teach.* Boulder, CO: Westview Press, p. 24.

"The World Factbook," www.cia.gov/.

Part 7: Love

Freire, P. (2004b). *Pedagogy of indignation.* Boulder, CO: Paradigm Publishers, p. 47.

Nieto, S. (2003). *What keeps teachers going?* New York: Teachers College Press.

Guevara. C. (1965). Notes on man and socialism in Cuba. Guevara wrote this piece in the form of a letter to Carlos Quijano, editor of *Marcha,* an independent radical weekly published in Montevideo, Uruguay. It bore the dateline "Havana, 1965." In addition to appearing in *Marcha,* it was printed by *Verde Olivo,* the magazine of the Cuban armed forces.

A Love Letter to Paulo: Kristen French

Freire, P. (1998c). *Teachers as cultural workers: Letters to those who dare teach.* Boulder, CO: Westview Press, p. 3.

Ibid., p. 57.
Ibid., p. 3.
Ibid., p. 68.

Learning to Love My Students: Alexis Nasdor-Jones

Freire, P. (1985). *The politics of education: Culture, power, and liberation.* South Hadley, MA: Bergin and Garvey, p. 197.

Teaching with Tenderness and Compassion: Ruth Harman

Freire, P. (1998a). *Pedagogy of freedom: Ethics, democracy, and civic courage.* Lanham, MD: Rowman and Littlefield, p. 62.
Hanh, Thich Nhat. (1992). *Peace is every step: The path of mindfulness in everyday life.* New York: Bantam.

Colonialism, the English Language, and a Teacher's Love: Kelley Crisp

Freire, P. (2004a). *Pedagogy of the heart.* New York: Continuum, p. 106.
Freire, P. (1974). *Education for critical consciousness.* New York: Continuum, p. 48.

Love as Daring: Jennifer Burk

Freire, P. (1985). *The politics of education: Culture, power, and liberation.* South Hadley, MA: Bergin and Garvey, p. 180.

Love, in Spite of It All: Steph Doyle

Freire, P. (1998a). *Pedagogy of freedom: Ethics, democracy, and civic courage.* Lanham, MD: Rowman and Littlefield, p. 94.
Freire, P. (1998c). *Teachers as cultural workers: Letters to those who dare teach.* Boulder, CO: Westview Press, p. 33.
Ibid., p. 27.
Ibid., p. 57.
Ibid., p. 56.

Teaching as Relationship: Mike Hayes

Freire, P. (1998a). *Pedagogy of freedom: Ethics, democracy, and civic courage.* Lanham, MD: Rowman and Littlefield, p. 125.

Time to Love: Tracy Walker

Freire, P. (1998a). *Pedagogy of freedom: Ethics, democracy, and civic courage.* Lanham, MD: Rowman and Littlefield, p. 71.
Babbitt, N. (2007). Tuck everlasting. New York: Square Fish Publishers.

Part 8: Study/Dialogue

Freire, P. (1985). *The politics of education: Culture, power, and liberation.* South Hadley, MA: Bergin and Garvey, p. 3.

The Need to Study: Tina Clark

Freire, P. (1998a). *Pedagogy of freedom: Ethics, democracy, and civic courage.* Lanham, MD: Rowman and Littlefield, p. 85.

Weekly Conversations: Martha Barquero-Checkwicz

Freire, P. (1998c). *Teachers as cultural workers: Letters to those who dare teach.* Boulder, CO: Westview Press, p. 18.

Critically Analyzing Paulo: Phil Lawrence

Freire, P. (1998c). *Teachers as cultural workers: Letters to those who dare teach.* Boulder, CO: Westview Press, pp. 30–31.
Ibid., p. 18.
Ibid., p. 23.
Ibid., pp. 24–25.
Ong, W. J. (2002). *Orality and literacy: The technologizing of the word.* London: Routledge.
Jain, S., and Jain, M. (Eds.) (2003). *The dark side of literacy.* Udaipur, India: Shikhanter.
Illich, I. (1970). *Deschooling society.* New York: Marion Boyers Press.

Re-reading the Text: Maria José Botelho

Freire, P. (1985a). *The politics of education: Culture, power, and liberation.* South Hadley, MA: Bergin and Garvey, p. 2.
McIntosh, Peggy. (1988). *White privilege and male privilege: A personal account of coming to see correspondences through work in women's studies.* Wellesley, MA: Center for Research on Women.
Gibson-Graham, J. K. (1996). *The end of capitalism (as we knew it): A feminist critique of political economy.* Malden, MA: Blackwell.

Beyond "Getting the Reading Done": Romina Pacheco

Freire, P. (1998a). *Pedagogy of freedom: Ethics, democracy, and civic courage.* Lanham, MD: Rowman and Littlefield, p. 3.
Freire, P. (1998c). *Teachers as cultural workers: Letters to those who dare teach.* Boulder, CO: Westview Press, p. 27.
Ibid., p. 3.

To Study Is a Revolutionary Duty: Jeff Duncan-Andrade

Freire, P. (1998a). *Pedagogy of freedom: Ethics, democracy, and civic courage.* Lanham, MD: Rowman and Littlefield, p. 79.

Freire, P., and Macedo, D. (1987). *Literacy: Reading the word and the world.* New York: Bergin and Garvey, p. 77.

Lazin, L. (2003). *Tupac: Resurrection.* United States: Amaru Entertainment.

Shakur, T. (1999). *The Rose that Grew from Concrete.* New York: Pocket Books, p. 3.

Shakur, T. (2002). *Better Dayz.* Los Angeles: Interscope Records, Disc 1, Track 7, 4:09.

Haberman, M. (2006). *Pedagogy of poverty: The pedagogy of poverty versus good teaching.* Retrieved November 14, 2006, from http://www.ednews.org/articles/610/1/Pedagogy-of-Poverty-The-Pedagogy-of-Poverty-Versus-Good-Teaching/Page1.html.

aha! Process. (2007). *A Platform for Economic Justice.* Retrieved July 10, 2007, from http://www.ahaprocess.com/files/PlatformForEconomicJustice.pdf, p. 4.

Freire, P. (2004b). *Pedagogy of indignation.* Boulder, CO: Paradigm Publishers, p. 20.

More than Turning Pages: Michael Greene

Freire, P. (1985a). *The politics of education: Culture, power, and liberation.* South Hadley, MA: Bergin and Garvey, p. 4.

Freire, P. (1998c). *Teachers as cultural workers: Letters to those who dare teach.* Boulder, CO: Westview Press.

Part 9: Freedom

Freire, P. (1998a). *Pedagogy of freedom: Ethics, democracy, and civic courage.* Lanham, MD: Rowman and Littlefield, p. 86.

Macedo, D., and Araújo Freire, A. M. (1998). Foreword, *Teachers as cultural workers: Letters to those who dare teach.* Boulder, CO: Westview, p. x.

Apple, M. W. (2006). *Educating the "right" way: Markets, standards, God, and inequality.* 2d ed. New York: Routledge.

Macedo, D., and Araújo Freire, A. M. (1998). Foreword, *Teachers as cultural workers: Letters to those who dare teach.* Boulder, CO: Westview, p. x.

Pedagogy of the Township: Bekisizwe S. Ndimande

Freire, P. (2007). *Daring to dream: Toward a pedagogy of the unfinished.* Boulder, CO: Paradigm Publishers, p. 7.

I would like to thank Sonia Nieto, Marcus Weaver-Hightower, and Alvaro Hypolito for their thoughtful comments on this letter.

*The research has since been published as Ndimande, B. S. (2005). *Cows and goats no longer count as inheritances: The politics of school "choice" in post-apartheid South Africa.* Dissertation Abstracts International, A 66/08 (UMI No. 3186245).

Freire, P. (1971). *Pedagogy of the oppressed.* New York: Herder and Herder, p. 150.

**I am mindful that Ngugi's and Fanon's work transcended the nations of Kenya and Martinique. Fanon, for instance, lamented the colonial behavior of black folks he came across in France.

Ngugi wa T. (1986). *Decolonizing the mind: The politics of language in African literature.* Portsmouth, NH: Heinemann.

Fanon, F. (1967). *Black skin white masks.* New York: Grove Press.

Freire, P. (1971). *Pedagogy of the oppressed*. New York: Herder and Herder, p. 39.

Feathers: Theresa Jenoure

Freire, P. (2004b). *Pedagogy of indignation*. Boulder, CO: Paradigm Publishers, p. 32.

Layers of Understanding: Margaret Allard

Freire, P. (1998a). *Pedagogy of freedom: Ethics, democracy, and civic courage*. Lanham, MD: Rowman and Littlefield, p. 87.

We Dare: Andrew Habana Hafner

Freire, P. (2004a). *Pedagogy of the heart*. New York: Continuum, p. 106.
Coelho, P. (1993). *The alchemist*. New York: HarperCollins Publishers.

Teaching and the Struggle for Democracy: Brahim Oulbeid

Freire, P. (1998c). *Teachers as cultural workers: Letters to those who dare teach*. Boulder, CO: Westview Press, p. 67.
Freire, P. (1985a). The act of study. In *The politics of education: Culture, power, and liberation* (pp. 1–4). South Hadley, MA: Bergin and Garvey.

New Beginnings and a Vision of Possibility: Maxine Greene

Freire, P. (1998a). *Pedagogy of freedom: Ethics, democracy, and civic courage*. Lanham, MD: Rowman and Littlefield, p. 72.
Horton, M., Kohl, J., and Kohl, H. (1997). *The long haul: An autobiography*. New York: Teachers College Press.

General Bibliography

aha! Process. (2007). *A Platform for Economic Justice*. Retrieved July 10, 2007, from http://www.ahaprocess.com/files/PlatformForEconomicJustice.pdf, p. 4.
Althusser, Louis (1971). *Lenin and philosophy and other essays*. New York: Monthly Review Press, www.marxists.org/reference/archive/althusser/1970/ideology.htm. Retrieved on 9/8/2007.
American Rage against the Machine. Available at http://www.musicfanclubs.org/rage/biographical.htm.
Angelou, Maya. (1996). *Life doesn't frighten me*. New York: Stewart, Tabori and Chang.
Apple, M. W. (2006). *Educating the "right" way: Markets, standards, God, and inequality*. 2d ed. New York: Routledge.
Babbitt, N. (2007). *Tuck everlasting*. New York: Square Fish Publishers.
Barab, S., and Roth, W-M. (2006). Curriculum-based ecosystems: Supporting knowing from an ecological perspective. *Educational Researcher* 35, n. 5, pp. 3–13.
Belpré, P. (1969). *Santiago*. New York: F. Warne.

Berliner, D. (2006). Our impoverished view of educational reform. *Teachers College Record* 108, no. 6, pp. 949–95.

Brown, K., Figueroa, E., and Sayers, D. (1997). Yet another path he blazed: Paulo Freire, the pedagogy of distancing, and technology. *Taboo: The Journal of Culture and Education* 2, pp. 154–56.

Brown, K., Cummins, J., Figueroa, E., and Sayers, D. (1998). Global learning networks: Gaining perspective on our lives with distance. In E. Lee, D. Menkart, and M. Okazawa-Rey (Eds.), *Beyond heroes and holidays: A practical guide to K–12 anti-racist, multicultural education and staff development*. Washington, DC: Network of Educators on the Americas.

Coelho, P. (1993). *The alchemist*. New York: HarperCollins Publishers.

Collins, M. (1995). Critical commentaries on the role of the adult educator: From self-directed learning to postmodernist sensibilities. In Welton, M. R. (1995), *In defense of the lifeworld: Critical perspectives on adult learning*. New York: State University of New York Press.

Colón-Muñiz, A., Park, P., and Wilson, T. (forthcoming). *Memories of Paulo*. Rotterdam. Sense Publishers.

Delpit, L. (1995). *Other people's children: Cultural conflict in the classroom*. New York: New Press.

Dickinson, E. (1960). I dwell in possibility. In T. H. Johnson, *The complete poems of Emily Dickinson*. New York: Little, Brown and Co.

Flores-Gonzalez, N. (2002). *School kids/street kids: Identity development in Latino students*. New York: Teachers College Press.

Freire, P. (n.d.). *The Ladoc "keyhole" series*. Washington, DC: Division for Latin America, United States Council of Churches.

———. (1970). *Cultural action for freedom*. Cambridge, MA: Center for the Study of Development and Social Change.

———. (1970). *Pedagogy of the oppressed*. New York: Seabury Press.

———. (1971). *Pedagogy of the oppressed*. New York: Herder and Herder.

———. (1974). *Education for critical consciousness*. Translated by Myra B. Ramos. New York: Continuum.

———. (1978). *Pedagogy in process: The letters to Guinea-Bissau*. Translated by Carman St. John Hunter. New York: Continuum.

———. (1983). The importance of the act of reading, *Journal of Education* 165, no. 1, pp. 5–11.

———. (1985a). The act of study. In *The politics of education: Culture, power, and liberation* (pp. 1–4). South Hadley, MA: Bergin and Garvey.

———. (1985b). *The politics of education: Culture, power, and liberation*. South Hadley, MA: Bergin and Garvey.

———. (1994). *Pedagogy of hope: Reliving Pedagogy of the oppressed*. New York: Continuum.

———. (1996). *Letters to Cristina: Reflections on my life and work*. New York: Routledge.

———. (1998a). *Pedagogy of freedom: Ethics, democracy, and civic courage*. Lanham, MD: Rowman and Littlefield.

———. (1998b). *Pedagogy of the oppressed*. New York: Continuum Publishing Co.

———. (1998c). *Teachers as cultural workers: Letters to those who dare teach*. Boulder, CO: Westview Press.

———. (2000). *Pedagogy of the oppressed*. (M. B. Ramos, Trans.). New York: Continuum.

———. (2002). *Education for critical consciousness*. New York: Continuum International Publishing Group.

———. (2004a). *Pedagogy of the heart*. New York: Continuum.

———. (2004b). *Pedagogy of indignation*. Boulder, CO: Paradigm Publishers.

————. (2005). *Teachers as cultural workers: Letters to those who dare teach.* Boulder, CO: Westview Press.

Freire, P., and Macedo, D. (1987). *Literacy: Reading the word and the world.* South Hadley, MA: Bergin and Garvey Publishers.

Freire, P., and Macedo, D. (1995). A dialogue: Culture, language, and race. *Harvard Educational Review* 65, no. 3: 377–402.

Freire, P., and Macedo, D. (1997). Scientism as a form of racism: Freire and Macedo. World Wide Web: http://www.Hb.wmc.edu/pub/researcher/issueXI-2/ freire-macedo.html. Date unknown (April 5, 1997).

Fromm, E. (1989). *The art of loving.* New York. Harper and Row.

Gannett, R. S. (1948). *My father's dragon.* New York: Random House.

Gibson-Graham, J. K. (1996). *The end of capitalism (as we knew it): A feminist critique of political economy.* Malden, MA: Blackwell.

Giroux, H. A. (1988). *Teachers as intellectuals: Toward a critical pedagogy of learning.* Granby, MA: Bergin and Garvey.

Giroux, H. A., and McLaren, P. (1994). *Between borders: Pedagogy and the politics of cultural studies.* New York: Routledge.

Guevara. C. (1965). "Notes on man and socialism in Cuba." Guevara wrote this piece in the form of a letter to Carlos Quijano, editor of *Marcha,* an independent radical weekly published in Montevideo, Uruguay. It bore the dateline "Havana, 1965." In addition to appearing in *Marcha,* it was printed by *Verde Olivo,* the magazine of the Cuban armed forces.

Haberman, M. (2006). *Pedagogy of poverty: The pedagogy of poverty versus good teaching.* Retrieved November 14, 2006, from http://www.ednews.org/articles/610/1/Pedagogy-of-Poverty-The-Pedagogy-of-Poverty-Versus-Good-Teaching/Page1.html.

Hanh, Thich Nhat. (1992). *Peace is every step: The path of mindfulness in everyday life.* New York: Bantam.

Heaney, T. (1995). Issues in Freirian pedagogy. Available at: http://nlu.nl.edu/ace/Resources/Documents/FreireIssues.html. June 20, 1995 (April 5, 1997).

hooks, b. (1994). *Teaching to transgress: Education as the practice of freedom.* New York: Routledge.

Horton, M., and Freire, P. (1990). *We make the road by walking: Conversations on education and social change.* Philadelphia: Temple University Press.

Horton, M., Kohl, J., and Kohl, H. (1997). *The long haul: An autobiography.* New York: Teachers College Press.

Illich, I. (1970). *Deschooling society.* New York: Marion Boyers Press.

Jain, S., and Jain, M. (Eds.) (2003). *The dark side of literacy.* Udaipur, India: Shikhanter.

Kahn, R., and Kellner, D. (2006). Resisting globalization. In G. Ritzer (Ed.), *The Blackwell companion to globalization.* Malden, MA: Blackwell Publishers.

Kalantzis, M., Cope, B. I., Noble, G., and Poynting, S. (1990). *Cultures of schooling.* London: Falmer Press.

Kohl, H. (1974). *Reading, how to.* New York: Dutton.

Kreisberg, S. (1992). *Transforming power: Domination, empowerment, and education.* Albany: State University of New York.

Kutz, E., and Roskelly, H. (1991). *An unquiet pedagogy; Transforming practice in the English classroom.* Portsmouth NH: Boynton/Cook Publishers.

Lazin, L. (2003). *Tupac: Resurrection.* United States: Amaru Entertainment.

Lester, J. (1998). *From slave ship to freedom road.* New York: Dial Books.

Lionni, L. (1982). *Let's make rabbits.* New York: Pantheon Books.

Lorde, Audre. 1984. *Sister outsider: Essays and speeches by Audre Lorde.* Freedom, CA: Crossing Press.

Marcos, Subcomandante Insurgente (2001). A land to harvest a future. In J. Ponce de León (Ed.), *Our word is our weapon: Selected writings*. New York: Seven Stories Press.

McIntosh, Peggy. (1988). *White privilege and male privilege: A personal account of coming to see correspondences through work in women's studies*. Wellesley, MA: Center for Research on Women.

Macedo, D., and Araújo Freire, A. M. (1998). Foreword, *Teachers as cultural workers: Letters to those who dare teach*. Boulder, CO: Westview, p. x.

National Commission on Excellence in Education. (1983). *A nation at risk: The imperative for education reform*. Washington, DC: U.S. Government Printing Office.

Ndimande, B. S. (2005). *Cows and goats no longer count as inheritances: The politics of school "choice" in post-apartheid South Africa*. Dissertation Abstracts International, A 66/08. (UMI No. 3186245).

Neruda, P. (1974). *Toward the splendid city*. New York: Noonday, pp. 33–35.

Nieto, S. (1995). From brown heroes and holidays to assimilationist agendas: Reconsidering the critiques of multicultural education. In C. E. Sleeter and P. L. McLaren (Eds.), *Multicultural education, critical pedagogy, and the politics of difference* (pp. 191–220). New York: State University of New York Press.

Nieto, S. (2003). *What keeps teachers going?* New York: Teachers College Press.

Nieto, S. (2004). *Affirming diversity: The sociopolitical context of multicultural education*. New York: Longman (2d edition, 1996; 3d edition, 2000; 4th edition, 2004, by Allyn and Bacon).

Ong, W. J. (2002). *Orality and literacy: The technologizing of the word*. London: Routledge.

Shakur, T. (1999). *The Rose that Grew from Concrete*. New York: Pocket Books, p. 3.

Shakur, T. (2002). *Better Dayz*. Los Angeles: Interscope Records, Disc 1, Track 7, 4:09.

Shor, I. (Ed.) (1987). *Freire for the classroom: A sourcebook for liberatory teaching*. Portsmouth, NJ: Boynton/Cook Publishers, Heinemann.

Shor, I., and Freire, P. (1987). *A pedagogy for liberation: Dialogues on transforming education*. Granby, MA: Bergin and Garvey Publishers.

Spring, J. (2007). *Deculturalization and the struggle for equality: A brief history of the education of dominated cultures in the United States* (5th edition). Boston: McGraw-Hill.

Vega de Jesús, R. (August 2004). Voices: A cross-cultural binational study of Puerto Rican circular migrant students (CMS). Unpublished dissertation, University of Connecticut, Storrs, CT. Dissertation Abstract International, 65, 4477.

Williams. S. (1990). *I went walking*. San Diego: Harcourt Brace Jovanovich.

Yolen, Jane (1992). *Encounter*. San Diego: Harcourt Brace Jovanovich.

About the Editor and the Contributors

Editor

For many years, Sonia Nieto taught prospective and practicing teachers in the Language, Literacy, and Culture Program at the University of Massachusetts, Amherst. She was first introduced to the work of Paulo Freire as a doctoral student and later had the privilege of helping coordinate his many visits to the campus during the 1980s. Currently professor emerita, she continues to speak and write on issues of multicultural education, the education of students of culturally and linguistically diverse backgrounds, teacher education, and educational equity.

Contributors

Sawsan Abbadi is currently a lecturer of Arabic within the tricollege system of Swarthmore, Haverford, and Bryn Mawr. She is working on her doctorate at the University of Massachusetts, Amherst.

As a lecturer at the University of Massachusetts in Amherst, Margaret Allard currently teaches English-as-a-second-language courses.

Daniela Alvarez-Bradley teaches English language learners in an elementary school in Massachusetts. She strives to weave the lessons she learned from Paulo Freire into her work every day.

Shakira Alvarez-Ferrer is a case manager at Big Brothers Big Sisters of Hampshire County in Amherst, Massachusetts.

Martha Barquero-Checkwicz was born in San José, Costa Rica, and grew up in Miami, Florida, and Pacayas, Costa Rica. She currently teaches fifth-grade ELL students at Frederick Harris Elementary School in Springfield, Massachusetts, and although she never met Paulo while he was living, she feels that she truly met him through his writing.

Born in Cuba, Berta Rosa Berriz, Ed.D., is a national board certified (2006) bilingual teacher, national faculty at Lesley University, a dancer, a writer, and storyteller. Her doctoral research at Harvard Graduate School of Education (2005) investigated the relationship between the cultural identity of Puerto Rican and Dominican second-generation students and their teachers' assessment of their academic performance.

Patty Bode is the director of art education for Tufts University in a program affiliated with the School of the Museum of Fine Arts, Boston. Years of experience as an activist, public school art teacher, and teacher educator inform her art making, research, and teaching.

Maria José Botelho is an assistant professor of literacy education at the Ontario Institute for Studies in Education of the University of Toronto. She teaches courses and conducts research in critical multicultural literacies, critical multi-cultural analysis of children's and young adult literature, and critical collaborative inquiry.

Linda Brodkey is a professor in the Department of Literature and director of the Warren College Writing Program at the University of California at San Diego. She is the author of two books (*Academic Writing as Social Practice* and *Writing Permitted in Designated Areas Only*) and numerous articles on writing and writing pedagogy.

Jennifer Burk is a middle school ESL teacher for the Beverly Public Schools in Beverly, Massachusetts.

Diana Caballero is presently clinical associate professor at Fordham University's Graduate School of Education and is still seeking to create a better world!

Tina Clark is an art teacher in the Greenfield, Massachusetts, public schools. She believes that to be a learner as well as a teacher is a statement that is easy to understand, yet difficult to execute; when executed, the effect is astounding.

Anaida Colón-Muñíz is an associate professor of education at Chapman University, Orange, California. Although she was introduced to Paulo's work in 1975 in a study group at Bank Street College, she got to meet and chat with him only many years later, at the University of California, Irvine, in the elevator, of all places!

Nancy Costa has been a social worker for twenty-seven years, with the last fifteen in the West Springfield Public Schools. Her work with three- to six-year-olds, their parents, and their teachers is focused on enhancing the students' educational experience by first meeting their emotional needs.

Mary Cowhey teaches second grade in Northampton, Massachusetts, and is the author of *Black Ants and Buddhists: Thinking Critically and Teaching Differently in the Primary Grades* (Stenhouse, 2006).

Kelley Crisp is currently supervising student teachers and working with adult language learners in and around Amherst, Massachusetts.

Laila M. Di Silvio currently teaches social studies to seventh graders in South Hadley, Massachusetts. A returned Peace Corps volunteer and avid traveler, she seeks to prepare her students to be compassionate, knowledgeable, and just global citizens.

Steph Doyle is a grade-three Sheltered English Immersion (SEI) teacher in Dorchester, Massachusetts. She does what she loves and she loves what she does.

Jeffrey Duncan-Andrade, PhD, is assistant professor in Raza Studies and the College of Education, and codirector of the Educational Equity Initiative at San Francisco State University's Cesar Chavez Institute. He also teaches a twelfth-grade English literature course in Oakland, California.

Andree Rose Catalfamo Fee, D.Ed., is a professor of developmental English and reading at Chesapeake College in Maryland. Reading *Pedagogy of the Oppressed* for the first time caused her months of cognitive dissonance but eventually changed not only her teaching but also her life.

Michelle Fine teaches psychology, women's studies, and urban education at the Graduate Center of the City University of New York. As a member of the Participatory Action Research Collective, her research interests focus on questions of injustice and resistance within prisons, schools, and youth movements.

Dawn Fontaine is an urban high school educator who has woven Paulo Freire's ideas of *conscientization* into her pedagogy in an effort to create greater participation for her students in their own learning.

Kristen B. French is director of the Center of Educational Pluralism and an assistant professor in elementary education at Western Washington University.

After thirty-six years of teaching in Massachusetts, Mary Ginley began again in North Port, Florida, teaching fifth grade. She met Paulo when she read *Pedagogy of the Oppressed* for a course in multicultural education in the mid-1990s.

Maxine Greene is professor of philosophy and education (emerita) at Teachers College, still teaching "Education and Aesthetic Experience." She is also philosopher-in-residence at Lincoln Center Institute for the Arts in Education, and her most recent book is *The Dialectic of Freedom*.

Michael Greene is a chaplain at the University of Massachusetts, Amherst. He also teaches ESL to adults and works part-time as a cabinetmaker/carpenter.

Andrew Habana Hafner is an educator and researcher who has heard Paulo Freire's call that dares us to teach with humility and hope. He brings Freire's guiding words in his work for community and social justice for the oppressed worldwide.

Deb Habib is the executive director of Seeds of Solidarity, a nonprofit organization in Orange, Massachusetts. She is a mother, school board member, and community organizer whose teaching and writing focus on the intersections of social justice, food, and environment.

Sarah Hamlett is a high school Spanish teacher in Leominster, Massachusetts. She has been teaching for six years.

Ruth Harman is an assistant professor at the University of Georgia, Athens. Previously, she was a part-time lecturer in language and literacy development at Smith College and at the University of Massachusetts, Amherst, and before that, a teacher of adult basic education in New Orleans, Louisiana.

Michael Hayes has taught middle school math for many years and has also served as an interim coprincipal of a middle school.

Toni Hochstadt has lived, worked, and studied in Canada, Germany, and Kenya, as well as the United States. She currently works in legal services and resides in Northampton, Massachusetts, with her two daughters, all of whom hula-hoop as frequently as possible.

Jason G. Irizarry is an assistant professor in the Neag School of Education at the University of Connecticut. His teaching and research focus on urban teacher recruitment, preparation, and retention with an emphasis on increasing the number of teachers of color, culturally responsive pedagogy, urban youth culture, and Latino students in U.S. schools.

Theresa Jenoure is a freelance musician, teacher educator at Lesley University, and director of Augusta Savage Art Gallery at the University of Massachusetts. She meets Paulo in that World where he still teaches.

Eugenie Kang has been a teacher educator and a middle and high school social studies teacher. She is currently working in Springfield, Massachusetts, where she teaches phenomenal students and works with educators who understand the transformative power of education.

Elena V. Khatskevich is a PhD student in the Department of Communication, University of Massachusetts, Amherst.

Herbert Kohl, author of many books on education including *36 Children, I Won't Learn from You,* and *Stupidity and Tears,* has taught for over forty years, working with young people from five to forty-five. In addition, he has been an activist for social justice and with his wife, Judith, collaborated with Myles Horton, one of the founders of the Highlander Center, on Myles's autobiography, *The Long Haul.*

Tzu-Pei Kuo is a part-time lecturer in four different colleges in Taiwan. From the moment she met Paulo in a graduate class, his words have accompanied her through every difficult moment of teaching.

Claire LaBonté is an ELL/ESOL instructional leadership specialist at Milton Bradley School for the Springfield, Massachusetts, public schools.

Phil Lawrence, M.Ed. (Umass, Amherst-2007) is a working artist and adjunct faculty in the Art Department at Holyoke Community College. He was introduced to Paulo's work through Sonia Nieto's final class at UMass before her retirement

Carlos REC McBride's work focuses on Hip Hop culture and critical literacy among urban youth. He is a doctoral student in language, literacy, and culture in the School of Education at the University of Massachusetts, Amherst, and also an adjunct professor at Greenfield Community College, where he teaches a class called "These Are the Breaks: A Critical Analysis of the History of Hip Hop Culture and Its Social Impact."

Kathy McDonough is a teacher educator in the Boston area and a graduate student at the University of Massachusetts, Amherst.

Amadee Meyer teaches English language learners in Massachusetts.

Adriana Castillo Morehouse has been a Spanish-as-a-second-language instructor for fifteen years, fifth to twelfth grades, in western Massachusetts. In her teaching, she emphasizes the integration of second language instruction with Latin American literature, history, culture, politics, and social justice issues.

Ernest Morrell is an associate professor in the Graduate School of Education and Information Studies at the University of California, Los Angeles.

Dalia Mostafa is principal of Madina Academy in Windsor, Connecticut, and a doctoral student at the University of Massachusetts, Amherst.

Bekisizwe S. Ndimande is assistant professor in the College of Education and Center for African Studies at the University of Illinois at Urbana-Champaign. From

2006 to 2008 he was a visiting fellow in the Faculty of Education, University of Pretoria, South Africa.

A French teacher originally from Morocco and now a graduate student in the French Department at UMass, Amherst, Brahim Oulbeid speaks four languages (Berber, Arabic, French, and English). He finds that Paulo Freire's writings about the conditions of teachers in Brazil are a mirror image of the conditions of teachers in all of the least economically developed countries.

Romina Pacheco was born and raised in Maracay, Venezuela. She is currently a doctoral student in the Higher Education Administration program at the University of Massachusetts, Amherst.

Jacqueline Pinn is a higher education administrator in student affairs whose work focuses on extending multicultural learning beyond the classroom, specifically in the areas of academic support and cultural enrichment. She incorporates wellness and spirituality throughout her work in order to help students achieve internal stability that enables them to make smart life choices.

After sixteen years as a public school teacher in diverse communities, John Raible now works in the Department of Teaching, Learning and Teacher Education at the University of Nebraska-Lincoln.

Elizabeth Rendón, a first-grade teacher in the Boston Public Schools, recalls reading about Paulo Freire's pedagogies and his belief that teachers can be agents of change when she was in graduate school. Although his writing sounded poetic and intellectual, as she studied his work, she not only began to understand it but, in addition, his ideals helped shape the teacher she is today.

Angélica Ribeiro teaches English language learners at Duggan Middle School in Springfield, Massachusetts.

Elizabeth Robinson is a doctoral student. Her interests are in the work of urban public school ESL teachers within the current "high-stakes" political context of U.S. schools.

Carolina Rothkegel, originally from Chile, studied for her master's degree in bilingual education in the United States. She teaches English language learner students from kindergarten to sixth grade in Amherst, Massachusetts. Paulo Freire has inspired her work in multicultural classrooms.

Wendy Seger is currently working in the public schools in Springfield, Massachusetts, as a Cornerstone literacy fellow. Cornerstone is a school reform initiative that helps build the literacy capacity of students and teachers through focused professional development and collaboration of staff and community stakeholders.

Ira Shor and Paulo Freire worked together from 1983 to 1997, coauthoring the first "talking book," *A Pedagogy for Liberation* (1986). Ira teaches at the City University of NY Graduate Center, and still misses Paulo.

After teaching diverse high school English language learners in New York, Lynn Sisco recently relocated to Austin, Texas, where she edits K–8 ESL textbooks. She also teaches beginning level ESL classes for adults.

Elaine Stinson, a board certified elementary school teacher in the Amherst, Massachusetts, Public Schools, has been teaching for fifteen years. She was greatly influenced by Paulo Freire while attending the University of Massachusetts as a graduate student.

Stacie Tate is currently an assistant professor at American University in Washington, D.C. She continues Freire's work by teaching courses on critical literacy and pedagogy.

Lisa Varandani has worked in the field of education since 1994. Currently she writes textbooks for teaching English to speakers of other languages.

Ramón Vega de Jesús, PhD, is an educational psychologist and assistant professor at California State University, Stanislaus. He first met Paulo Freire in Puerto Rico as a preservice teacher in the late 1970s, and today he employs Paulo's legacy in all of his courses.

Tracy Walker has been teaching English for nine years, first in Portland, Oregon, and more recently in Ludlow, Massachusetts. A graduate of the Language Literacy and Culture program in the School of Education at the University of Massachusetts, she has also taught English as a foreign language in Oaxaca, Mexico, and currently works for the Western Massachusetts Writing Project.

Kerri Warfield has been teaching for seven years as an art educator in Westfield, Massachusetts, where she currently resides. She has a bachelor's degree in fine art, with a concentration in art education and a master's degree in multicultural education, both from the University of Massachusetts, Amherst.

Sara Young is a teacher educator whose research and courses focus on critical multicultural pedagogy. She currently teaches preservice teachers at Marlboro College in Vermont and at the University of Massachusetts, Amherst.

Hera Zinno has an M.A.T. in foreign languages and is a Spanish teacher in Fort Lauderdale, Florida.

DATE DUE

MAY 1 4 2014	
	PRINTED IN U.S.A.